THE
UNWRITTEN
RULES
OF
FRIENDSHIP

NATALIE MADORSKY ELMAN

The Special Educator's Almanac: Ready-to-Use
Activities for a Resource Room or a Self-Contained Classroom

Super Sayings: Super Ways to Teach Idioms to Kids

The Resource Room Primer:
Teaching Techniques for Developing, Implementing,
or Improving a Resource Room Program

EILEEN KENNEDY-MOORE

Expressing Emotion: Myths, Realities,
and Therapeutic Strategies
(with coauthor Jeanne C. Watson)

Twelve Ways to Get Your Parents' Attention
(Other Than Hitting Your Sister),
a book for children

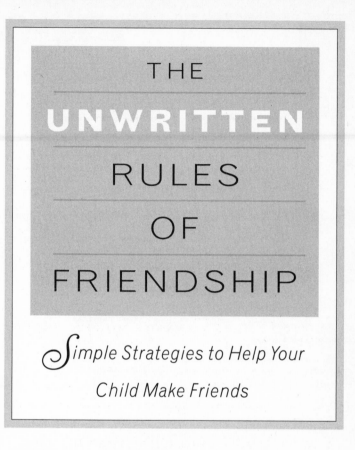

THE
UNWRITTEN
RULES
OF
FRIENDSHIP

Simple Strategies to Help Your Child Make Friends

NATALIE MADORSKY ELMAN, Ph.D.

and

EILEEN KENNEDY-MOORE, Ph.D.

LITTLE, BROWN AND COMPANY

Boston New York London

Copyright © 2003 by Natalie Madorsky Elman and
Eileen Kennedy-Moore

First Edition

The authors are grateful for permission to reprint
"Ten Ways to Resolve Conflict" © 2000 National Liberty Museum.
By permission of the National Liberty Museum,
America's Home for Heroes, 321 Chestnut Street,
Philadelphia, PA 19106.

Library of Congress Cataloging-in-Publication Data

Elman, Natalie Madorsky.

The unwritten rules of friendship: simple strategies to help your child make
friends / by Natalie Madorsky Elman and Eileen Kennedy-Moore.
p. cm.

Includes bibliographical references and index.

ISBN 0-316-91730-3

1. Friendship in children. 2. Social skills in children. 3. Child rearing.
I. Kennedy-Moore, Eileen. II. Title.

BF723.F68 E45 2003
649'.1 — dc21   2002040611

10 9 8 7 6 5 4 3 2 1

Q-MART

Printed in the United States of America

This book is dedicated to Freda Lafcovitz Madorsky, whose beautiful memory has made an indelible imprint on the ideas of this book.

N. M. E.

To my children,
Mary, Daniel, Sheila, and Brenna

E. K-M.

"TELL ME, I FORGET;

SHOW ME, I REMEMBER,

INVOLVE ME, I UNDERSTAND . . ."

Confucius

CONTENTS

Why We Wrote This Book

Natalie

It was during my first year as a teacher of learning disabled children that I realized how misunderstood children with social skill deficits can be. The kids whom I saw with reading or math difficulties garnered sympathy and lots of instructional support, but the children with social problems were often met with irritation and rejection from both staff and students. And they received little or no help.

One little boy, whom I'll call Bobby Murphy, really stands out in my memory. One day, it was my turn to be "on duty" as the teacher responsible for dealing with discipline problems at our public elementary school. I'd just gotten back from lunch, when I heard a buzz from the principal's office. "Bobby Murphy was causing trouble on the bus again," the secretary said over the intercom. "We're sending him down for you to deal with him." I'd heard about Bobby Murphy. Everybody in the school had. The word in the teachers' lounge was that he was a holy terror — the meanest, toughest kid in the school. I took a deep breath, straightened my spine, and prepared myself to deal firmly with this future hoodlum. When I heard a knock, I strode to the door expecting the worst. What I saw was a skinny little freckled boy with a tear-stained face. The "bad boy of the school" stood trembling in the doorway of my classroom.

I invited Bobby in, and together we began unraveling what had happened on the bus. The story was one that I have heard repeatedly since then. Like many children with social skill deficits, Bobby was totally unaware of his role in causing all the mayhem. He claimed he was "just kidding." He was mystified by the angry responses he elicited from both adults and children. He was miserable and very much alone.

I'm an educator, a speech therapist, and a learning consultant in private practice. As the founder and director of the Summit Center for Learning, I've been leading social skills training groups for more than two decades. I've helped hundreds of children learn the *Unwritten Rules* about how to get along with their peers. Teaching the Unwritten Rules directly gives children like Bobby Murphy the crucial social knowledge that they haven't managed to pick up on their own. It opens the door to social success for children who have always felt like outsiders.

The flash of understanding that I've seen in the eyes of children when they grasp an Unwritten Rule is what inspired me to write this book. I wanted to be able to share with parents the tried-and-true techniques that I've used in my groups. I know these techniques work, and I wanted to give parents a chance to dramatically change their children's lives for the better.

Eileen

My work involves providing psychotherapy to individual children, adults, and families. One of the most common concerns that parents mention is their children's friendship problems. Just about every child struggles socially at some point. They grapple with being teased, being the odd one out in a threesome, trying to find a buddy to play with at recess, or feeling lost in a new classroom where they don't know anyone. Although these kinds of problems are "normal," they can be very painful. As a parent, I can understand my adult clients' desire to do whatever they can to help their children make and keep friends.

Sometimes social difficulties go beyond occasional glitches to become more enduring problems. Through my work, I know how hurt and lonely elementary school children can feel when they are stuck in the role of "outsider." When children are rejected again and again by their peers, they generally start to see themselves as unlikable.

This book offers a message of hope. It says that you can help your child learn to get along better with others. Once you understand how and why your child is stumbling socially, you can take steps to smooth the way for him or her. You can work *with* your child's personality rather than against it, and help your child grow and develop socially in ways that fit with his or her unique strengths.

As a therapist and a mother, I've seen how painful it is for children when they feel like they have no friends. But I've also seen how the right kind of coaching can make it possible for children to feel more capable, comfortable, and confident in social situations. Natalie and I wrote this book because we care about children, and we share a commitment to helping children gain the knowledge and skills they need to build fulfilling relationships.

THE
UNWRITTEN
RULES
OF
FRIENDSHIP

CHAPTER 1

The Unwritten Rules of Friendship:

Simple Strategies Every Child

Needs to Know

$\mathcal{I}$t's happening again. Your child runs into the house and cries,

"Mommy, nobody wants to play with me."
"All the kids are picking on me."
"Nobody likes me."

Remarks like these break a parent's heart. You see how crushed your child feels. You worry and wonder, *Why don't the other kids like her?* Or maybe you have some inkling that your child is doing something to drive other kids away. You feel frustrated and think, *If only she weren't so shy, or so bossy, or so aggressive, or such a sore loser . . .* Mostly, you feel helpless. As much as you'd like to, you know you can't make friends for your child, and you can't protect her from teasing or unkind remarks. But you wish there were *something* you could do to make it easier for your child to get along with others.

THE CONSEQUENCES OF FRIENDSHIP PROBLEMS

Almost every child has trouble with social relationships in some way, at some time. Having an argument with a friend, dealing with teasing, being excluded from a group, and trying to find a buddy in a new classroom are painful but typical childhood experiences. While some kids sail through social situations, weathering these normal friendship glitches fairly easily, others constantly struggle and flounder.

When children have trouble relating to their peers, they suffer. Other kids reject, ridicule, or ignore them. They feel lonely and isolated. Moreover, children rarely just outgrow social problems. Elementary school children who don't have a best friend tend to become lonely young adults.

Friendship problems are painful and can often lead to far-reaching consequences. If your child has problems with math, he can always use a calculator when he is older. If he is a poor speller, he can rely on a dictionary or the spelling checker on a computer. However, as Dr. Melvin Levine of the University of North Carolina Medical School points out, if your child has social deficits, the effects continue to be crippling long after graduation and in just about every area of life. Problems making friends can persist into adulthood, keeping your child trapped in the role of "outsider." Social difficulties can also limit your child's future professional opportunities by compromising his or her ability to work effectively with bosses, clients, and coworkers. Social problems can even interfere with your child's ability to find a loving spouse, to build a strong marriage, and to raise children.

The good news is that you can help your child learn to get along with others. Using this book as a guide, you can pinpoint your child's particular social strengths and weaknesses. You can spell out for your child the *Unwritten Rules* that underlie social situations. With these rules as an essential foundation, you can teach your child the necessary skills for building, sustaining, and repairing friendships.

WHAT ARE THE UNWRITTEN RULES?

Every social interaction is governed by Unwritten Rules. These rules explain how to interpret social cues and how to act appropriately in social situations. They describe the implicit knowledge, the unspoken subtext, that flows like a current through social relationships. They can be as simple as "Greet people you know" or as complex as "In every good negotiation, both sides win something."

The Unwritten Rules are guidelines rather than restrictions. They make human interactions proceed smoothly and comfortably. Knowing these rules is essential in navigating the social world capably.

Unwritten Rules are culturally based. For instance, in American culture, direct eye contact is expected when conversing with others. It's a sign of interest, honesty, and sincerity. In other cultures, direct eye contact is disrespectful. Even within the United States, there are variations in the Unwritten Rules. People from New York City tend to speak quickly, whereas a more leisurely pace of speaking is the norm in other parts of the country. In this book, we focus on the rules that seem most critical for children's relationships, but depending on where you live, you may need to modify them somewhat.

Unwritten Rules are everywhere, in every social situation. In a restaurant, you know to listen politely while the server describes the specials for the evening. That's an Unwritten Rule. At work, you know that it's not a good idea to ask the boss for a raise right after she's chewed you out for missing a deadline. That's another Unwritten Rule. If you think about it, you can probably come up with hundreds of Unwritten Rules that guide your behavior every day.

These rules are rarely stated, but most people have an intuitive understanding of them. When you get into an elevator, the first thing you do is turn around and face the doors. You probably never had any specific lessons in elevator etiquette, but somehow you learned this Unwritten Rule. If you were to break this rule and remain standing with your back to the doors, people would think you were strange.

The Unwritten Rules of social situations are so ingrained that the idea of breaking them seems peculiar, even laughable. You know that to get the attention of the person in line ahead of you, you should tap her on the shoulder, not pat her on the head. You know never to ask an acquaintance how much money she earns. You know not to describe your hemorrhoids to a stranger.

WHY CHILDREN NEED TO KNOW THE UNWRITTEN RULES

The key factor that determines how smoothly children (and adults) get along with others is whether or not they understand and can follow the Unwritten Rules that guide social relationships. Some children pick up these rules automatically; others are oblivious to them. Like rudderless ships, they easily veer off course in social situations. They come on too strong, or they are too passive, or they stick out in a way that makes others reject them. They are targets for bullies. They feel awkward in groups because they don't recognize the social cues influencing everyone else's behavior. They wish desperately for friends but don't understand the nuances of cultivating relationships. They may feel lonely and isolated, as if they were strangers in a foreign country where they don't speak the language.

Sometimes children have social problems when they move to a new town or a new school. They may have been getting along fine in their old environment, but suddenly the rules change, and they are at a loss. For instance, if your child recently moved from the city to the suburbs, the rules about how to dress, how to spend time together, and even how to talk may be very different in his or her new community. Also, the kids who knew your child since nursery school may have accepted his or her idiosyncrasies, but new classmates may be less tolerant.

The Unwritten Rules for children are not identical to those for adults. For instance, a firm handshake is essential for adults but irrelevant for children. Asking the age of a new acquaintance is rude for adults but is a friendly overture for children. Making disgusting burping noises is an admirable skill only among boys of a certain age.

The Unwritten Rules that we present in this book are drawn, as much as possible, from research studies of children interacting in ordinary settings, such as camp or the local playground. These observational studies help us understand how socially adept children actually relate to other children so we don't have to rely on our adult ideas of how children *should* behave.

Unless they know the Unwritten Rules of social situations, children cannot possibly use social skills appropriately. Teaching children about social skills without placing these skills in the context of Unwritten Rules is like teaching children to sail on dry land. They may learn the mechanics perfectly, but they don't really understand when and how to use them. What difference does it make if a child has learned to make "I" statements (e.g., "I feel . . . when you . . .") if she doesn't understand the rules about which topics are acceptable to discuss in which situations? What good is it if a child can list all the steps in problem solving but doesn't know that new relationships cannot tolerate conflict? Social skills training tells children how to act. The Unwritten Rules go beyond this basic training by helping children understand social roles and expectations so that they can choose behaviors that fit the situation.

By explicitly teaching the Unwritten Rules of how to get along with others, you can provide your child with essential guidelines for navigating the social maze. You can unveil for your child the unspoken social conventions that everybody else seems to know. You can give your child the knowledge necessary for making and keeping friends.

A WHOLE-CHILD PERSPECTIVE

Our goal in this book is to help each child gain a sense of social comfort and connection in a way that complements his or her own unique personality. We've drawn upon research, as well as clinical experience, to come up with vivid and compassionate descriptions of nine prototypical children with friendship problems. These nine children are *normal* kids who struggle to be accepted by their peers. We highlight the particular Unwritten Rules that each type of child needs to learn, and we offer easy-to-use, targeted suggestions for teaching these rules and enhancing social interactions both at home and at school.

We use a whole-child perspective, which recognizes that children with specific social problems also have corresponding strengths that can be cultivated. The Shy Child can become a good listener and a loyal friend. The Vulnerable Child might acquire a highly developed sense of justice and a special empathy for the downtrodden.

Our whole-child perspective works *with* rather than against children's enduring tendencies. Not every child can or wants to become an effervescent Mr. or Ms. Popularity who is the life of every party. And this is fine. A quieter style of relating can also lead to friendship. The Born Leader may always be more comfortable leading than following a group, but she can learn how to temper her take-charge tendencies so that other people respond to her ideas with enthusiasm rather than resistance or resentment. The Different Drummer may always have an offbeat, quirky sense of humor, but learning the Unwritten Rules can help her decide when and how to use that humor.

The brief descriptions of children in the table of contents and the questions at the beginning of each chapter can help you identify which sections of this book are most relevant for helping your child learn to relate well to others. You will probably recognize your child in *several* different chapters. At the end of each chapter, we list related chapters that you may want to read. Keep in mind that the nine children in this book are composites of the many children we've known. We offer these descriptions to help you understand rather than just label your child. Whether your child is having trouble resolving an argument with a friend or even making a friend in the first place, whether your child is painfully shy or a bit rambunctious, this book gives you the tools you need to nurture your child's social well-being.

HELPING YOUR CHILD RELATE WELL TO OTHERS

Children need friends. Friends are a source of fun and companionship. Building a fort in the backyard is more fun if you have a buddy to help. Friends also help children develop a sense of who they are: "Jason and I both love soccer"; "Karen's favorite color is purple, but I like yellow." Children's friendships are a critical training ground for learning how to get along with other people. When two small girls negotiate who gets to wear the sequined dress and who gets to wear the feather boa, they are learning skills that they will use in all future relationships. Through their friendships, children learn about leading and following, arguing and making up, sharing and feeling empathy.

Having friends helps children feel happy, confident, and connected, but children aren't born knowing how to build friendships.

They learn it. When your child was two years old, she probably played alongside another child without interacting. At three, she probably began cooperative play, working with another child toward a shared goal. At four, maybe she could share or take turns without shrieking.

Now, in elementary school, friendships are more complicated, and the rules governing how to fit in can be subtle. Very young children tend to identify their friends as whomever they happen to be with at the moment, but elementary school children can identify best friends and begin to form bonds. For preschoolers, the key challenges of social relationships usually involve remembering not to hit or snatch toys. Your elementary school child needs much more complex social knowledge and abilities, such as how to blend in to a group, how to behave differently in a beginning versus an established friendship, and how to resolve conflicts.

Each chapter in this book describes specific strategies that address particular social difficulties common among elementary school children (approximately ages six through twelve). We offer many exercises for learning the Unwritten Rules so that you can choose the ones that seem best suited to your child's needs, interests, and maturity level. You should also keep the following general guidelines in mind while teaching your child to relate well to others.

1. Talk with your child's teacher.

If your child is having social problems, it is essential that you talk with his or her teacher to get an objective opinion on the matter. Your child might complain, "Everybody hates me!" but the teacher might paint a very different picture. Maybe there is just one particular classmate who squabbles with your child. Maybe your child is generally well-liked but hangs back in group situations. The teacher sees your child "in action" every day and could give you important information about your child's behavior around other kids. What you see at home may not be typical of how your child acts at school. Your son might be a little chatterbox with the family but completely silent with classmates. Or maybe your daughter is doing something that classmates find off-putting. You need to know the whole picture if you're going to help your child learn to get along better.

The teacher can also be a wonderful ally in helping your child learn the relevant Unwritten Rules. At the end of each chapter, we feature a section called "The Home-School Connection," which offers doable suggestions that you might want to discuss with your child's teacher.

2. Provide opportunities for socializing.

In previous generations, children learned social skills by hanging out with the kids in the neighborhood and by interacting with large and extended families. Today, many parents are too concerned about safety to allow their children to roam the neighborhood unsupervised. Most children have many structured activities and lessons, leaving them less time to simply play with others. Families are generally smaller and more transient, so children have fewer siblings and relatives with whom to practice their social skills. All of this means that it is harder for today's children to learn through hands-on experience how to get along with other children.

You need to give your child the opportunity to practice relating to peers. Usually this means scheduling one-on-one play dates. In our experience, short play dates that focus on a planned activity, such as going bowling or going out for ice cream, work best for children who are struggling socially.

You may also need to help your child find potential friends outside of school. If your child is having trouble with classmates, he or she might fit in better with kids from your church or synagogue, or with the members of a club that focuses on special interests, such as chess or horseback riding. Some children feel more confident interacting with kids a little bit younger than they are. If your child has cousins around his or her age, they could be a great source of support. Because they are family members, cousins may be a little more tolerant of your child than the kids at school are, and they can give your child a sustaining sense of belonging. Being included in the activities of a more socially savvy cousin could also help your child smooth some rough edges.

3. Proceed slowly and consistently.

Once you see how learning the Unwritten Rules could help your child, you may be tempted to sit your child down and go through a chapter or two with him or her in one sitting. Don't. You're better off taking a more gradual approach. Children have short attention spans (some more than others). If you try to teach too much too fast, your child is likely to become bored, anxious, or overwhelmed. Give your child a chance to get comfortable with one idea or strategy before you move on to another. Try taking a low-key, fun approach when you do the exercises with your child. Learning to make and keep friends is important, but you don't want it to dominate your interactions with your child. Your child needs your social coaching, but your child also needs to feel your love and acceptance, and to spend time with you just playing or hanging out.

Keep in mind that there are no quick fixes for helping your child relate better to others. Don't try just one activity and conclude, "This book doesn't work." For many children, learning the Unwritten Rules is like learning a foreign language. It takes time and experience to master the material. Your child will need ongoing exposure to the rules, practice using them, and reminders before entering specific difficult situations. You may also need to revisit the Unwritten Rules as your child gets older and social situations become even more complex. Learning to get along with others is a lifelong process. With every new relationship and every new stage of life, we all need to learn and change.

4. Share your confidence.

Children often have trouble with perspective. If someone doesn't invite them to a birthday party, they react like it's the worst thing in the world. If kids are mean to them, they assume that this will always be the case. As adults, we know that circumstances change, that people grow, and that there's a big wide world outside of this year's elementary school class. So, when your child comes home crying because "everyone" was mean to him or her, listen, empathize, try to understand your child's point of view, but also express your confidence that, with help, your child will be able to find a way to deal with the situation.

As you work on the exercises in this book, keep the focus on success rather than failure. Applaud when your child is able to implement the techniques in the book. Comment on how he or she is becoming more comfortable socially. Warn your child that it may take a while for other kids to notice the changes he or she is making, but assure your child that these efforts will pay off. Avoid what Dr. Michael Thompson and his colleagues, authors of *Best Friends, Worst Enemies: Understanding the Social Lives of Children,* call "interviewing for pain." If you greet your child every day after school by asking, "Was anyone mean to you today?" your child is going to come up with something to report.

It's hard to respond calmly when your child is hurting. Seeing your child suffer can make you want to leap into action to protect him or her. Sometimes parents of children who are the brunt of ridicule or rejection wonder if they should call the parents of the other child. In general, we don't recommend this. If your child is truly in danger, of course you need to take steps to ensure his or her safety, but this is usually best accomplished by talking to school authorities. Contacting the other child's parents carries the risk of spreading the conflict to the parents. It also says to your child, "You can't handle this. I need to solve it for you." You should only give this message if it really is a situation that your child can't manage alone. Otherwise, focus on giving your child the knowledge, skills, and support he or she needs to solve the problem.

5. Emphasize kindness.

At their core, the Unwritten Rules are about kindness and civility. They emphasize talking and listening to one another, respecting and caring about one another, and reaching out to help one another. True friendship grows from a sense of connection. The best thing you can do to help your child learn to get along with others is to place a high value on kindness. Don't tolerate cruelty between siblings. Point out the impact of your child's words and actions on others. Insist that family members speak to one another in a respectful tone of voice. Let your child experience the joy of giving. Avoid putting other people down. Talk about how you can understand someone else's point of view even when you don't agree with it. Express appreciation when your child does something thoughtful or helpful. These actions demonstrate the fundamentals of social relationships described in the Unwritten Rules.

CHAPTER 2

The Vulnerable Child

Does your child . . .

feel frightened and helpless because another child is making his or her life miserable?

always manage to be singled out to get picked on?

dread going to school or group activities because other kids are so mean?

cry frequently about being hurt by others for no reason?

have trouble realizing when he or she is annoying other children?

Do you . . .

dread new group situations, knowing it's just a matter of time before your child gets picked on?

feel desperate to protect your child and furious with the child or children who pick on him or her?

feel exasperated that your child seems to go out of his or her way to provoke other children?

wish you could take on the bully yourself?

worry that your child will never be able to stand up for him- or herself?

feel embarrassed by your child's weakness and wish he or she had the guts to fight back?

Some kids are magnets for bullying. Wherever they are, whomever they are with, these Vulnerable Children manage to get picked on. They are always the ones who are called nasty names, who are deliberately tripped as they walk down the hall, who get beaten up, or who are generally humiliated by other kids. It happens all the time: at the playground, at Sunday school, at summer camp, or at Scout troop meetings. No child deserves to be treated cruelly, but it's almost like there is something about these kids that attracts abuse.

Other Vulnerable Children are bullied in only one specific setting, by one particular child. Usually it happens during times with less structure and less supervision, such as at recess or on the way home from school. They somehow become the target of abuse by an Intimidating Child. They feel trapped and helpless to stop it.

As parents, seeing a blow to our child strikes at our heart. Sometimes it brings out the mother lioness in us, and we feel a ferocious desire to protect our child against the "mean kid." Sometimes it keeps us up at night, worrying about how our child is suffering. Sometimes our child gets over the hurt faster than we do.

Most kids are resilient enough to handle occasional incidents that make them feel embarrassed or upset, but being regularly intimidated and humiliated can leave lifelong scars. So, although we don't want to overreact to every little slight our child receives, we must not minimize the pain of being bullied. Recent events such as the Columbine school shooting have alerted parents and teachers to the potentially devastating effects of bullying. No child should have to endure being continually threatened, harassed, or ostracized. Being bullied does not build character or toughen kids up. It is a frightening and crushing experience.

WHAT IS BULLYING?

Bullying involves (1) deliberate hurtful behavior *plus* (2) an imbalance of power between the victim and the bully that makes it hard for the victim to defend him- or herself. Bullying is often repeated over time, but sometimes a single severe incident can qualify.

When we think of bullying, most of us picture a big kid beating up a little kid. However, bullying can also involve threats, vicious teasing and name-calling, or constantly ostracizing someone. Both girls and boys can bully, although girls are more likely to do it in a nonphysical way.

It is sometimes hard to draw the line between ordinary meanness and bullying. Not every scuffle or unkind remark constitutes bullying. All children get teased or taunted. At some point most children will have to cope with the sting of being rejected or excluded from a group. Many children get involved in an occasional angry shoving match or in wrestling play that gets out of hand. Sporadic incidents like these can be very upsetting for children and parents, but they don't have the devastating long-term consequences for both the victim and the aggressor that bullying does.

Bullying is more than meanness; it's peer abuse. Bullying involves a pattern of systematic, targeted intimidation and harassment. If the victim regularly feels frightened, threatened, or humiliated rather than occasionally mad or embarrassed, it is probably bullying. If the aggression is frequent, severe, or enduring, it is bullying. If the action would be a serious criminal offense if committed by an adult (e.g., assault, extortion), it is definitely bullying.

It's tempting to blame bullying completely on the aggressive child. Cruel behavior certainly shouldn't be excused or tolerated. But research observations of pairs of children playing games show that *both* Vulnerable and Intimidating Children contribute to the pattern of bullying. These children bring out the worst in each other. When bullies and victims are paired, they each play their classic domineering and submissive roles. Bullies act bossy and reject victims' suggestions, while victims passively comply with bullies' orders. However, when bullies and victims are paired with other children, they behave in less stereotypical ways. Bullies are less likely to oppose their partners' ideas, and victims are more likely to assertively ask for help or explanations. In other words, it takes two to tango. Bullying requires the interaction of an Intimidating Child and a Vulnerable Child.

WHO GETS BULLIED?

Children often believe that they are bullied because they are different somehow or because they have a less-than-perfect physical appearance. It's true that differences are often the topic of taunting, but all children have something that sets them apart from others. Research and our own clinical experience say that it's primarily what's going on *inside* a child that determines whether or not that child faces ongoing bullying.

Some of the "coolest" kids we know are chubby or thin, short or tall, academically gifted or struggling. What these well-liked children have in common is an inner sense of security that enables them to shrug off ridicule.

In contrast, children who are targeted by bullies are anxious kids who care too much about being accepted and somehow broadcast a message to other kids that says "Here I am — pick on me!" Too often, these are children with few, if any, friends who will come to their aid. Other kids usually stand passively by while these children get harassed, grateful that it's not them. Intimidating Children view this as approval and encouragement to do more. Each time Vulnerable Children are bullied, they become more entrenched in the victim role in the eyes of other children and in their own eyes.

Once children become targets of bullying, how they respond has a big impact on whether the bullying continues. One study of kindergartners found that at the beginning of the school year, 22 percent of children reported being victimized frequently. By the end of the school year, only about a third of these children were still being regularly bullied. Our experience suggests that children who bully try out a variety of victims and stick with the ones who provide the most satisfying responses.

ON THE POSITIVE SIDE

Children who have been victims of bullying are likely to develop an endearing tendency to understand and root for the underdog. They may acquire a great sense of fairness and a concern for justice. With appropriate guidance, these children may become astute in avoiding and defusing conflict. Vulnerable Children sometimes develop a keen sense of humor and an ability to laugh at themselves.

SO, WHAT CAN WE DO?

The best way to stop bullying is through comprehensive school or community programs that (1) educate people about bullying, (2) foster a value of kindness and an intolerance for cruelty, and (3) address the needs of individual children — both those who bully and those who are victimized. However, these kinds of programs take time and coordinated effort to establish.

As the parent of a Vulnerable Child, you undoubtedly want to do something *now*. You can do this by taking steps to ensure your child's safety and by helping your child learn to be less of a target for bullying.

Vulnerable Children need the support and protection of adults. If your child's safety is at stake, you may need to make different arrangements for getting him or her to and from school. If the bullying is taking place at school, you may need to alert school personnel so that they can help put a stop to it. In addition, Vulnerable Children need to learn the Unwritten Rules about dealing with bullying. They must understand that the more vulnerable they appear, the more they will be picked on. They have to identify and eliminate the things they might do to irritate others. Vulnerable Children also must learn options for avoiding or escaping dangerous situations.

It is easy to hate a child who hurts your child. But as you read over the examples and exercises in this chapter, try to keep in mind that no matter how awful their behavior is, children who bully are still children. These kids require a different kind of help than your child does, but they are also suffering and deserve compassion. You may want to read chapter 3, "The Intimidating Child," if you want to understand the other side of bullying.

In this chapter, we talk about strategies for helping two kinds of Vulnerable Children: Allen is an Unassertive Child who gives in to threats; Phillip is a Provocative Child who asks for trouble by antagonizing a tougher kid. We also discuss strategies for coping with transient meanness, which is a painful but unavoidable part of childhood.

Allen: Giving In to Threats

Allen stood by the school door, hiding behind a column, praying for the bell to ring. He checked his watch for the fourth time — still five more minutes of recess. He pushed himself more tightly into the space behind the column, wishing he could be invisible, so Ben wouldn't spot him.

A voice from behind shattered his hopes. "Hey, creep, where's my math homework?"

Allen gulped. He turned around and saw Ben and his two friends looming over him. "Um . . . I couldn't do it. I had to go to the orthodontist right after school, and then I had a lot of my own homework, and my mom wouldn't let me stay up late . . ."

"Tomorrow you'd better bring today's *and* tomorrow's homework or you're dead meat," said Ben, poking Allen in the chest. His friends snickered. Ben gave Allen a parting shove and walked away.

Allen sighed and leaned his head against the column. The bell finally rang, too late to help him. Allen joined the other children lining up to go inside, wondering how he would ever manage to do his own homework plus double homework for Ben.

THE UNASSERTIVE CHILD

Allen is a classic example of one kind of Vulnerable Child: the Unassertive Child. He is anxious, he has low self-esteem, and he responds passively to threats. The other boys can get away with picking on him because he's an easy target.

Unassertive Children feel trapped and helpless in the face of bullying. Like Allen, they spend a lot of time wishing that the bullying would magically end, but they are too paralyzed by fear to try to do anything to stop it. They may have some vague idea about standing up for themselves, but they have no idea how to do this. So instead they cower and give in, making them magnets for further intimidation.

As the bullying continues over time, Unassertive Children feel more and more humiliated. They may even start to believe that they deserve to be treated cruelly. If someone deliberately treats them badly, most adults have a lifetime of experience and enough positive relationships and accomplishments to say to themselves, *This is not right. I don't deserve this.* But children are more vulnerable to cruelty. Their sense of who they are is still forming, and they draw upon their interactions with others in learning about themselves. In a corner of their minds, Unassertive Children may start to think, *If people treat me badly, there must be something wrong with me.*

Although some children readily complain to their parents about being bullied, others, especially Unassertive Children, are reluctant to say anything because they are ashamed or fear retribution. Your child may be a silent victim of bullying if he or she

- is uncharacteristically reluctant to go to school
- avoids previously enjoyed activities involving other children
- avoids the school lunchroom or playground
- is suddenly reluctant to walk to or from school
- seems moody, anxious, or depressed
- has changes in sleep patterns
- frequently complains about vague, unexplained physical problems such as headaches or stomachaches
- comes home with torn clothing or is mysteriously missing valued possessions

When they find out that their child is being bullied, many parents feel so outraged and so protective of their child that they want to leap in right away and solve the problem. If your child is in immediate danger, you *must* intervene and demand that the school take precautions to keep your child safe. (In general, it is more effective to talk to the teacher and the principal than to try to confront the aggressive child or his or her parents directly.) But be careful about stepping in too quickly — you may unintentionally confirm your child's belief that he or she is weak and inadequate. If the aggression is not too severe, giving children the chance *and the tools* to handle the situation on their own can boost their confidence and help them learn what to do if it happens again.

Some parents are quick to urge their children to stand up to bullies. But Unassertive Children feel frightened and intimidated. They don't know how to stand up for themselves. Moreover, some situations are too dangerous for children to handle on their own.

Sometimes parents of Unassertive Children wonder if they should teach their child to fight back. It seems everyone has a friend or a relative who knows of a case in which a child gave the bully one good punch and that was the end of it. Perhaps this does work in rare instances, but in general, we don't recommend teaching Vulnerable Children to use physical force. First, it's unlikely to work, because children who bully usually pick unfair fights. Intimidating Children tend to be bigger, stronger, or just plain tougher than their victims, so it's unlikely that Vulnerable Children will be able to overpower them. Second, an aggressive response may be exactly what their tormentor is hoping for. Children who bully are trying to get a big reaction out of their victims. Getting someone fighting mad and squashing them anyway is very satisfying for Intimidating Children. It's entertaining for them and for their audience. Third, fighting back can easily lead to an escalation that ends with someone getting seriously injured. The idea of lashing out and really hurting someone who hurts them can be very appealing to children . . . until they get hit back. Intimidating Children attack others because they are trying to cover up their own sense of powerlessness. They are not going to back down easily. If their intended victim tries to retaliate, odds are they will do something even worse to save face.

What about teaching Vulnerable Children martial arts, which stress defending oneself without attacking back? Martial arts can help children stand up straight and feel more confident so that they are less of a target for bullying. Practicing the movements is a great way for children to be physically active and to feel strong. Learning to use their bodies in a coordinated way and earning new belts can be wonderful for children's self-esteem. Martial arts doesn't require precise eye-hand coordination or large physical size, so even children who are generally not athletes can excel. However, don't expect your child to suddenly be able to fend off tougher kids. This scenario works in the movies, but in real life, it rarely happens. Also, we don't want to give children the impression that they should try to handle a truly dangerous situation on their own.

If you have an Unassertive Child who is being victimized, tell your child that his or her safety is the most important concern. Explain that it's okay to run away or to ask an adult for help if he or she is in danger. At some point, when your child is not too upset and is open to learning new strategies, go over the Unwritten Rules about how to avoid being picked on. Practice the following activities, focusing on those that seem most relevant for your child.

THE UNWRITTEN RULES

- Vulnerable body language attracts bullies.
- Giving in to a bully's demands has no end.
- Each time you allow yourself to be taken advantage of, you shrink a little inside.
- There is safety in numbers.
- Some situations require intervention by teachers or parents.

ACTIVITIES FOR LEARNING THE
UNWRITTEN RULES

1. Changing Vulnerable Body Language

Many victims of chronic bullying can be spotted a mile away because of their body language, which practically screams, "Pick on me! I'm easily intimidated!" Stand in front of a mirror with your child and practice the differences between the confident and vulnerable body language characteristics listed in the following table. Practice sitting, standing, and walking confidently.

Confident Body Language	Vulnerable Body Language
• Looking people in the eye when they are talking (without staring)	• Looking at the floor or everywhere except the person talking
• Shoulders down and back, but not stiff	• Shoulders high, tight, and curved forward
• Head back, so ears are aligned with shoulders	• Head ducked down
• Arms and legs relaxed, elbows away from body (for boys, legs apart when sitting)	• Arms and legs wrapped around body as if feeling cold
• Moderate, relaxed walking pace	• Hurried or tentative walking

Once your child recognizes the difference between vulnerable and confident body language, use games to help him or her break the slouching habit. The old exercise of walking with a book on one's head can be a fun way to reinforce standing tall. Try making a game out of using good posture at the dinner table. Give everyone at the table twenty-five pennies. If they slouch, they lose one; if they don't lose any pennies through the whole meal, they win an extra twenty-five cents. If you don't want to use money, use points or stickers instead. The game will be more fun if you include yourself. You might be surprised at how vigilant you become of your own posture.

2. Practicing Assertive Responses to Bullying

Help your child understand the difference between passive, aggressive, and assertive behavior. *Passive* behavior means being a doormat. It means submitting to what other people want regardless of what you want or need. *Aggressive* behavior means being a steamroller. It involves hurting or intimidating other people to get what you want. The middle ground is *assertive* behavior. This involves taking care of yourself while treating other people with respect.

Passive responses perpetuate bullying. Giving in or doing nothing essentially grants a child who bullies permission to continue. Aggressive responses escalate bullying. Hitting Intimidating Children or yelling threats or insults at them can goad them into being meaner. So, your child's best option is an assertive response.

Have your child practice saying assertive statements in a confident (not angry) voice, using strong body language, and then walking away calmly. You can use your own statements or the ones we've listed below. Assertive statements allow your child to preserve his or her dignity without putting anyone down. Emphasize that this is just practice. Your child does not actually have to use any of these statements; you just want him or her to try them and to see how it feels to say them.

ASSERTIVE RESPONSES TO BULLYING

I'm not going to do that anymore.

No, it's mine. I'm not going to give it to you.

No, thank you.

Think what you want. I know differently.

So?

So what?

You're entitled to your opinion.

The message in all of these statements is "I'm not going to let this ridicule or intimidation get to me." Discuss which of these statements works best with the taunts that your child usually hears. You and your child may be able to come up with other assertive statements that fit his or her particular situation. Try to come up with several options so that your child has the opportunity to choose one that feels right.

Alternatively, if your child is too frightened to risk using any of the assertive statements, or if your child easily gets tongue-tied, he or she may prefer to be assertive *without words*. Have your child role-play with you, looking the Intimidating Child in the eye with a bored expression, and then looking away. Another good nonverbal assertiveness technique for your child to try is rolling his or her eyes in disgust. In either case, the message is "I'm not letting you get to me." You may want to use a mirror to help your child perfect that bored or disgusted expression, but most elementary school children are very good at looking bored and disgusted!

Talk with your child about how it feels to say assertive statements or to use nonverbal assertiveness. Would your child feel the same way after yelling insults at the Intimidating Child? Would your child feel the same way after bursting into tears or running away instead of walking away calmly? Try acting out those responses as well so your child can feel the difference. Unlike the aggressive or passive responses, the assertive responses can give Unassertive Children a new sense of inner strength, even when they are scared. These responses may or may not stop bullying, but they can build your child's sense of dignity and self-respect.

As you and your child evaluate possible statements and techniques, bear in mind that what works for you may not be right for your child. For instance, you may have been able to avoid trouble as a child by joking, but if your child is the serious type, he or she probably can't do this and will feel more inadequate if you insist on it. Help your child decide which strategies seem right for him or her.

Be sure to explain that nonverbal assertiveness does *not* include trying to physically hurt another child. That's aggression, and it is usually not a good strategy for Unassertive Children because they could get seriously hurt.

You should also discuss with your child the fact that there are some situations in which assertiveness is not a good idea. If your child is in danger or if he or she is being threatened by a group of bullies, getting away and getting adult help are better choices.

3. Building Confidence and Finding Allies

Because bullying can be so crushing, Unassertive Children need to have experiences that make them feel good about themselves. We can't give children self-esteem; they have to build it themselves by working hard and accomplishing something that matters to them. Encourage your child's interests, acknowledge his or her achievements, and praise his or her efforts. Learning and doing new things can help your child feel capable.

For instance, if your child is a good swimmer, sign him or her up for the local swim team. If your child is a jumper and a climber, look for a good gymnastics class. If your child has a flair for the dramatic, a local drama group might be just the thing. If your child loves math and science, you may want to look into enrichment programs at local colleges.

Your child may be reluctant to try new activities for fear of being picked on. However, a structured situation with close adult super-vision is usually a safe environment. Joining a different group can give your child a chance to play a new role and perhaps make some additional friends. Try to get your child to agree to stick with the chosen activity for some reasonable trial period. After your child is comfortable in the group, you should follow up with more unstruc-tured and one-on-one socializing.

Being alone during unstructured school time makes children sit-ting ducks for bullies. Hanging out with other children during lunch and recess and just before or after school can make your child less of a target. Emphasize that these other children don't have to be your child's bosom buddies — they just have to be there. When your child is not interacting with other children, simply staying near the teacher or other responsible adults is a good option.

Phillip: Asking for Trouble

Phillip walked into the cafeteria and made a beeline for Bruno and his friends. He tapped the older boy repeatedly on the shoulder. Bruno swatted at Phillip's hand and snarled, "What's your problem, weirdo?"

Phillip leaned in close to Bruno's face. "Don't even think about picking on me today," he said in a sanctimonious voice. "Because if you do, I'm going straight to the principal's office and then, boy, will you be in trouble."

"Oh, I'm so scared," Bruno said sarcastically, turning back to his lunch. His friends snickered.

"I mean it," Phillip insisted. "I really mean it."

Bruno stood up slowly, towering over Phillip. He carefully poured his remaining milk over Phillip's head, then shoved him backward so that he crashed into several empty chairs.

"Oops," Bruno said.

"I'm telling!" Phillip shrieked.

THE PROVOCATIVE CHILD

Phillip is an example of another type of Vulnerable Child: the Provocative Child. Certainly, no one deserves to be bullied, no matter what they do, but Provocative Children seem to ask for trouble. Instead of avoiding aggressive kids, they seek them out. Instead of trying to defuse a tense situation or get away, they persist, practically waving a red flag in the faces of Intimidating Children. They then complain bitterly about being picked on. These children seem totally unaware of how annoying their actions are and frequently get into situations that are over their heads. They egg other children on and don't know when to stop or how to handle it when the other children retaliate. They may start a wrestling match and then wail when the other child fights back. They crowd other children and then feel outraged when someone shoves them away. They might chase a child or blatantly snatch someone's hat or pen and then become upset when the other child turns around and swats them. They might laugh at someone's haircut and then feel hurt when the other child retorts with a nastier insult. If we were to talk to Phillip about the incident with Bruno, he would probably insist, "I didn't do anything!" Or he might protest, "I had to tell him. I made up my mind about what I was going to do, and I had to tell Bruno how much trouble he was going to be in so he would leave me alone."

Sometimes Provocative Children act silly or obnoxious because it's the only way they know to get their peers' attention. For instance, they may grab a ball that a group of boys is playing with and refuse to give it back. They wrongly assume that negative attention is better than no attention. They may also secretly enjoy the excitement and the power of getting everyone riled up. Provocative Children's behavior often stems from impulsiveness and an inability to anticipate other people's reactions. They are honestly surprised that other children find their taunts irritating.

Provocative Children have trouble seeing the link between their behavior and other children's annoyance because there is a delayed reaction. They might provoke and provoke and provoke another child and get no reaction. But then, at some point, they use up their "reserve" of tolerance with that child. They provoke him or her one more time, and they trigger a furious response. The other child reacts to the fifteen times that his chair was kicked before, but the Provocative Child only sees the final event: "I accidentally bumped him just a tiny bit, and he hit me!"

Despite the fact that Provocative Children seem to bring a lot of their troubles on themselves, they still have a fundamental right to be safe. If you suspect that you have a Provocative Child, talk with him or her about the importance of trying to avoid trouble, recognizing a dangerous situation, and getting away and finding help if necessary. You may also need to talk to school officials about ensuring your child's safety. Don't hesitate to do so, even if your child has gotten into trouble in the past with the teacher or the principal.

Don't assume that your child will "learn his or her lesson" from other children. Provocative Children seldom do. We've known children who have been repeatedly and cruelly victimized, and they still don't understand how they antagonize other children. Provocative Children need to have this spelled out for them. Your child needs your help to see his or her behavior as others see it. Choose an appropriate moment to go over the Unwritten Rules with your child. Some or all of the following exercises can help your child become better at anticipating the consequences of different actions. These activities underscore the Unwritten Rules about picking up on social cues and avoiding trouble.

THE UNWRITTEN RULES

- Never provoke someone bigger or tougher than you.
- You don't have to announce your intentions.
- Staying out of harm's way is wise.
- Respect other people's space.
- Keep your hands to yourself.
- When someone says "Stop," stop.
- If you hit someone, odds are they'll hit you back harder.
- If you call someone names, they are likely to call you something worse.

ACTIVITIES FOR LEARNING
THE UNWRITTEN RUL ES

1. Identifying Provocative Behavior

Provocative Children often don't realize what they are doing that annoys others. If you're not sure either, your child's teacher may be able to help you identify some possibilities. We've listed some of the most common provocative behaviors and some options for learning to avoid them.

Provocative Behavior: Invading other children's space.

Possible Remedies: Emphasize to your child that kids need to keep their hands and feet to themselves. Poking or tugging on other children or kicking them under the table is always annoying. In addition, starting around third grade, hugging and holding hands with peers becomes inappropriate. Kids who don't realize this seem weird to other children and often get picked on.

To help your child learn not to invade the space of other children, you could try sitting in the car with your child at a nearby park and watching the school-age children play. Point out to your child how the children are playing together without getting on top of one another.

You may want to post a vivid note about respecting others' space on your refrigerator. It could be a motto such as Hands off! If you are artistic, you could even draw a picture of a hand inside a circle with a diagonal slash. If your child has siblings, the rule should apply to them as well.

Give your child plenty of hugs but don't let him or her get your attention in annoying ways. Tell your child, "I don't like to be poked (or tugged on, or repeatedly tapped). Please use your words."

Another way to help your child learn to respect other people's space is to give a concrete example. Get two hula hoops and place them next to each other on the floor. Have your child stand in the center of one while you stand in the center of the other. Explain to your child that people have an invisible comfort circle around them. Mom, Dad, Grandma, and Grandpa welcome hugs and close contact from your child, but if he or she invades other people's comfort circle, they will become irritated and instinctively back away. Now, each of you pick up your hula hoops and hold them at waist height. Wander around, making sure that the hula hoops never overlap so your child can get a feeling for what is an acceptable degree of closeness with acquaintances. For fun, you may want to put on some lively music as you do this.

Once your child is good at respecting body space with the hula hoops, try it without them. This time, you stand still and have your child approach you in various locations, from all directions, until he or she can reliably estimate a socially appropriate distance. Check the distance by having both of you hold out your arms to make sure that you are two arm's lengths apart (your child's arm, and your own).

When children are standing in line at school, back to front, it's okay to be closer than usual, but remind your child not to shove others or to jump or hang on anyone's back. Warn your child never to get in someone's face. The natural response to having someone's hand or face directly in front of one's own face is to want to swat it away. Try it with your child so he or she can experience how annoying this can be.

Provocative Behavior: Talking in a high, shrill, or too loud voice.

Possible Remedies: Tape-record your child and yourself talking in different tones of voice and at different volumes. Point out that shrill or loud voices hurt other people's ears and make it hard for them to listen. Provocative Children need to be especially careful of their voice when they are feeling nervous, angry, or excited because that's when they are most likely to talk in an irritating manner. With your child's help, come up with a quick, nonembarrassing gesture or comment that you can use to remind him or her to use a pleasant voice. It may be tapping your ear or your throat, or it may be a simple phrase like "voice" or "volume."

Be sure to notice when your child uses the proper tone. Saying, "I like the way your voice sounds now," helps your child know what to aim for. Only remark on your child's voice when others are not around so that you don't embarass him or her.

2. Picking Up on Annoyance Cues

One of the biggest problems that Provocative Children have is that they ignore or are oblivious to other children's expressions of annoyance. Point out to your child that other people's irritation can quickly build to anger or dislike if your child doesn't respond appropriately. Help your child make a list of possible signs of annoyance in others. Your list might look something like this:

ANNOYANCE CUES

Facial cues: Squinting eyes
                Sneering mouth or pursed lips
                Red face

Body cues: Turning away
                Shaking head
                Hands on hips

Vocal cues: Deep sighs
                Disgusted click of tongue ("Tsk!")
                "Stop it!"
                "Cut it out!"
                "Go away!"
                "Get off me!"
                "You're so annoying!"

To help your child become adept at noticing and responding appropriately to signs of annoyance, practice at home. When your child is doing something to irritate you or other family members, say, "Freeze!" Tell everyone not to move his or her body or face. Ask your child, "What are the signs that say you need to stop? What do you need to stop doing?" If you have more than one child, you can also call "Freeze!" when your Provocative Child is being bothered by a sibling. Have that sibling answer the same questions. This not only helps your Provocative Child feel less singled out but also gives him or her a chance to understand what it's like to be on the receiving end of exasperating behavior.

3. Seeing a Chain of Events: Pond Ripple Stories

In the story at the beginning of this section, we can readily see how Phillip's actions triggered Bruno's bullying, but for Phillip, the chain of events began when Bruno poured milk on him. If we asked Phillip why he thought Bruno poured milk on him, he would probably say, "I have no idea. He just all of a sudden did it. He is always picking on me." Provocative Children need to learn to recognize their role in inviting aggression. They need to see that other people's reactions don't usually come out of the blue. Every effect has at least one and often several causes.

In helping these children understand chains of events, our goal is *not* to blame them for being bullied but to give them a new sense of power and control. It must be terrifying for them to feel that they are suddenly and unpredictably attacked (verbally or physically). If Provocative Children become aware of chains of events, they won't feel so helpless.

One way to explain chains of events to your child is to make up what we call a Pond Ripple Story. These stories show how a little action, such as throwing a pebble in a pond, can create many ripples. Write an event involving some minor misbehavior in the center of a large piece of paper and circle it. For instance, you could write, "Tom went to see Mike's new puppy instead of going straight home after school, as he had promised." Explain to your child that every action causes ripple effects. Ask your child to think of what happens next and then write his or her response in a larger circle around the first event. Take turns with your child, thinking of consequences for more and more ripples. We've provided an example of a Pond Ripple Story. You and your child can come up with additional story starters or use some of these: "Jane threw sand in Margaret's face"; "George left his bike in the driveway"; "Grace told the teacher that Carla took her pencil"; "Stuart left his math homework on the bus."

A POND RIPPLE STORY

Tom went to see Mike's new puppy instead of going straight home after school, as he had promised.

Tom's mother became worried and called the school.

The principal said that Tom had left on time and that he was very concerned that Tom hadn't arrived home.

Tom's mother called several of his friends. None of them knew where he was. They offered to go out looking for Tom.

Tom's mother called his father at the office; he said he would come right home and suggested that she call the police.

Tom's mother called the police.

A police officer came to the house to get a description of Tom, then began to canvass the neighborhood.

The police officer found Tom at Mike's house and notified Tom's parents.

Tom's mother and father had to notify the principal and all of Tom's friends and neighbors that Tom was safe.

Tom was in deep trouble.

After your child creates some Pond Ripple Stories, you can use this idea to talk about events in his or her life. When your child complains, "It just happened" or "He did it for no reason," remind him or her about the pond ripples. Help your child identify the earlier ripples by asking, "What happened just before that? And before that? And before that?" Keep asking until you have the full story. Provocative Children focus only on the end of a series of events. They need help to spell out the full sequence and to discover their role in what happened.

Alternatively, when your child talks about doing something with short-term benefits but long-term costs, you can ask him or her to enumerate what the likely future ripples will be. You may want to actually write out the ripples on paper to make the consequences more graphic.

4. Discussing Likely Consequences of Possible Responses to Bullying

Provocative Children often act impulsively, without thinking about the likely consequences of their actions. Make a list with your child of potential responses to bullying. First, just write down alternatives that your child suggests, without commenting. Allow your child to consider any response, no matter how inappropriate. Be sure to include the following on your list.

Possible Responses to Bullying
- Ignoring it
- Running away
- Calling the other child names
- Threatening to beat up the other child
- Warning the other child about what you are going to do
- Pushing or hitting the other child
- Telling the teacher
- Staying near the teacher
- Staying near friendly kids
- Giving a strong retort
- Crying
- Telling the other child your feelings are hurt

- Avoiding the other child
- Using humor

After you've come up with a list of possible responses, help your child guess the likely consequences of each one. Ask your child the following questions:

Which responses will make it more or less likely that the bullying will continue?
Which responses will lead to an escalation of the aggression?
Which responses will get you in trouble with the teacher or other adults?
Which responses will be hardest or easiest for you to use?

This exercise could be eye-opening for both you and your child. Your child may be surprised to learn that there are so many options for responding to bullying. You may be surprised at how hard it is for your child to come up with possible strategies and to anticipate likely consequences. This exercise gives your child a chance to think in advance about how his or her responses come across to other children.

Emphasize that choosing the best strategy depends on the circumstances. Some children who bully will stop if they are ignored, but others won't. Sometimes it's safe to stay and give a strong retort; other times it's necessary to run for safety. Crying or saying that your feelings are hurt is almost always a mistake. Intimidating Children will probably react with laughter or indifference and take it as encouragement to continue being mean.

Try acting out some of the responses. You be your child and have your child take the role of the aggressor. We have found that role-play is an excellent way to help children understand other people's perspectives and anticipate the consequences of their own actions.

Your child may have some revenge fantasies about getting even with the Intimidating Child. He or she might say, "I could learn karate and kick him and chop him and break his bones," or "I could steal her backpack and throw it away," or "I could tell everyone lies about her." While the two of you are brainstorming solutions, just write these suggestions down without comment. When you go back to evaluate, acknowledge your child's feelings by saying something like "When you've been hurt by someone, it's very tempting to hurt them back." Then talk about the consequences of giving in to the temptation to get even. If your child does something unkind, what's to prevent the other child from doing something worse to retaliate? You may also want to ask how your child would feel about him- or herself after doing something as mean as the other child did.

TRANSIENT MEANNESS

Kids are mean to each other. There is no getting around it. We've talked about the extreme case, in which a child is continually cast in the role of a victim, but more subtle and more transient forms of meanness happen every day: a girl is excluded from a club that her friends just formed; a boy is the only one in his class not invited to a birthday party; bigger kids steal a younger child's lunch and play Monkey in the Middle, tossing it over his head; kids taunt a girl in gym class by calling her fat and saying she is too slow to play on their team. There is no question that these actions are unkind. The targets of this type of cruelty can be deeply hurt. If you are a parent of a child who has been mistreated in this way, you may feel justifiably outraged or protective.

However, there is just no escaping ordinary childhood aggression. We can't guarantee that siblings will always behave kindly toward one another. We certainly can't guarantee that schoolmates will always treat one another well. That doesn't imply that we accept or condone nastiness. We need to step in and teach our children about compassion, empathy, and acceptable behavior. At the same time, we need to recognize that teasing and churlishness are usually temporary. Today's victim is often tomorrow's perpetrator, and vice versa.

When children say that someone was mean to them, it's important to acknowledge their hurt or angry feelings, but it's also important not to overreact. If it's a minor or isolated event, you may want to encourage your child to "see how things go tomorrow." It is not uncommon for parents to stew and fret over their child's troubles with a fellow classmate only to find out the next day that the situation has been resolved.

The following Unwritten Rules and activities are designed to help children cope with the day-to-day friction that comes their way.

THE UNWRITTEN RULES

- You don't have to stay around people who are unkind to you.
- Relationships ebb and flow.
- It's easier to make friends one kid at a time than to take on a whole group.
- If one friend or group doesn't work out, consider others.

ACTIVITIES FOR LEARNING THE UNWRITTEN RULES

1. Weathering Unkindness

When your child has been the target of unkind words or actions, listen to him or her. Acknowledge how painful it is to be excluded or to be the brunt of teasing, but also tell your child to remember what this feels like so that he or she will be less likely to do the same thing to another child.

You may need to help your child put transient meanness in perspective. Explain to your child that all relationships have ups and downs. That's one good reason for having a variety of friends. If your child isn't getting along with one friend, he or she can hang out with someone else for a while. Your child doesn't have to stay around children who are unkind to him or her. On the other hand, it's silly to end a friendship over a minor tiff or transgression. Remind your child that there is no such thing as a "perfect friend." Sometimes it's best to ignore or laugh off mean behavior. Other times it helps to tell the other person, "Cut it out!" or "I don't like that!" If you think your child tends to overreact to teasing, you may want to read chapter 8, "The Sensitive Soul."

2. Seeing the Individuals in a Group

Sometimes children come home from school and complain, "Nobody likes me! Everybody hates me!" In most cases this is not true. If your child says this, he or she is probably focusing on the mean behavior of a few children and assuming that all the other children feel the same way. Facing an unfriendly group would be daunting for anyone, so you need to encourage your child to concentrate on individual children instead. You may even want to pull out your child's class roster or picture. Did every single child on that list call your child names, or was it just some kids? Which children seem nice? Whom would your child like to get to know better? One mother we know told her children, "Somewhere in your class is a child who is just waiting to be your friend. You need to figure out who it is." The one-at-a-time strategy can also help if your child has been rejected by a group of his or her former friends. Chances are that not everyone in the group feels strongly about excluding your child. Playing with the more accepting group members individually and building up those friendships can help patch things up. If your child has trouble initiating friendships with other children, you may want to look over some of the exercises in chapter 5, "The Shy Child."

THE HOME-SCHOOL CONNECTION

If you have a Vulnerable Child who is continually being picked on, you should definitely enlist the help of your child's teacher. Having the teacher keep a closer eye on the situation can prevent trouble. Also, the teacher can be an important source of information about what is really going on. He or she may be able to provide answers that your child can't. How does your child usually respond to bullying? Is your child doing something provocative to irritate other children? Is your child overreacting to ordinary meanness?

Providing Information About Bullying: You may want to volunteer to help your child's teacher put together a program for the whole class about minimizing bullying. At any given time, 80 percent of children are *not* involved in bullying or being victimized. These children can play a key role in defusing conflict and sticking up for the victims of aggression. Your school program can emphasize the following key points:

- Bullying means cruelty *plus* a power difference that makes it hard for victims to defend themselves.
- Not all bullying is physical.
- Nobody deserves to be bullied.
- When people watch bullying without doing anything to try to stop it, they are telling the child who bullies that it's okay to be cruel.
- *Tattling* means telling on someone just to get them in trouble. *Reporting* means telling on someone to protect a person's safety.

With your support, the teacher may be willing to introduce additional classroom activities to discourage bullying. You could offer to help the teacher make posters of class rules that encourage kindness, such as NO NAME-CALLING or YOU CAN'T SAY ANYONE CAN'T PLAY. The teacher could also write down students' acts of kindness on the board or make a special kindness bulletin board. When a goal is reached, such as a hundred acts of kindness, you can help organize a party so the whole class can celebrate. The child who contributed the most acts of kindness can win a prize.

If you are very concerned about bullying at your child's school, you may want to start a schoolwide initiative to decrease bullying, perhaps through the Parent-Teacher Association.

Fostering Peer Support: If the teacher prefers not to take a classroomwide approach, there are still things he or she can do to help your child. You may want to ask the teacher to assign a temporary buddy to stay near your child during lunch and recess and just before and after school. This will make your child less of a target for bullying. The buddy could be a popular child or a particularly kind child, or both.

Avoiding Provocative Behavior: If your child tends to be provocative, the teacher may be able to talk to him or her privately about the situation and perhaps use some prearranged signal to remind your child not to engage in a particular annoying behavior.

Meeting with the Intimidating Child: The teacher or the school counselor may be willing to have some weekly conferences with your child and the child who is bullying. These meetings can work wonders when they emphasize compassion for *both* children. Vulnerable Children feel empowered when they can safely talk to their aggressors about what they are going through. Intimidating Children gain compassion when they understand their victims' feelings. These conferences can even result in the Intimidating Child becoming the protector of the Vulnerable Child.

IF YOU TOO . . .

Bullying problems elicit very strong reactions from parents, especially parents who have been bullied themselves. If you were a Vulnerable Child, your past can provide you with a special understanding of what your child is going through. You've been there. You know how painful it is to be constantly intimidated or humiliated by peers. However, your experiences could lead you to identify too closely with your child. You may be extremely protective of your child. You may want to leap in and solve the problem before your child has had a chance to try to solve it. Empathize with your child but bear in mind that your child's feelings and capabilities are not necessarily the same as yours. You need to help your child find the solutions that are right for him or her.

You may also need to consider if the vulnerable role has continued for you into adulthood. Are you still unassertive? Is it hard for you to say no and mean it? Do you give in to avoid arguments? If you tell your child that it's important to stand up for oneself but then let other people intimidate you, your child is not going to learn self-respect. For your own sake and your child's sake, you may need to deal with these issues.

SUMMARY

Vulnerable Children are often the targets of bullying. For parents, there is nothing more wrenching than seeing their child get hurt, either physically or verbally. Vulnerable Children need the support and protection of adults. Their safety is the first concern, but we also need to give them coping strategies so that they can feel less vulnerable. They need to understand that the more they cringe or overreact to other children's taunts, the more they will get picked on. They need to learn how to avoid trouble and how to respond if they are threatened or harassed.

You Will Also Want to Read:

THE UNWRITTEN RULES FOR THE VULNERABLE CHILD AT A GLANCE

- Vulnerable body language attracts bullies.
- Giving in to a bully's demands has no end.
- Each time you allow yourself to be taken advantage of, you shrink a little inside.
- There is safety in numbers.
- Some situations require intervention by teachers or parents.
- Never provoke someone bigger or tougher than you.
- You don't have to announce your intentions.
- Staying out of harm's way is wise.
- Respect other people's space.
- Keep your hands to yourself.
- When someone says, "Stop," stop.
- If you hit someone, odds are they'll hit you back harder.
- If you call someone names, they are likely to call you something worse.

- You don't have to stay around people who are unkind to you.
- Relationships ebb and flow.
- It's easier to make friends one kid at a time than to take on a whole group.
- If one friend or group doesn't work out, consider others.

CHAPTER 3

The Intimidating Child

Does your child . . .

get in trouble for picking on weaker or younger children?

intimidate playmates?

seem not to care about other people's feelings?

get into a lot of fights but always insist that it's the other child's fault?

brag that he or she can beat up other kids?

justify being mean to others by saying, "They were asking for it" or "I had to teach them a lesson"?

Do you . . .

feel embarrassed when your child picks on younger or more vulnerable children?

feel shocked by how mean your child can be?

feel exasperated with your child's apparent lack of remorse?

worry that your child acts tough and disrespectful in elementary school and wonder what he or she will be like in high school?

wish your child would have more compassion for others?

feel glad that your child can defend him- or herself but worry that your child gets in trouble too often?

know your child has a good heart, even though he or she keeps
getting into trouble?

*I*t's hard to be the parent of an Intimidating Child — a child
who threatens or bullies weaker kids, and who comes across as un-
caring and belligerent. Parents of children who are picked on get
lots of sympathy. Other adults are quick to support their righteous
indignation. They feel sorry for victimized children and are eager to
help protect them. In contrast, parents of Intimidating Children
are judged guilty by association. Other adults are angry at these
parents for "allowing" their children to be cruel. They are quick to
criticize these parents and look down on them for having raised a
"bad" kid.

But the truth is that nobody *wants* to raise a child who is unkind.
Parents of Intimidating Children need support as much as parents of
victims do. Most parents are horrified when they hear that their child
is bullying someone. They often feel helpless to stop their child's
aggression. Most bullying takes place when the parents aren't even
around, and lecturing or punishing doesn't seem to help. Sometimes
the parents of an Intimidating Child are coping with major stressors
such as illness, marital conflict, or financial problems. Their child's
bullying may be a reaction to these difficulties. It's also yet another
thing that these parents have to deal with when they are already feeling overwhelmed.

As difficult as it is to be the parent of an Intimidating Child, it's even
harder to be that child. People are quick to dislike, dismiss, or condemn
Intimidating Children. They see them being deliberately cruel to other
children who can't defend themselves, and they forget that Intimidating Children are kids too. They think of them as villains rather than as
youngsters in need of help and guidance. Adults may even be tempted
to give children who bully a taste of their own medicine.

Intimidating Children don't help matters because, when confronted about their bullying, they behave in ways that discourage sympathy. They seem to enjoy hurting others, and they rarely admit to mistakes. Although some of these children are very smooth when dealing with adults, most tend to be argumentative and disrespectful. Intimidating Children often blame others for their misbehavior, and they can have an infuriating attitude of entitlement and superiority.

However, the "toughness" that Intimidating Children show the world is just a facade. These children are actually *more* likely than others to feel depressed, lonely, and inadequate. Intimidating Children try to control others because, inside, they feel vulnerable. Sometimes they feel overwhelmed by family changes or difficulties. Sometimes their sense of powerlessness comes from feeling personally flawed. Many of these children believe that they don't fit in with other kids, that they can't keep up academically at school, or that they aren't capable of meeting parental expectations. Often, children who bully have been bullied themselves. Acting aggressively gives them a temporary sense of control — a brief respite from their own feelings of helplessness. The more inadequate they feel, the more they will try to cover up these feelings by intimidating other children. This is a desperate coping strategy that provides a false and fragile sense of worthiness.

The feelings of inferiority that Intimidating Children work so hard to camouflage don't necessarily reflect reality. Children often overestimate their role in situations or overinterpret the significance of events. It's common, for instance, for children to see their parents' divorce as somehow their fault. They may see their struggles with math as a sign that they are completely stupid. They may have an exaggerated idea of parental expectations. They may hear an older brother jokingly call them "wimpy" or "ugly" and really believe it.

On the other hand, children often learn to hurt and intimidate because they have been treated harshly themselves. Children who are physically hurt by parents, caretakers, siblings, or other children don't learn to respect authority or to stand up for themselves — they learn that "might makes right." Children who are regularly subjected to put-downs don't "toughen up" or "straighten out" — they learn that ridicule is acceptable and that intimidation gets you what you want.

ON THE POSITIVE SIDE

With intervention, Intimidating Children can become assertive leaders or even passionate defenders of the weak. Once they gain better self-understanding, improved self-control, and a greater sense of self-worth, they are capable of having more compassion for others. They can learn to redirect their "fighting spirit" away from hurting others and toward achieving positive goals.

SO, WHAT CAN WE DO?

Intimidating Children need to learn that bullying gives them a *false* sense of power. It makes others afraid of them rather than connected to them. Often, children who bully are copying the aggressiveness that they themselves have experienced and trying to mask an inner sense of helplessness and inadequacy. Simply punishing Intimidating Children doesn't work. While they need clear limits on their aggressive behavior, they also need help identifying and remedying the source of their feelings of vulnerability, and learning better ways of relating.

In this chapter, we describe three Intimidating Children. Jason gets into trouble with school authorities because he resorts to physical aggression to try to get respect from a peer. Dolores leads a group of girls in excluding another child. Jennifer bullies her younger sister.

Jason: Believing "Might Makes Right"

"Thank you for coming in today on such short notice, Mrs. King," the principal, Dr. White, began. "As I told you on the phone, I'm very concerned about the fact that Jason has been bullying another child. Today's incident was particularly distressing."

Mrs. King glanced at her son, who sat next to her, staring at his shoes. This was not the first time that the principal had called her in to talk about Jason's aggressive behavior. She sighed and turned back to the principal. "What did he do this time?"

"He shoved a younger child on the playground and caused him to have a bloody nose." Dr. White looked sternly at Jason. "Well, young man? What do you have to say for yourself?"

"He started it . . . ," Jason began.

The principal interrupted, "Our school policy says that violence is never acceptable."

"Rob was calling me 'butthead,' and I couldn't take it any more. He can't get away with calling me names!" Jason said.

"Jason," Dr. White said, "this is not an isolated incident. I am afraid a pattern is developing here. This is the fourth time since the beginning of the school year that you have been sent to my office for fighting on the playground. This has to stop."

Mrs. King sighed again. "I just don't know what to do. I've tried talking with Jason . . . I've tried punishing him . . . I've even taken away his Nintendo. Nothing helps."

Intimidating Children aren't born to bully others. They *learn* to do it. They do it because they can, because it works, and because it temporarily makes them feel powerful.

About half to two thirds of children who bully are ringleaders who initiate aggression. The rest are followers — they don't start the bullying but readily join in. They like the feelings of excitement and power they get from hanging out with ringleaders. In early elementary school, some children may look up to these tough kids because they seem powerful and get what they want, but by high school, most kids dislike and avoid Intimidating Children.

Bullying is not usually something that children outgrow on their own. Children who are identified as bullies by their classmates in elementary school are likely to continue to be aggressive as adults. If your child intimidates others, he or she needs your help *now* to change what could otherwise be a lifelong pattern that can cause personal, professional, and even legal problems.

The immediate goal in working with children who bully is to stop their hurtful behavior. These children need clear limits and closer supervision, particularly before and after school, which are prime times for bullying. If your work or other commitments prevent you from watching your child at these times, you may need to enlist the help of a friend, relative, or sitter, or consider an extended care program. Intimidating Children need to know that the adults in their lives won't let them hurt other people *and* won't let other people hurt them. Refuse to listen to any excuses that your child might offer to justify his or her cruelty. Bullying other children is simply unacceptable.

Intimidating Children are trapped in an unhealthy pattern of behavior that in the long run hurts them as much as it hurts their victims. On some level, they are often frightened by what they have done and by what they have been able to get away with. Your child may complain about additional supervision and strictly enforced rules, but knowing that an adult is willing and able to step in and set limits can be immensely reassuring.

For your child's sake, you need to establish a cooperative effort between home and school. Arrange for the school to notify you promptly if your child hurts or intimidates another child. Decide on some reasonable consequences for aggressive behavior that you can enforce immediately and consistently, and inform your child of them *in advance*. These should be meaningful to your child but of relatively short duration so that your child can have the chance to try using more acceptable behaviors soon. A logical consequence for being unkind is not being allowed to be around other children for a while. One to three days of being grounded, doing without play dates, or having phone privileges revoked are good possibilities. Longer or more severe punishments make children focus on the punishment rather than their misbehavior. You may also want to require that your child make amends by replacing broken possessions or by writing an apology. Remember, once the punishment is over, it's over. Let your child start again with a clean slate.

To really help children who bully, however, we need to address the underlying problems. (This may require therapy with a mental health professional.) We need to figure out what is going on in their lives that makes them feel powerless or inadequate, and remedy it if possible. We also need to teach them better ways of relating to people that don't involve dominating or submitting. The Unwritten Rules and the following exercises can help.

THE UNWRITTEN RULES

- Violence creates more problems than it solves.
- Real control is self-control, not control of others.
- Being feared is not the same as being liked or respected.
- To get respect, show respect.

ACTIVITIES FOR LEARNING
THE UNWRITTEN RULES

1. Valuing Kindness

The best antidote for bullying is to teach your child to value kindness. Encouraging kindness not only shows children more satisfying ways of relating to others but also helps them to feel happier and to like themselves more. Helping others is one of the best ways to improve mood and self-esteem.

Catch your child being kind. When he or she entertains a younger sibling or holds the door open for someone at the mall or brings you your glasses, say, "Thank you. That was kind of you." Read Conari Press's *Kids' Random Acts of Kindness* with your child or check out the Web site www.actsofkindness.org. Both emphasize that little acts of kindness add up to make a better world.

Consider participating in charitable activities as a family. You could spend a day working together on a Habitat for Humanity project. You could visit a nursing home and bring treats or even put on a show for the residents. You could volunteer to help out at the Special Olympics or at a clean-up day in a nearby park. You could even have a garage sale and give a portion of the proceeds to charity. Let your child help choose which charities receive donations of family time or money. All of these ideas teach your child about kindness and compassion for others.

2. Offering a New Role

Amazingly, only one sixth of children whose classmates think they are bullies see themselves in that role. Most of them see themselves as protectors of other children. This suggests that a good strategy for helping children who bully is to encourage them to use their strength and cleverness to help others.

Read William J. Bennett's *The Children's Book of Heroes* with your child. Talk about what makes someone a hero. Which hero does your child admire most? Why? Tell your child about the people you admire and describe their heroic qualities. Stories about ancestors or older relatives who behaved in heroic ways can be especially inspiring because these people seem closer to home than celebrities do.

Talk with your child about the difference between *fear* and *respect*. True heroes inspire respect rather than fear. We admire them, seek them out, and want to be like them. When we fear someone, we may go along with what they want, but we secretly resent them. We hope someone will come along and "put them in their place." Some children who bully do so because they believe others will respect them if they fear them. Explain that the best way to get respect is to treat others with respect.

Tell your child that people have the opportunity to be heroic every single day. Rescuing a frightened toddler from the top of a jungle gym, helping someone with a homework assignment, and speaking up to stop unkindness to others are all acts of heroism. Anything that helps someone in trouble is heroic. Who in your child's school or neighborhood needs protection? Which classmate has no friends and could use a sponsor? You may want to give your child the opportunity to tutor younger children (other than siblings) so he or she can feel like a hero.

While you are promoting true heroism, it's a good idea to minimize how much time your child spends watching violent television shows or playing violent video games. These promote a false idea of heroism based on aggression. Seeing hours of violence also dulls your child's empathy for other people's pain. Children who already have problems with being too aggressive are particularly vulnerable to the negative influence of violent media.

3. Avoiding Power Struggles

Avoiding power struggles is a good idea with any child but is especially important with Intimidating Children, who tend to see all interactions in terms of dominance and submission. We've listed some tips for fostering cooperation below.

Avoiding Criticism: Try not to criticize your child. A brief descriptive statement such as "The trash is overflowing" or "Coats belong in the closet" will produce more cooperation and less resentment than a barked order such as "Go do it this instant!" or a resentful tirade along the lines of "What's the matter with you? How many times do I have to tell you?"

Offering Choices: Give your child choices, when possible, about which task to do and when or how to do it.

Emphasizing the Positive: Emphasize what your child *can* do rather than what he or she can't do. Try to turn your no into a yes. "Yes, you can go over to John's house after you pick up your room."

Working Together: Do chores together. It's more fun to tackle a job as a team than to do it alone.

Avoiding Threats: Avoid using threats. Statements beginning with the word *if* are threats. "If you don't make your bed, you're going to school without breakfast." This statement can make a child feel resistant and resentful. It makes them dig in their heels and think, *You can't make me!* Try using the word *when* instead of *if.* "When your bed is made, you may have breakfast." This statement expresses the same idea as the earlier statement, but it has a very different tone. It implies confidence that your child will have the good sense to do what has to be done.

Avoiding Interrogation: When your child misbehaves, don't take the role of prosecuting attorney. There is no benefit in wringing a confession out of your child ("Did you do that?") or demanding that he or she explain the misbehavior ("Why did you do that?"). Being interrogated about their "crimes" makes children feel defensive. It tempts them to lie and to look for excuses. You both know what your child did. It doesn't matter why he or she did it because it's unacceptable behavior. Go from there. Enforce reasonable consequences. Look for ways for your child to make amends. When you are both feeling calm, talk about different ways your child could have handled the situation.

Having Fun with Your Child: Play with your child. Laugh together. Be silly. Too often, we get so caught up in the daily grind that we forget how important it is to just enjoy each other and have fun together. Don't wait for elaborate outings or carefully planned occasions. Try to make fun part of your everyday life. Use a goofy accent when you ask your child what he or she wants for lunch. Tell jokes. Dance. Teach your child the twist or the bunny hop. Have a kids-versus-adults pillow fight. One of our favorite books, *Simple Fun for Busy People: 333 Ways to Enjoy Your Loved Ones in the Time You Have* by Gary Krane, has hundreds of silly ideas, all of which are completely incompatible with the grim power struggles in which Intimidating Children are often trapped.

Dolores: Excluding Another Child

Dolores walked into the coatroom, saying in a loud voice, "Ewww, there's Creepy Clara! Don't put your coat near hers or you'll get cooties." The other girls quickly scrambled to move their coats to hooks that were farther away. "Courtney, you touched her! You have cooties now!" Dolores pronounced.

"No, I didn't!" Courtney protested, dancing around. "I wouldn't go near her with a ten-foot pole!"

Clara stood silently, enduring the ridicule, with her back to the other girls. Tears came to her eyes.

"Quick, everyone!" Dolores commanded. "Let's run before Cootie Girl touches us." Snickering, the girls scampered into the classroom, leaving Clara behind.

Adults overhearing this kind of teasing and taunting are likely to dismiss it as childhood foolishness and not even respond. Who cares about cooties? They aren't real. However, when teasing is targeted and persistent, when it routinely separates a child from the group, it can wound a child even more deeply than physical blows. Dolores's remarks make Clara feel worthless and ostracized. The other girls don't dare to question Dolores because each one is afraid that she'll be the next victim. Whenever groups of children gang up on a single child, either physically or verbally, it constitutes bullying and must not be tolerated.

Why is Dolores picking on Clara? How can she be so unkind? If we talked to Dolores about this incident, she would probably say that it was no big deal. She was just kidding around.

Adults often find it exasperating or even infuriating when children who bully trivialize the suffering of their victims. But these children are out of touch with even their own feelings. They readily talk about how "ticked off" they are, but they find it hard to acknowledge feeling sad or lonely or hurt, even to themselves. These feelings are too frightening for them to think about or even recognize. Instead, they use aggression to cover up their inner sense of powerlessness and inadequacy.

Intimidating Children are drawn to less-powerful children, but they are also put off by them. At some level, they identify with the vulnerability of the child they pick on, but they also want to push this weakness away. Dolores truly can't explain why she picks on Clara, but she does know that Clara bugs her. She also knows that she gets a kick out of having all the other girls go along with her in tormenting Clara. Intimidating Children want to prove that they are nothing like their victims. It's almost as though they believe that if they can stomp on other people's weakness, they will stomp out their own.

The Unwritten Rules and the following activities are about compassion. Most Intimidating Children don't realize that feelings matter. They need help learning to understand and to respect other people's feelings *and* their own.

THE UNWRITTEN RULES

- Do unto others as you would have them do unto you.
- Words can wound.
- Just because you don't like some people doesn't mean you should be nasty to them.
- You can't build yourself up by putting other people down.

ACTIVITIES FOR LEARNING THE UNWRITTEN RULES

1. Decreasing Meanness

If you see your child being unkind to another child, talk to him or her about it privately. Sometimes children don't even realize they are being mean. One girl we know, speaking about a former friend, told her mother, "I'm not being mean to her; I'm just completely ignoring her." Explain to your child how his or her actions probably make the other child feel. Mention any signs you notice of the other child's distress: "Her face just crumbled after you said that"; "Did you see how he kind of hunched over and walked away slowly after you told him he couldn't play?" Talk about treating people with courtesy, even if you don't like them. Be specific about what that means. You may want to make a list with your child of dos and don'ts for minimum acceptable behavior: "Don't call people names"; "Do greet people who greet you"; "Don't push anyone."

Make sure your child knows that being unkind makes him or her seem *less* attractive to other kids. Nobody thinks, *Oh, I'd like to be friends with her because I've seen her be so nasty,* or *He seems like a great guy because he's always pushing people around.*

2. Acknowledging Feelings and Cultivating Empathy

Although a baby will burst into tears when other babies cry, true empathy develops over a lifetime. Children don't fully develop the cognitive ability to put themselves in another person's shoes until around nine years of age. Adults are generally better at understanding other people's feelings when they are thirty-eight than when they are eighteen because they have more of their own life experience to draw upon in guessing how others feel. However, this doesn't mean that you should wait until age nine or thirty-eight to teach your child to care about others.

Children need lots of exposure and coaching to learn to understand other people's feelings. Although they won't fully master this skill for a while, you can begin teaching your children about empathy when they are less than a year old. A young baby has no concept of other people's feelings, but when you take her hand and say, "Nice," and show her how to stroke your cheek gently instead of swat at it, you are beginning to show her how other people want to be treated. A four-year-old can't fully grasp his younger brother's yearning to be included in his play, but he can learn that you expect him to take turns and that his brother will shriek if he doesn't. He will also understand when you point to his sobbing sibling and say, "Look, his feelings are hurt."

By elementary school, children are ready to label feelings, to guess at how other people might be feeling, and to begin to understand causes and consequences of feelings and behavior. You can help your child learn to become more empathic by talking about characters in books or on TV. Start by just commenting on a character's reaction to an event: "She sure is mad!"; "He seems excited." Work up to asking your child questions about characters' feelings: "How are they feeling?"; "How do you know they feel that way?"; "Why are they feeling that way?"; "What could they do to make themselves feel better?"; "Do the characters like each other? Why or why not?" One or two questions at a time is plenty, and you don't have to do this every time you and your child open a book or turn on the TV. If your child seems irritated by your questions, stop.

Talking about characters' feelings can be helpful, but the most important thing you can do to help your child become more empathic is to help your child talk about his or her own feelings. The basis of empathy is an awareness of our own feelings. Talking with children about their feelings not only helps them to understand these feelings better but also shows them that their feelings matter and that they will be treated with compassion. Many children give one-word answers when asked "How was your day?" You may find that specific questions work better: "How was the math test?"; "Whom did you play with at recess?"; "What did you do in gym?" Avoid "why" questions because they often make children feel defensive. You may want to create a dinnertime ritual in which each family member gets a turn to report the best and worst things that happened to him or her that day.

Keep in mind that some children need time to open up. It's common for children to start out by giving one-word answers to questions about a big event and then to fill their parents in on their thoughts, feelings, or experiences later, a dribble at a time, over the course of a day or several days. Dr. William S. Pollack, author of *Real Boys: Rescuing Our Sons from the Myths of Boyhood,* describes how boys often need a period of silence before they feel ready to share their feelings. They are also more likely to talk while doing some activity rather than in response to direct questions.

As your child talks about the day, try to make comments that acknowledge his or her feelings: "How frustrating!"; "Boy, that must have been scary!"; "You seem kind of down."; "It sounds like you're really mad at her!"; "I bet that hurt your feelings." Be careful not to be heavy-handed or judgmental about this. Lecturing or getting upset will discourage your child from sharing in the future.

Sometimes children are worried or upset about something but don't know how to bring up the topic or don't want to discuss it in front of their siblings. If you suspect this is the case for your child, you may want to set up a little mailbox in your room, where your child can slip you a note. Some children find it easier to write rather than talk about things that make them feel worried, sad, or angry. If your child sends you a note, find a private time to talk about it. Acknowledge your child's feelings ("You're really upset about this."; "I can see why that bugs you."). Try to hold off on giving advice; just give your child a chance to see that you understand how he or she is feeling and that you care.

If you can manage it, it's wonderful to spend ten minutes or so one-on-one with your child at the end of the day, when you tuck him or her in bed. If you can't do it during the week, maybe you can fit it in on the weekends. For many children, this quiet time gives them a chance to confide in you. But even if they don't share any earth-shattering secrets, this time lets them feel cared about. Turn the lights off. Stroke your child's hair, give him or her a back rub, or just snuggle together. They may be embarrassed to admit it, but "big" elementary school kids need cuddling just like babies and toddlers do.

Jennifer: Bullying a Sibling

Lois was watching her favorite cartoon, when her older sister, Jennifer, sauntered into the room, plopped down on the couch beside her, and casually clicked the remote to a different channel. "Hey! I was watching that!" Lois protested, lunging for the remote.

"So what?" Jennifer responded, elbowing Lois out of the way and tucking the remote securely under her arm.

"You're making me miss my favorite show!" Lois cried.

"It's a stupid show, anyway," Jennifer replied in a bored voice, not even bothering to look at Lois.

"Turn it back!" Lois screeched. "I was here first!"

"Get lost, brat," Jennifer said, snatching the bag of potato chips that Lois had in her lap.

"I'm telling!" Lois cried.

"Go ahead. Run to Mommy like the baby that you are," taunted Jennifer as she continued to watch her show.

What Jennifer did to Lois is more than ordinary sibling squabbling — it's bullying. She is taking advantage of the fact that she is bigger and stronger than Lois, and she is treating Lois like a nonentity.

It is astonishing how unkind siblings can be to each other. They are adept at knowing each other's most vulnerable points and using this knowledge to hurt each other. They may tease each other mercilessly, lie to get each other in trouble, steal or destroy each other's things, pinch or hit each other, or threaten and demand outrageous "service." Familiarity breeds insensitivity. It's almost as if children believe that it doesn't "count" if they hurt a sibling. Brothers and sisters don't seem like real people with real feelings to them. In some ways, sibling bullying is even worse than schoolyard bullying because it is inescapable.

You can't make your kids like each other, but you can insist that they treat each other with respect. Recognize that people who live together are going to get mad at each other. Talk with your children about good ways of resolving grievances. Get the kids involved in (1) deciding what kind of family you all want to be and (2) setting up some family rules to make sure this happens.

Be very careful not to compare siblings or to assign them to roles, such as the "good kid" and the "bad kid." If you see patterns developing, you need to go out of your way to give your children opportunities to break out of their roles. Both the "helpless victim" role and the "cruel bully" role are terribly limiting and self-destructive.

All children need their parents to give them a chance to behave in kind and considerate ways. Put your child in charge of holding the baby gently or pushing a toddler safely on a tricycle or teaching a sibling the right way to throw a football. You show your confidence in your child when you give him or her responsibility and say, "I know you can do this." Praise your children's kindness lavishly. Let them overhear you mentioning their kind deeds to other adults. Be sure not to spoil your praise by bringing up past mistakes or suggesting that it's about time that they did something nice.

Sibling squabbles are the bane of any parent with more than one child, but they are also a golden opportunity for learning to deal with the power issues that are so difficult for Intimidating Children. When you have two angry or upset children, you can help them both learn about negotiation and compromise. When you have one angry or upset child and one gleeful or indifferent child, it's a chance to teach compassion.

THE UNWRITTEN RULES

- Getting along with siblings is good practice for getting along with others.
- Sibling relationships are lifelong.
- A younger sibling will grow up and remember.

ACTIVITIES FOR LEARNING
THE UNWRITTEN RULES

1. Learning About Negotiation and Compromise

Parents are often advised to let siblings work their problems out on their own. However, this advice only makes sense if siblings already know how to solve their problems. The truth is that often you *do* need to step in on your children's quarrels to prevent cruelty and to teach your children constructive ways to resolve conflicts.

You need to draw the line for your children concerning what is or isn't acceptable behavior. If your children are physically hurting each other, say, "Stop! It's not safe for you two to be near each other now," and then separate them. When they are shrieking insults at each other, say, "Stop! In this family we don't scream at each other, and we don't call each other names." If you are not sure whether your kids are fighting or just wrestling, ask them, "Are you both enjoying this?" If either child says no, put an end to it.

You may need to help your children to express their viewpoints constructively. "Use your words to tell your sister what you want, in a calm voice." Sometimes it helps to describe the problem for your children and to establish an expectation of peaceful resolution: "I see two kids who want to watch two different television programs. What can we do that's fair to everyone?" When the problem is laid out objectively, children can often come up with reasonable solutions. If they really have no ideas, offer several suggestions and let them agree on one. Don't let your children put you in the role of final judge and arbitrator. Help them with the process of problem-solving, if necessary, but make it clear that choosing and implementing a solution is up to them. Sometimes all your kids require is for you to say, "I'm sure you two can come up with a fair compromise."

2. Finding Compassion

Sibling conflicts can also provide a chance to teach empathy and compassion or at least to show that cruelty doesn't pay. Suppose a younger sibling deliberately breaks an older sibling's elaborate Lego construction, or suppose an older sibling teases a younger sibling to the point of tears by squirting the younger sibling's favorite toy with water. When only one of two children is feeling angry or upset, console the injured party (thereby preventing that sibling from doing something equally nasty to retaliate). As you do so, make a point of describing in detail how that child is feeling, *without* criticizing the perpetrator. "You worked so hard on those Legos! It took you days to build that tower and make it so fancy. It's so frustrating to see it broken up now." Or, "Oh, look at that sad face! You're so upset that your favorite toy is all wet." Then, turn to the perpetrator and, without accusing him or her, ask, "What can you do to help your sister / brother feel better?" If the perpetrator decides to do something kind to remedy the situation, thank him or her and point out how much better the injured sibling feels. There is no need to mention that the perpetrator caused the upset in the first place. If the perpetrator says there is nothing he or she can do to help, remark casually, "Oh, I'm sure you could think of something if you tried." For a younger child, you may want to offer a suggestion (e.g., help rebuild, get some paper towels), but for an older child who really knows how to help, say nothing more. Go back to consoling the injured party for a moment, giving the perpetrator one more chance to help, then take care of the situation yourself with no further comment. The perpetrator has plenty to think about — much more than if you had simply scolded or demanded, "How could you do that?" He or she can make a different choice next time. When you do all of this, you help your child to see that cruelty hurts, induce some healthy guilt, and, most important, give your child a chance to choose to behave in a kind way.

THE HOME-SCHOOL CONNECTION

If your child is getting into trouble at school for bullying or intimidating other children, it is essential that you talk to the teacher. You should reassure the teacher that you take this behavior seriously and that you are willing to do whatever is necessary to stop it. Ask the teacher to inform you promptly if your child is unkind to another child so that you can follow up at home. The teacher may be able to tell you exactly what your child is doing and with whom. Knowing the circumstances under which your child hurts others is essential for knowing how to prevent it. Talk with the teacher about ways to keep your child apart from the classmate he or she picks on and from other children who encourage bullying (as either ringleaders or followers). Include your child in the teacher conference if you can so that he or she sees the seriousness of the issue and understands that cruel behavior will not be tolerated.

You shouldn't make excuses for your child's actions, but you may want to talk with the teacher (when your child is not present) about what is going on in your child's life that makes him or her feel powerless. This can help the teacher develop a sympathetic view of your child. Alternatively, if you don't know why your child is feeling helpless or inadequate, the teacher may have some ideas about what is wrong and how to help. Academic difficulties are common among children who bully, and you may need the school's help to deal with learning problems.

Offering a New Role: Brainstorm with the teacher about ways to offer your child a new role with more satisfying ways of relating to others. What responsibilities could the teacher give your child? Are there other children whom your child could be assigned to help somehow?

Could your child be a tutor in reading, writing, or math for a child in a younger grade? We have been deeply touched by how gentle and patient "tough" kids can be when they are given the chance to work with younger children. If the teacher is involved in setting up your child's new role, he or she is more likely to notice and praise your child's progress.

Communicating with the Vulnerable Child: The teacher or the school counselor may be willing to have some weekly conferences with your child and the child he or she has picked on. The point of these meetings is to give *both* children an opportunity to clear the air. When Intimidating Children have a chance to hear directly about the pain that their actions have caused, they can begin to see their victims as people. They may feel guilt or remorse for the suffering they have caused. Feeling guilty can be a healthy internal signal that tells us we need to do something differently or make amends. If Intimidating Children are able to understand the impact of their behavior, they'll want to change. Sometimes these conferences result in the Intimidating Child becoming the protector of the Vulnerable Child, creating a win-win situation for both kids.

IF YOU TOO . . .

If you were also an Intimidating Child, you may have a tendency to minimize or justify your child's actions. This can be a mistake. It alienates school personnel and keeps your child trapped and isolated in a role that can have devastating long-term consequences.

You may need to ask yourself whether your childhood role has continued into adulthood. No one sets out to be intimidating, but sometimes, especially when we are under a lot of stress, old, unhappy patterns of relating can resurface. Maybe you are just copying the way your parents acted because that's what's familiar to you. If you don't like what you see, you owe it to yourself and your child to learn new ways of relating.

Listen to how you talk to your family. Are there too many orders and threats? Is it hard for you to admit it when you are wrong? Do you sometimes "lose it" when you get mad and resort to name-calling or even get physical? Take an honest look at your parenting style. Do you tend to be too lenient or too harsh? too inconsistent? too grim? Do the consequences of your child's behavior depend more on your mood than on what your child has done? What about your relationship with your spouse (or ex-spouse)? Is there too much conflict or too little respect?

These are difficult questions to ask yourself, but your child's well-being may depend on your willingness to face the answers. Children's understanding of relationships comes from what they see us do rather than what we tell them. If you talk about the value of kindness but then ridicule others, your child won't learn compassion. If you talk about the importance of self-control but hit your child when you are angry, your child won't learn restraint. If you talk about taking turns but then cut into a long line of waiting people, your child won't learn to respect others. As parents, it's our job to show children that relationships are about caring rather than power.

In addition, you may need to do a better job taking care of yourself so that you can take better care of your child. You can't be a good parent if you are constantly feeling overwhelmed. Being a parent is a demanding job for anyone, but it can be especially so for the parents of Intimidating Children. You may have to make real changes in your life, involving work, relationships, or child care, to reduce your stress level. You should definitely do something to sustain yourself. This could be a relaxing hobby, exercise, meditation, or a regular night out with friends or your spouse. Maybe you just need to take a few minutes before you pick up your child from school or before you come home from work to center yourself by remembering how much you love your child and by thinking about the kind of parent you want to be.

SUMMARY

Intimidating Children threaten or bully weaker kids in order to cover up their own sense of vulnerability. To help them, we need to address the source of their feelings of powerlessness or inadequacy. We also need to teach them more satisfying ways of relating to others. Once they learn to have compassion for themselves, they are better able to have compassion for others.

You Will Also Want to Read:
   Chapter 6, "The Short-Fused Child"
   Chapter 9, "The Born Leader"
   Chapter 10, "The Pessimistic Child"

THE UNWRITTEN RULES FOR THE INTIMIDATING CHILD AT A GLANCE

- Violence creates more problems than it solves.
- Real control is self-control, not control of others.
- Being feared is not the same as being liked or respected.
- To get respect, show respect.
- Do unto others as you would have them do unto you.
- Words can wound.
- Just because you don't like some people doesn't mean you should be nasty to them.

- You can't build yourself up by putting other people down.
- Getting along with siblings is good practice for getting along with others.
- Sibling relationships are lifelong.
- A younger sibling will grow up and remember.

CHAPTER 4

The Different Drummer

Does your child . . .

often act silly or obnoxious around other kids?

tend to barge in, disrupting classmates' games or conversations?

talk nonstop?

frequently irritate other children?

sometimes scare away potential friends by coming on too strong?

feel jealous when a friend has another friend?

complain that other kids avoid him or her?

tend to be oblivious to other people's reactions?

Do you . . .

wonder why your child always seems like an outsider in a group?

wish your child would act his or her age?

fear that your child's irritating habits might drive other children away?

find yourself frequently telling your child, "Don't do that! It's annoying."

feel exasperated because your child is so clueless about how his or her behavior affects others?

feel sad because your child is a nice kid who really wants friends but keeps getting rebuffed?

*D*ifferent Drummers are the children who always seem to be out of step with their peers. They have trouble fitting in because they don't pick up on the general rhythm of social interactions. Their behavior seems jarring. Different Drummers have trouble predicting and understanding other people's responses, so they consistently show poor social judgment. They always seem to make bad decisions about what to do, and when and where to do it.

Most Different Drummers want to make friends, but they go about it all wrong and end up pushing others away. Because they don't know how to relate to other children appropriately, they resort to self-defeating tactics. They might interrupt an ongoing game or do gross things in public. They might ask overly personal questions or talk on and on in endless detail about a topic that bores listeners. They often think they are being friendly or funny, but their peers find them annoying. Their out-of-sync behavior can prevent them from fitting in with their peers. Other children feel uncomfortable around them and may even avoid them. Sometimes, Different Drummers are targets of bullying. (If this is the case with your child, see chapter 2, "The Vulnerable Child.")

Different Drummers are *not* simply children who have unusual interests or who like spending time alone. There are children who seem content being apart from the crowd, but they usually have one or two friends who share their interests, as well as a sense of self-confidence that enables them to go off the beaten path. Although they might benefit from learning some new ways to relate to their peers (see chapter 7, "The Little Adult"), they generally seem comfortable creating their own niche. In contrast, Different Drummers stand out, not by choice but because of their social blunders. These children are lonely. They don't realize that their behavior places a wedge between them and their peers, so they feel hurt and bewildered when other children reject them.

Different Drummers often struggle with what Drs. Marshall P. Duke and Stephen Nowicki Jr., authors of *Helping the Child Who Doesn't Fit In*, call "dyssemia," which they define as "difficulty understanding and using nonverbal signs or signals." These children don't know how to read other people's body language, and they routinely send the wrong nonverbal message themselves. They stand too close to people; they tap people repeatedly in an irritating way to get their attention; they talk too loudly; they laugh when everyone else is being serious. According to Dr. Albert Mehrabian, a pioneering researcher in the field of nonverbal communication, 55 percent of the emotional meaning of a message is carried through facial expression, posture, and gestures. Another 38 percent of meaning comes from tone of voice. The actual words we speak convey only 7 percent of meaning. So, when Different Drummers fail to register nonverbal cues, they miss about 90 percent of social communication. This puts them at a tremendous disadvantage in relating to others.

Underneath it all, Different Drummers are usually nice kids who want to have friends. They generally have good intentions. Even when they do unkind things, like snatching someone's toy or scribbling on someone's artwork, they usually do them out of ignorance rather than malice. It's not that these children don't care about other people's feelings — they just have a hard time predicting how others will react and don't know any other way to get kids to notice them. If they can get over the initial hurdle of establishing a relationship, Different Drummers often settle down and behave more appropriately. Given a chance, they can be good friends. Unfortunately, they rarely get this chance because their annoying behaviors keep their peers away. Seeing these children who so desperately want to be liked get rejected again and again is heartbreaking.

ON THE POSITIVE SIDE

Once they get past their initial difficulties, Different Drummers can be loyal and caring companions. They treasure their friends, and they can be exceptionally warm and giving to the people they care about.

Some Different Drummers are very creative. Not being part of the crowd may foster a unique ability to think "outside the box." Some of our most celebrated artists, writers, musicians, entrepreneurs, and scientists had trouble fitting in as children. Many Different Drummers have an offbeat, quirky sense of humor that can be very entertaining. Some of these children are full of ideas and have a special exuberance that makes them fun to be around.

Once they understand how to connect with others in positive and appropriate ways, Different Drummers can develop healthy, reciprocal friendships. They can learn to make thoughtful choices about who would make a good friend. Moreover, as they develop a greater sense of inner confidence, they will have less need to resort to annoying behaviors.

SO, WHAT CAN WE DO?

The goal with Different Drummers is to help them gain a clearer understanding of how their behavior is viewed by others. They don't have to give up all of their uniqueness, but they will have an easier time socially if they can find a way to be their own person without turning everyone off. Different Drummers need to learn to express liking for other children without annoying or overwhelming them. They need to learn how to blend in to a group and how to recognize signs that enough is enough. They need to understand that lasting friendships build gradually. They also need to accept that their friends will have other friends, and to understand that this is not a betrayal.

As you discuss the Unwritten Rules and work on the exercises in this chapter, you may need to caution your child that it will take time for peers to notice any changes in his or her behavior. Unfortunately, Different Drummers have already established a reputation for being annoying. One instance of being appropriately friendly won't instantly change their peers' perceptions, because reputations die hard. However, a consistent effort will definitely pay off. As your child's behavior improves, he or she can gradually build a base of support by having one-on-one play dates with different children. As more classmates come to know and like your child, his or her reputation will gradually improve.

Your child should think carefully about which classmates seem appealing and would be most open to friendship. Someone who has been especially vocal in expressing irritation with your child would not be a good choice — no matter how "cool" that classmate is. Someone who already has many friends might not be available. Someone who seems kind or tolerant and who isn't already paired up with a best friend offers your child the best chance for a relationship. There are many nice kids who aren't part of the "in crowd" who could be wonderful friends for your child.

In this chapter we describe three Different Drummers. Eric tries to engage other children by acting obnoxious. Spencer talks nonstop, which is confusing and off-putting to others. Chelsea wants an instant and exclusive best friend. She comes on too strong, in a way that is likely to be overwhelming to her peers.

Eric: Seeking Negative Attention

"He's doing it again," Ana informed her friend Emily as the two girls unpacked their lunches.

With a disgusted noise, Emily looked over at the next lunch table and saw Eric watching her fixedly. "Quit staring at me, Eric!" she snapped.

"Quit staring at me!" Eric mimicked.

"Cut it out!" Emily said.

"Cut it out!" Eric repeated.

"You're so weird, Eric!" Ana said.

"You're so weird, Eric!" he repeated.

"You're acting like a kindergartner," Ana scolded.

"You're acting like a kindergartner," Eric echoed.

"Let's just go sit somewhere else," Emily said, gathering up her lunch. She and Ana quickly moved to a table on the other side of the room.

Why is Eric antagonizing the girls? Why doesn't he stop mimicking them when they ask him to stop? Eric wanted the girls to notice him and, most likely, was trying to engage them by being funny, but he only succeeded in annoying them.

Different Drummers often try to be the class clown, but because they have such poor social judgment, their humor usually falls flat. For instance, they might make a comment that no one finds funny, and instead of just letting it go, they repeat the comment five more times. Even if they get a laugh the first time, they repeat the joke until it is annoying rather than amusing. They may resort to bathroom humor long after their peers have outgrown it. Different Drummers also laugh inappropriately. They might snicker to themselves for no apparent reason or laugh loudly when someone falls. Sometimes they have an especially raucous or unusual laugh. Their peers view their humor as babyish, disgusting, or just plain weird.

Many Different Drummers do obnoxious things because it's the only way they can think of to get their peers to notice them. They might sit blocking the bottom of a slide, ignoring other children's shouts to get out of the way. They might deliberately knock over someone's project or snatch the soccer ball from a group of kids in the middle of a game, then run away. They might refuse to pass the pencils until everyone at their table is screaming at them. These children don't just join a group — they barge in, disrupting whatever activity is going on, bringing conversation to a crashing halt, and drawing everyone's attention to them. It's as if they've unconsciously decided that any attention is better than none. They truly want to connect with their peers, but their actions only serve to dig them deeper into their role as outsiders.

For some Different Drummers, their odd or outrageous behavior is actually a cover for their underlying feelings of shyness and insecurity. However, instead of hanging back like Shy Children, they can't resist leaping into the fray. Although they fear that other kids won't like them, they act in ways that practically beg others to reject them. If you suspect that your child struggles with inner feelings of shyness, you may also want to read chapter 5, "The Shy Child."

Some Different Drummers draw negative attention to themselves because they act in ways that are more appropriate for younger children. For example, they might come to school wearing a Superman cape, or they might insist on carrying a favorite baby doll everywhere they go. This kind of behavior is adorable in nursery school, and it might even be okay in kindergarten, but by grade school, when most of their peers have moved on to older activities, it makes these children seem odd. They need to find a way to pursue their interests without creating a barrier that separates them from their classmates.

Learning the Unwritten Rules and doing the following exercises can help your child fit in more easily with peers.

THE UNWRITTEN RULES

- You can't make friends with people by annoying them.
- Even if something is funny the first time, the second time, it's not.
- If people tell you that what you are doing is not funny, stop doing it.

- When someone says, "Stop," stop.
- Joining a group means blending in *without* interrupting the action or the conversation.
- To make friends, become interested in others and their ideas. Don't worry about making them notice you.

**ACTIVITIES FOR LEARNING
THE UNWRITTEN RULES**

1. Being Able to Stop

Different Drummers don't just do an annoying behavior once — they *keep doing it,* regardless of how many times people tell them to stop. This is extremely exasperating for their peers, their teachers, and their parents. It is essential that you teach your child to notice and comply when someone tells him or her to stop.

Often the initial motivation when Different Drummers do something outrageous is to get their peers to laugh or think they are clever. However, because they have such poor judgment about how to win approval, their efforts usually misfire. When the other kids start yelling at them, they don't know how to extract themselves from the situation and still save face. So they continue acting up, further alienating their peers.

Different Drummers' problems with stopping stem partly from impulsiveness — once they get going, it's hard for them to put on the brakes — but mostly from failure to understand how their behavior affects others. It's almost as if they believe that people don't really mean it when they ask them to stop, or maybe they think that if they keep doing whatever it is, people will change their minds and start to like it. Explain to your child that this never happens. Doing something annoying once is a forgivable mistake; persisting despite requests to stop seems like deliberate provocation, and it makes people furious.

Tell your child that he or she needs to listen the first time someone says stop. Give your child some specific strategies for doing this. Saying, "Sorry!" is a good start. Then your child should return the ball, cross his or her arms, sit on his or her hands, cover his or her mouth, or just walk away — whatever it takes to stop the behavior. Role-play using these stopping strategies.

At home you can use a small object as a stop signal. Have your child choose something that can fit in the palm of his or her hand — a nice smooth rock, a marble, a seashell, or even a small plastic figure could work well. Explain that this object tells your child "enough is enough." When you notice your child doing an unacceptable behavior relentlessly, hand him or her the object without saying anything. You might use the stop object when your child is teasing a sibling, making obnoxious noises, or bothering you with incessant questions. Holding the stop object gives your child something to do in place of the irritating behavior, and it pulls you out of the role of verbally nagging and being ignored. With practice, your child may come to internalize this signal and think of it when a classmate asks him or her to stop.

2. Identifying Annoying Behavior

Different Drummers need specific pointers about what they are *not* supposed to do. As unlikely as it might seem to parents, teachers, or classmates, these children just don't figure out on their own that something they are doing is annoying. No matter how many times other kids scream at them, they simply don't make the connection between their behavior and their classmates' ire. They don't understand how people can be so mad at them when they were "just kidding."

You will do your child a favor if you help him or her understand that some behaviors *never* get a positive response from others. We've compiled a list of some of the most common examples of universally disliked behaviors. Some of these behaviors are unpleasantly noisy or distracting. Some of them are intrusive because they invade other people's personal space or privacy. Some are frustrating because they disrupt peers' activities or prevent them from doing what they want to do, and some are simply unkind. You may want to add your own items to the list. Your child's teacher may also be able to offer some suggestions of specific behaviors your child should avoid. Go over the whole list with your child, then choose no more than five problem areas to work on. Make sure your child understands why other kids don't like these behaviors. Create a personal list for your child. Keep the list in an accessible place as a reminder.

Annoying Behaviors to Avoid

Noisy or Distracting Behaviors
    Mimicking others
    Making distracting noises
    Talking in a loud or shrill voice
    Using baby talk
    Singing or humming when people are working
    Kicking someone's chair
    Talking or making noise when people are trying to listen

Intrusive Behaviors
    Tapping or poking people to get their attention
    Standing too close to someone
    Putting something (an object, your hand, your face) directly in
        front of someone's face
    Staring at someone
    Eavesdropping on a private conversation

Shouting out someone's secrets or personal information

Interrupting people before they have finished talking

Frustrating Behaviors

Disrupting someone's game or project

Knocking someone's book, paper, or pencil onto the floor

Deliberately blocking someone's way

Refusing to share or take turns

Cutting in front of classmates in line

Grabbing more than your fair share of supplies or treats

Deliberately doing something slowly so that other people won't get a turn

Calling people repeatedly on the phone and hanging up when they answer

Unkind Behaviors

Snatching someone's possessions

Breaking or wrecking something that doesn't belong to you

Tripping someone on purpose

Pushing or shoving someone who is in your way

Being too rough or hurting someone to get a laugh or to get what you want

Playing practical jokes on someone

Laughing when something bad happens to someone

3. Observing Well-Liked Kids

Your child is less apt to resort to doing annoying things if he or she knows positive ways of relating to peers. Research shows that well-liked children use specific friendly behaviors to engage their peers. The Friendly Behaviors Checklist describes some of these. Go over this checklist with your child and then have him or her observe a popular classmate. After school, your child can tell you which of the items on the checklist were used by that classmate and describe how he or she did each behavior. Your child probably never noticed these social niceties or realized how important they are.

Once your child understands what friendly behaviors look like, he or she can try using them. Have your child pick one friendly behavior and practice it with you until he or she can do it naturally. Remember to start small. For instance, your child might want to practice greeting one or two classmates by name. Tell your child that if a classmate doesn't respond to the friendly overture, that's okay. It's still a step in the right direction for improving your child's reputation. The other child might just be startled because your child has never done this before. Your child might want to try the same behavior the next day with the same classmate, or he or she might want to try a different behavior or a different classmate.

FRIENDLY BEHAVIORS CHECKLIST

Yes	No	Relaxed, friendly smile
Yes	No	Greets others by name
Yes	No	Shows interest when others are speaking by listening carefully, not interrupting, and asking relevant questions
Yes	No	Invites others to join him or her
Yes	No	Offers sincere compliments
Yes	No	Shares with others
Yes	No	Talks in a friendly way to lots of different people
Yes	No	Volunteers to help others
Yes	No	Dresses appropriately; doesn't call attention to him- or herself with peculiar clothing or accessories

---

4. Handling Young Interests

Children should not be pushed to grow up sooner than necessary. So, if your child still wants to play with young toys, that's fine. However, have him or her play with them at home. Bringing these toys to school is like issuing a public announcement saying, "I'm different from you!" It's off-putting to other children, and it causes your child unnecessary grief.

While you allow your child to pursue young interests at home, you should also make sure that he or she has some age-appropriate toys or games. This gives your child the opportunity to play with these toys when he or she is ready and provides attractive choices when classmates come over for play dates. If you are not sure which activities are age-appropriate, ask other parents for ideas. Buying "age-appropriate" toys for your child doesn't mean you want him or her suddenly to turn into a mini-teenager. There are a lot of options between playing with baby dolls and experimenting with makeup. Most grade-school children enjoy bikes and scooters, board games, Foosball, air hockey, sports, or arts and crafts.

5. Having Activity-Based Play Dates

Different Drummers are often at their worst when they are in a group of kids and when they don't know what they are supposed to do. They do better in one-on-one situations in which the agenda is clear and the end time is known. You might want to try inviting (or having your child invite) some classmates, one at a time, to go on some fun outings. Even if other children aren't sure they like your child, if the outing seems interesting enough, they are likely to give your child a chance. Possible activities include going out for ice cream, attending a sporting event, seeing a movie, going bowling, flying kites, or visiting a pottery studio. At-home play dates are also a possibility if you plan compelling activities, such as baking cookies or building and painting birdhouses. Keep the play date fun and short so that the other child leaves wanting more. Anticipate possible trouble spots and talk with your child about how to handle them. Every time your child has a positive interaction with a classmate, it's another step toward improving his or her reputation and possibly making a new friend.

6. Blending In to a Group

The goal in joining a group is to do so without drawing attention to oneself or interrupting ongoing activity. This means that your child needs to observe carefully what the other kids are doing and then blend in.

Blending in to an established group is one of the most difficult social skills (even for adults), so your child is likely to need plenty of practice to be able to do it smoothly. Use puppets or plastic figures to act out with your child several kinds of group activities and how someone might blend in with the group. The general strategy is to watch for a while to understand what the kids are doing, and then to find a way to contribute without disrupting the action. For instance, if the characters are playing ball, the new person could wait until someone misses the ball and then kick or throw it back. If the characters are building something out of sticks, the newcomer can bring over some leaves to make a flag or a moat. A sincere compliment can be a way of contributing to group enthusiasm. For example, if the others are playing marbles, the new person can admire a good shot or an especially nice marble.

Tell your child that it's *not* a good idea to ask other kids, "Can I play too?" This question stops the game, as everyone in the group turns to consider whether they want your child to join. It also gives other kids an opportunity to say no.

If your child is having trouble understanding why it's important to blend in to a group, you may want to have your child play the characters in the group, while you play the newcomer who snatches the ball, wrecks the group project, or yells, "That's a stupid building! I could do it much better!" When a new person calls attention to him- or herself, the activity comes to a crashing halt, and the group members may even turn against the intruder. Have your child suggest better ways for the newcomer to join in the fun.

Spencer: Talking Up a Storm

"Okay, Spencer. You can go first for Show and Tell," Mrs. McKinley announced.

Spencer walked to the front of the classroom carrying his skateboard. "Well," he began, "I really hurt myself. This is my skateboard that I got for my birthday. It's much faster than my brother's. My Aunt Belinda has three kids, and they really like this kind of skateboard. You used to only be able to get it in Washington, but now you can get it on-line. There are ten models. Model LXZ-2875 has a pintail, sixty-two-millimeter wheels, and an Extra Gloss Finish with fabric-inlay options. Model LXS-2879 has the Super Gloss finish, wide trucks, and Deluxe Optimum wheels. Those are seventy-millimeter. Model RT-5994 has sixty-five-millimeter wheels with an eleven-millimeter stringer in between the trucks, the Jump Master Sport back with racing stripes, and . . ."

"Um, Spencer," Mrs. McKinley interrupted, "you said you hurt yourself. Are you okay, now?"

"Oh, yeah. I'm fine," Spencer said.

"Well, that's good," Mrs. McKinley said, looking a little confused. "You can sit down now, Spencer."

Spencer is addressing the entire class, but it's as if he's talking to himself. He has no sense of his audience's reaction. His presentation is an endless, muddled monologue that contains a mixture of relevant and irrelevant facts, in fairly random order, followed by an unnecessary list of incomprehensible details. Spencer isn't conveying information to his classmates; he's just talking at them in a stream of consciousness. His classmates are probably so bored by his verbiage that they don't even try to follow it.

Spencer's monologue was supposed to be a presentation, but some Different Drummers talk this way even in casual conversation. An adult might take the time to ask questions to fill in the missing links ("How did you hurt yourself?"; "Did your Aunt Belinda give you the skateboard?"; "Does Aunt Belinda live in Washington?"; "Which model do you have?"), but other children usually won't. They lose patience, get bored, and just walk away.

A variety of topics can fuel Different Drummers' unrelenting one-way conversations. Some of these children are quasi-experts on a particular subject, and given half a chance, they will go on at length about it, continuing to talk even after their listeners' eyes have glazed over. They may also interrupt others and maneuver the conversation to their favorite topic. Some Different Drummers brag endlessly. Most have trouble distinguishing the main point of a story from the details. Many Different Drummers show poor social judgment by sharing personal information in excruciating detail. If they have an injury or an operation, these children regale acquaintances with all the grisly facts ("You could see the bone . . ."; "And there was blood and pus . . ."), completely ignoring their listeners' expressions of revulsion. If they get a stomach virus, you can be sure that they will describe the symptoms in vivid detail to everyone at the lunch table.

Parents of nonstop talkers spend day after day hearing their child's monologues, and before long, they might find themselves only half listening. They might give the occasional "uh-huh," but really their child's talking has become background noise. If your child is having trouble with run-on talking, it is essential that you *don't* pretend to listen. Your child can tell when you aren't really paying attention, and if this happens a lot, it could hurt your child's self-esteem. Pretending to listen also gives your child the message that it's okay to talk *at* someone, and it prevents your child from learning important inter-action skills. Moreover, if you let your child follow you around, talk-ing incessantly about some topic regardless of whether you are engaged in what he or she is saying, your child will do the same thing to classmates. Only their responses won't be as tolerant as yours.

It's more helpful to your child if you are honest about your reac-tions. Sometimes Different Drummers start conversations or make requests at the worst possible moments: you are rushing to get every-one out the door, the dishwasher is overflowing, the baby needs a diaper change, you can't find your keys, and he or she wants to give you a blow-by-blow description of the latest episode of a favorite TV show. If you are too busy to listen, say so, and point out all the rea-sons why it isn't a good time. Promise you will discuss the matter at some specific later time. When you are ready to listen to your child, turn and face him or her, make good eye contact, and give your child your full attention. If you don't know what your child is talking about, say, "You lost me," or "Start at the beginning. What happened first?" If your child brings up a gross topic, say, "I don't want to hear about this. Let's talk about something else." If your child is includ-ing a lot of irrelevant details, ask, "Is this the main point you want to tell me?"

If your child tends to give monologues rather than have conversa-tions, going over the Unwritten Rules and doing the following exer-cises can help him or her learn appropriate conversation skills.

THE UNWRITTEN RULES

- Think about whether your listener would be interested before you say something.
- If you give too many details, listeners won't be able to see your main point.
- A conversation means two or more people *taking turns* talking.

- If no one is looking at you or asking questions while you are talking, no one is listening to you.
- When you see that someone is no longer listening, you need to stop talking.
- Think of questions to ask rather than things to say.
- Nobody wants to be grossed out.

ACTIVITIES FOR LEARNING THE UNWRITTEN RULES

1. Getting to the Point and Leaving Out Irrelevant Facts

Many Different Drummers go on at length because they have trouble summarizing information. One way to teach your child to get to the point is by subscribing to a magazine, such as *Time for Kids,* and having him or her read an article and report one interesting fact or idea at dinnertime. Or you may want to have each family member report the one best and one worst thing that happened that day. Insist that your child stick to one idea. This gives your child practice selecting his or her contributions to the conversation. It also gives your child a chance to see that he or she can get listeners' full attention by sharing one idea and to understand that bombarding listeners with a barrage of words will only bore them. It's also a good idea to insist that your child stop talking and listen while other family members speak.

Another technique you might want to try is giving your child a specific format for relating an experience. The following list shows the format we suggest for helping children organize their thoughts when they are telling someone about their experiences.

Format for Organizing Thoughts
1. "First . . ."
2. "Then . . ."

3. "After that . . ."
4. "Finally . . ."

Write this format on an index card for your child. See if he or she can use it to describe a recent experience, such as a field trip or even an episode of a television show.

You can also help your child learn not to go on at length by arranging a signal that tells him or her to stop talking. You may want to use a discreet nonverbal gesture, such as tapping your lips or touching your ear, or you may prefer a simple phrase. In social skills groups, we use the term *TMI,* which stands for Too Much Information, or the palm-on-fingertips time-out sign used by referees. You can use your own "stop talking" signal when your child is providing more detail than listeners can process (such as Spencer's list of model numbers) or when your child is discussing something private that listeners don't need to know.

2. Listening Rather than Telling: Conversational Ping-Pong

When a topic comes up, Different Drummers state everything they know about that topic, regardless of listeners' interest or reactions. For instance, if someone says, "I'm from Puerto Rico," instead of following up that statement by asking questions such as "How long have you been in this country?" or "What are the main differences you've noticed between Puerto Rico and here?" or "Do you speak Spanish?" Different Drummers are likely to launch into a monologue about what they know about Puerto Rico — even if they know very little. They might say, "Puerto Rico is part of the United States, but it isn't a state," or, worse, "I used to think Puerto Rico was spelled P-O-R-T-O, but it's really P-U-E-R-T-O." It doesn't occur to them that it is inappropriate to lecture a Puerto Rican person about Puerto Rico. They just say whatever comes to mind.

Help your child understand that in a conversation the issue isn't "What do I know?" but rather "What can I learn about this person?" or "What would my listener like to know?"

Explain to your child that a conversation is like a game of Ping-Pong: one person asks a question, then the other person answers and returns the serve with a question. If one person hogs the conversational ball by giving a long answer and not returning a question, the game gets very boring, and the other player is likely to leave. The game is also ruined if one person snatches the ball out of turn by interrupting before the other player has finished speaking.

You can show your child how to keep a conversation moving by tossing an actual Ping-Pong ball or even a crumpled ball of paper back and forth while you talk. Each player must ask a question in order to pass the ball. "What" and "how" questions work best. Limit your child to answers of only one or two sentences. Possible topics for your conversation include favorite music groups, favorite TV shows, and favorite sports.

You may need to inform your child that some sensitive topics, such as grades, money, religion, or physical characteristics, are better not discussed outside the family. Questions like "How come you have that weird bump on your chin?" are rude, embarrassing, and potentially hurtful.

3. Using Ending Statements

Sometimes Different Drummers get caught up in monologues because they don't know how to stop. They just keep talking and talking until listeners get fed up and walk away, and even then, they tend to follow after them, still talking. Once Spencer brought up the ten models of skateboards, he felt he had to describe each of them. If the teacher hadn't stopped him, he would have described all ten. If he noticed kids rolling their eyes, he might have talked faster, but he wouldn't have seen any alternative except to get all the way through the list. Teaching Different Drummers specific statements to end their monologues can give them a way out of this trap.

Help your child to be aware of the signs that show whether someone is listening or not. If your child sees that a listener is looking away, sighing, and no longer commenting or asking questions, that means the listener is bored and that your child needs to stop talking quickly or risk irritating the listener. Your child can use one of the statements below, or alternatives you come up with, to end a monologue, to invite the listener to have a turn speaking, or to end the conversation. These statements work either in person or on the phone. Discourage your child from saying, "To make a long story short . . ." People who say that rarely do it.

Ending Statements

Stopping Gracefully
　　"Well, you get the idea. I'm stopping now."
　　"Well, that's enough about that. I'm done talking."
　　"I won't bore you any further. I'm done."
　　"Sorry, I think I'm going on too long."

Giving the Listener a Chance
　　"What do you think?"
　　"Has that ever happened to you?"

Ending a Conversation
　　"Well, I have to go now."
　　"I'll let you go now."
　　"It was nice talking to you."
　　"See you soon."

4. Avoiding Bragging

Some Different Drummers are prone to bragging. They go on and on about their great accomplishments, experiences, or possessions. They aren't trying to offend anyone or put anyone down. By touting their good points, they think they are impressing others, but instead they are annoying them. Sometimes, Different Drummers don't even realize that they are bragging. They think they are merely providing information, and they don't understand why their peers respond so negatively. Teaching your child the difference between reporting and bragging is the first step toward getting him or her stop bragging.

Have your child take the Is It Bragging? Quiz. If your child doesn't recognize an instance of bragging, explain why saying that statement could hurt someone's feelings. Bragging conveys the message "I think I'm better than you."

Sometimes when we tell Different Drummers that a statement is bragging, they object, "But it's true!" It may be true, but if it could be seen as tooting their own horn, they shouldn't say it. Help your child understand that he or she will make a more favorable impression by complimenting others rather than complimenting him- or herself.

IS IT BRAGGING?

Yes No 1. Telling someone how much money you have in your savings account

Yes No 2. Telling someone your middle name

Yes No 3. Telling someone you got an A on the spelling test

Yes No 4. Telling someone your Dad can beat up their Dad

Yes No 5. Telling someone you have a toy at home that's better than his or hers

Yes No 6. Telling someone your family is rich

Yes	No	7.	Telling someone your address
Yes	No	8.	Telling someone how old you are
Yes	No	9.	Telling someone you can build a better tower than they can
Yes	No	10.	Telling someone who has been to Disney World once that you have been there three times

Answers:

1. Yes; 2. No; 3. Yes; 4. Yes; 5. Yes; 6. Yes; 7. No; 8. No; 9. Yes; 10. Yes

Sometimes Different Drummers go beyond bragging to telling outright "fish tales." The motivation is the same: they want kids to like them and to think they are cool and interesting. However, the social cost of lying is even worse than that of bragging because other kids will come to view Different Drummers as untrustworthy and to doubt everything they say.

A lot of kids lie to get out of trouble. While this isn't desirable, it's understandable. The best way to deal with this is simply not to put your child in the position of having to admit to or deny wrongdoing. If you know they did it, go from there. Confessions are unnecessary.

Some children tell stories that aren't true because they have a vivid imagination. If your child does this, compliment his or her creativity but tell him or her to warn listeners when a story isn't real. For instance, you can teach your child to say "What if . . ." or "Wouldn't it be cool if . . ." to preface a fantasy. When you suspect that your child is concocting a tall tale, interrupt and ask, "Is this real or is it imaginary? If it's imaginary, you need to tell me."

5. Disagreeing Respectfully
Many Different Drummers have trouble disagreeing respectfully. We know one boy who raised his hand in class, and when the teacher called on him, he yelled out, "WRONG!" He didn't understand why

the teacher was furious with him for saying that — after all, he raised his hand.

Explain to your child that disagreeing by putting down someone else's ideas makes the other person feel ridiculed. No one ever responds well to that. People will refuse to listen if your child states his or her opinions in a harsh or condescending way.

Sometimes the best way of handling disagreement is to say nothing. Explain to your child that in some cases it's simply not necessary or appropriate to share his or her opinion. For instance, if a parent, teacher, or other adult has already made up his or her mind about something, arguing won't help — it's just annoying. If the disagreement concerns a minor point, your child shouldn't quibble, because this will come across as nitpicking. Warn your child that public questioning of an authority figure can backfire.

If your child really wants to disagree, and there is time and opportunity to do so, he or she must do it in a respectful manner. A private discussion is usually best. Before mentioning a contrary opinion, your child should first find some point of agreement or at least say that he or she can understand the other person's point of view. When stating his or her opinion, your child should use a tone of voice that is calm, humble, and curious rather than confrontational. Your child should acknowledge either silently or in words that he or she could be wrong or that there may be more than one way of viewing the situation. For example, your child could say, "I agree that's important, but I think . . ."; "I can see why you think that. That makes sense, but what about . . . ?"; "That's a good point. I hadn't thought of that, but is it possible . . . ?"; or "I understand what you're saying. I could be wrong, but I thought . . ."

Use role-play to give your child some practice disagreeing respectfully. The following list describes some opinions that your child is likely to oppose. Say these statements and see if your child can see that they have some validity, before disagreeing. Encourage your child to state his or her own opinion in a friendly rather than belligerent way. You can also try this exercise using your family's "hot" topics.

Can You Disagree Respectfully with These Statements?
"I think kids should go to school year-round so they learn more and don't forget things over the summer."

"I think everyone should wear dull gray uniforms to school."

"Snails are much better pets than cats or dogs."

"Halloween should be banned because giving children candy causes tooth decay."

"People should not be allowed to drive until they are twenty-five years old because before that age they are too reckless and immature."

Chelsea: Coming On Too Strong

Chelsea's mother poured her a glass of milk. "So, did you play with Allison at recess today?"

"No," Chelsea answered with her mouth full of cookies. "She wanted to play with Belinda. I just read my book."

"You know, honey, you can play with more than one kid at a time . . . ," Chelsea's mother began.

"No," Chelsea insisted. "I only want to play with Allison. She is my friend."

"But, if you only have one friend . . ." Her mother tried again.

"The other kids don't want to play with me, Mom. Allison is the only one who likes me," Chelsea said. "Can Allison stay over Saturday and Sunday night? Then we could be together the whole weekend, just the two of us. I want to show her all my stuffed animals, and we could make friendship bracelets for each other . . ."

"Let's have Allison over for an afternoon play date before we talk about spending the night," Chelsea's mom suggested.

Chelsea wants an instant best friend. She wants to be joined at the hip to Allison, spending every day and night with her chosen buddy. There is a desperate quality to her pursuit of Allison. Because the other kids don't want to play with her, Chelsea clings to Allison for dear life. Fortunately, Chelsea's mother realizes that her daughter will scare Allison off unless she allows the friendship to build gradually.

Different Drummers like Chelsea tend to push people away because they come on too strong too quickly. They crowd others, both physically and emotionally. They stand too close when speaking to someone. They might even try to sit on the same chair as a potential friend. They are often overly affectionate — hugging people within minutes of meeting them or wanting to hold hands long after it's age-appropriate to do so. They are so eager to have a buddy that they are apt to ask a new acquaintance, "Will you be my best friend?" They plan numerous activities, trying to guarantee that they and their friend will be together continuously: "After school we can do this, and then you can stay for dinner and maybe your mom will let you spend the night. And tomorrow we can . . ." They call on the phone every night, and they are excessively interested in their friend's comings and goings so that they can arrange to see them as much as possible. If their friend signs up for ice-skating, they will want to do it too, even if they've never been interested in that activity before. These children are often jealous — they want their friend all to themselves. They feel threatened if their friend seeks out someone else's company. If another child tries to join in their play, Different Drummers might say to their friend, "Let's run away from him / her!"

Initially, some children may be flattered by Different Drummers' effusive desire to be with them all the time. However, they soon come to feel uncomfortable with the invasion of their space, privacy, and independence. Few children can tolerate Different Drummers' possessiveness. Even kids who like them find themselves drawing back. Usually, this makes Different Drummers push even harder, compounding the problem. When Different Drummers don't pick up on cues to slow down and give people breathing space, peers end up avoiding them and might even come to actively dislike them. Sometimes the parents of other children end up stepping in and telling Different Drummers not to call so often.

For many Different Drummers, their encroaching behavior stems from their fear of being rejected. They hug and hold hands to reassure themselves that the other child really is their friend. They worry about losing their friend if he or she spends time with someone else or participates in an activity that doesn't involve them. Their relationships tend to be all or nothing. They are too anxious to let friendships develop naturally over time, so they go straight to extreme intimacy. They don't understand that the tighter they cling, the more other children will pull away. The things they do to try to prevent being rejected actually cause them to be rejected.

The Unwritten Rules and the following activities focus on building relationships gradually and learning to feel comfortable alone.

THE UNWRITTEN RULES

- Leave when people are still wishing you could stay longer.
- Wait for new friends to invite you over before inviting them a second time.
- Acting too needy scares people off.
- Most people like to have more than one friend.
- People who need people are *not* the luckiest people in the world.
- Alone time helps you gain independence and learn to enjoy your own company.

ACTIVITIES FOR LEARNING
THE UNWRITTEN RULES

1. Showing Appropriately Friendly Behaviors at Different Stages of a Relationship

In order to avoid coming on too strong, Different Drummers need to understand that relationships progress through stages and that different types of behavior are appropriate at different stages of a relationship. Define the terms *acquaintance, friend,* and *close friend* for your child and write each definition on a large index card. You can use our definitions or your own words. Put names of people your child knows on the back of each labeled card. Your child might want to list everyone he or she knows on the "close friend" card, so you need to help him or her make some distinctions. ("You only see Cara at ballet class, so she counts as an acquaintance.") Emphasize that most people have a large number of acquaintances, a handful of friends, and only a few close friends. If your child seems distressed that he or she doesn't have enough friends or close friends, explain that all close friends start out as acquaintances and that relationships build over time.

THREE KINDS OF FRIENDS

Acquaintances: You know these children casually and think they are nice, but either you've just met them or you haven't had much one-on-one time with them.

Friends: You sometimes spend one-on-one time together, but not always. You know each other pretty well and enjoy each other's company, but you both have other friends. You invite them over about as often as they invite you over.

Close Friends: You've known each other for a long time, and you've had a lot of play dates at each other's homes. You prefer each other's company, but you both still have other friends. You spend enough time apart that you can look forward to seeing each other.

Once your child knows that different levels of friendship exist, he or she needs to understand what kinds of behavior are appropriate with each type of friend. Write the items from the following Possible Friendship Activities List on three-by-five-inch index cards (one item per card). Place the written definitions of the three kinds of friends on three stairs, with "acquaintance" at the bottom, "friend" in the middle, and "close friend" at the top, to represent building relationships. (If you don't have stairs, use the floor, a chair, and a table). Use a small box or basket to make an additional discard category for behaviors that are just "too much" at any stage of friendship. Help your child sort the activity cards into the appropriate piles. The divisions we've indicated aren't written in stone, so use your own judgment if you think an activity belongs in a different category. The main point is to get your child to make some distinctions and to understand that he or she needs to behave differently with different kinds of friends.

Explain to your child that it's fine to do a lower-level activity with a friend or close friend, but that the reverse is not true. Trying to do a close-friend activity with an acquaintance is like putting the roof on a house before the walls are built. It comes across as overwhelming and could scare off the other child. To build a friendship, your child needs to engage in plenty of the acquaintance activities first, then gradually add the friend activities, do these for a while, and then decide whether to add the close-friend activities. Help your child understand that many relationships stay at the acquaintance or friend level, never progressing to the close-friend level — and that's okay. While it's nice to have close friends, other friends and acquaintances also enrich our lives.

Possible Friendship Activities

Acquaintances

Smile at them.

Greet them by name.

Play with them in a group of other children at recess.

Share a treat with them.

Help them carry something heavy.

Pick up and give them something they dropped.

Tell them the homework assignment they missed.

Spend time together at an after-school activity.

Friends

Sit with them at lunch.

Offer to be their partner on a school project.

Invite them over to your house for an after-school play date.

Go to their house for a play date.

Call them on the phone.

Send them e-mail messages.

Invite them to your birthday party.

Close Friends

Pick them first for your team in gym.

Offer to share your turn on the class computer with them.

Help them understand schoolwork.

Let them borrow something of yours.

Spend the night at their house or invite them to sleep over at your
house.

Behaviors to Avoid at Any Stage of a Relationship

Continuing to invite them over, even though they show little
interest in you.

Calling them several times in one evening for no good reason.

Asking, "Will you be my (best) friend?"

Trying to monopolize all of their free time.

Acting jealous when they play with someone else.

Giving away money or favorite toys to try to get them to like you.

2. Learning to Enjoy Being Alone

Learning to enjoy being alone is an essential life skill. Cultivating the ability to be comfortable alone creates a positive sense of self-sufficiency. It allows us to get to know ourselves and grow as individuals. It also helps us cope with the inevitable times when we can't rely on someone else for entertainment. If your Different Drummer knows how to have fun alone, he or she may feel less compelled to relentlessly pursue the company of others.

Make "alone time" an explicit part of the weekly schedule. Start small — maybe as little as one hour, once a week. Insist that your child spend this time entertaining him- or herself. You can plan ahead by making a list with your child of possible fun activities, such as listening to music, reading, drawing, playing computer games, doing puzzles, building with Legos, or making crafts. However, during the actual alone time, insist that it's your child's job to decide what he or she wants to do.

ADDRESSING PROBLEMS WITH UNPLEASANT PERSONAL HABITS

Sometimes children have social problems because of their off-putting personal habits. They may have unpleasant body odor. They may have unappealing table manners (e.g., deliberately opening their mouths to show fellow diners their half-chewed food). They may engage in gross things, such as picking their nose, biting their nails, or chewing on their hair. They may engage in rude behaviors in public, such as passing gas or burping loudly. Sometimes children are unaware that they have these habits. Often they just don't realize how offensive these behaviors are to others.

These habits have nothing to do with who your child really is as a person, so it would be a shame to allow them to interfere with your child's ability to form friendships.

Educate your child about what kind of behavior is appropriate around others. Reading books about manners can help. We recommend *A Little Book of Manners for Boys* (by Bob and Emilie Barnes) or *Oops! The Manners Guide for Girls* (American Girl Library, by Nancy Holyoke). To give you some ideas of what types of behavior are appropriate at what age, you may want to read *Elbows Off the Table, Napkin in the Lap, No Video Games During Dinner: The Modern Guide to Teaching Children Good Manners* by Carol McD. Wallace.

Manners will be easier for your child to learn if you maintain the standards at home that you want him or her to use in public. To encourage your child to improve his or her personal hygiene, you may want to use a daily checklist or a simple reward system. Physical reminders such as wearing cotton gloves or ponytail holders can help break unattractive habits. Sometimes just placing a mirror in front of your child while he or she is eating can increase awareness and dramatically improve behavior.

THE HOME-SCHOOL CONNECTION

Unfortunately, teachers are often irritated by a Different Drummer's behavior, so your immediate goal is to be your child's public relations representative and paint a picture of your child as well-meaning but struggling. Help the teacher understand that it's poor social judgment rather than malice or disrespect that causes your child's misbehavior. Explain that your child really does want to get along with others but just doesn't understand how to do so appropriately. When your child resorts to desperate measures, other kids are turned off. If you have a particularly poignant example of how hard your child tries to be accepted, you may want to share it with the teacher. Your goal is to help the teacher see how difficult it is for your child to fit in so that the teacher can move beyond his or her own irritation and want to help make things better.

Having the teacher's help is essential for getting a complete picture of what your child does to push others away. The teacher sees your child in action with peers every day, so he or she has probably noticed some specific behaviors that your child needs to avoid. The teacher may be willing to set up a secret signal to remind your child to stop talking or to refrain from an annoying behavior. If the teacher can have regular private conferences with your child to discuss improvement and perhaps set new goals, this can be a great source of both practical and emotional support. It can give your child a sense that there is someone in his or her corner during the school day. The teacher may also be able to suggest some classmates who might be open to getting to know your child better through individual play dates.

IF YOU TOO . . .

If you recall having some of the difficulties that your Different Drummer is currently struggling with, you know how painful it is to be rejected for no apparent reason. How wonderful that you can offer your child not only compassion but also help in understanding and solving these problems.

Be careful that your sympathy for your child's problems doesn't lead you to be too tolerant of his or her out-of-sync behaviors. This could perpetuate your child's social difficulties. It would be a shame to allow your child's lack of social awareness to push away potential friends and prevent them from getting to know what a nice kid your child really is.

Try to observe your child as if you were someone meeting him or her for the first time to get a sense of what your child might be doing that could be off-putting. Talk with your child's teacher, Scout leader, or any other adult who can give you objective insight into what your child might be doing with peers that prevents him or her from fitting in. Share this knowledge with your child in a gentle and compassionate way. We have all outgrown some of the off-putting behaviors of our youth, but don't count on your child being able to do the same without help. You can save your child a lot of misery if you step in now and teach him or her how to relate to peers more appropriately.

SUMMARY

Different Drummers act in ways that are out of sync with their peers. They have trouble predicting and understanding other people's reactions, so they do annoying things like barging in to groups, talking nonstop, or monopolizing a friend's time. They are then mystified by their peers' rejection. Once Different Drummers learn appropriate ways of connecting with others, they are less likely to resort to self-defeating strategies and can develop their true capacity for friendship.

You Will Also Want to Read:
Chapter 2, "The Vulnerable Child"
Chapter 5, "The Shy Child"
Chapter 7, "The Little Adult"

THE UNWRITTEN RULES FOR THE DIFFERENT DRUMMER AT A GLANCE

- You can't make friends with people by annoying them.
- Even if something is funny the first time, the second time, it's not.

- If people tell you that what you are doing is not funny, stop doing it.
- When someone says, "Stop," stop.
- Joining a group means blending in *without* interrupting the action or the conversation.
- To make friends, become interested in others and their ideas. Don't worry about making them notice you.
- Think about whether your listener would be interested before you say something.
- If you give too many details, listeners won't be able to see your main point.
- A conversation means two or more people *taking turns* talking.
- If no one is looking at you or asking questions while you are talking, no one is listening to you.
- When you see that someone is no longer listening, you need to stop talking.
- Think of questions to ask rather than things to say.
- Nobody wants to be grossed out.
- Leave when people are still wishing you could stay longer.
- Wait for new friends to invite you over before inviting them a second time.
- Acting too needy scares people off.
- Most people like to have more than one friend.
- People who need people are *not* the luckiest people in the world.
- Alone time helps you gain independence and learn to enjoy your own company.

CHAPTER 5

The Shy Child

Does your child . . .

prefer to play alone because he or she feels awkward and embarrassed around other children?

avoid fun activities if they involve being with unfamiliar people?

want to skip school a lot?

desperately wish for friends but assume other people won't like him or her?

worry excessively about meeting new people or being in new situations?

freeze in panic when someone outside the family speaks to him or her, not knowing how to respond?

get so scared in new social situations that he or she has physical symptoms such as stomachaches, dizziness, or shortness of breath?

remain silent when asked simple, friendly questions and look to you or a sibling to respond instead?

Do you . . .

feel baffled that ordinary experiences like going to a birthday party are so terrifying for your child?

feel sorry for your child because he or she is so miserably anxious in social situations?

vacillate between wanting to shelter your child from scary social situations and wanting to push him or her to get over these fears?

feel exasperated that your child claims to want friends but avoids interacting with other children?

feel embarrassed when your child mumbles and looks away or just stands there speechless when you introduce him or her to people?

worry that your child will miss out on a lot of life experiences if he or she doesn't get over this shyness?

For Shy Children, being around unfamiliar people is like tiptoeing through a minefield. They are not just uneasy — they are terrified. They are convinced that everyone is staring at them and that they will somehow make a big mistake. They are constantly alert to the danger of humiliating themselves. Ordinary activities, like going to a birthday party, having to ask where the bathroom is, or eating in front of others, fill them with dread. They can be so anxious in social situations that they become paralyzed with fear. They may even feel physically sick.

Shyness comes in many different forms. Some children feel shy all the time, whereas others are only shy in certain situations. You may be surprised to hear that your child, who is talkative and outgoing at home, is quiet and withdrawn at school. Perhaps your child relates well to adults but gets tongue-tied around other kids. Or maybe your child is comfortable one-on-one but feels intimidated by groups. Some Shy Children can easily get up and sing or recite memorized lines in front of an audience but can't manage a casual conversation.

What all forms of shyness have in common is feeling painfully torn between the desire to connect with others and the need to stay safe by avoiding them. If Shy Children truly didn't want friends, they could live happily as hermits. The problem is that they do want friends — desperately — but they are terrified of being ridiculed or rejected. Shy Children want people to notice and admire them, but they also wish they were invisible. They will stare longingly at a group of children playing but then shrink in fear if anyone approaches them. They may beg to sign up for ballet or karate lessons but then sob hysterically that they can't do it once they arrive at the class. This waffling between conflicting desires can be maddening for parents, but keep in mind that your child did not choose to have these crippling fears and self-doubts that prevent him or her from relating to other children.

For some Shy Children, the strain of being around unfamiliar people is so overwhelming that they explode in tantrums. Although most of their tantrums take place at home, Shy Children sometimes "lose it" in public. Suddenly, they just can't take it anymore, and they erupt in what we call a "spillover tantrum." Parents are often amazed and appalled that the same child who hides behind their legs or stands silently when introduced to a stranger can carry on in front of the whole world. Shy Children are likely to feel mortified afterward if anyone outside the family sees them screaming and crying, but while they are in the throes of a tantrum, they are unable to think of anything except how overwhelmed they feel. If your child is prone to tantrums, you may want to look at the section on stress-related tantrums (under "Malcolm") in chapter 6, "The Short-Fused Child."

About 40 percent of children are shy. Some are born with this tendency; others become shy as they get older and begin to interact more with people outside the family.

According to Jerome Kagan, a developmental psychologist at Harvard University, one out of five children is born with what he calls an "inhibited temperament." As infants, these children are easily overstimulated. Other babies look happy or interested when they encounter colorful mobiles, new voices, or unusual smells, but inhibited children feel overwhelmed. They become extremely distressed; they cry, flail their arms and legs, and arch their backs. As toddlers, inhibited children tend to freeze in unfamiliar situations. They often refuse to talk to or even look at a strange child or adult. They may even hide their faces in their mothers' laps. Dr. Kagan believes that the brains of inhibited children are especially sensitive to perceived danger and therefore prone to fear.

But temperament doesn't necessarily determine a child's destiny; it's merely a starting point. Life experiences can influence whether children's innate tendencies are intensified or mellowed. About one third of inhibited babies do *not* grow up to be shy toddlers. These children somehow encounter experiences that lessen their tendency to fear the unknown and to withdraw when they feel frightened. Most of these children have parents who encourage them to gradually build their confidence by facing rather than avoiding new situations. On the other hand, some outgoing babies become shy. Perhaps their experiences teach them to fear new situations.

Both children who are born shy and those who become shy are trapped in a cycle, which is represented in figure 5.1. Shy Children feel anxious around other kids, so they avoid social situations. But avoiding social situations means that they have fewer opportunities to learn how to make friends. Shy Children typically haven't learned key social skills, such as how to join a group, how to greet people, or how to respond to the friendly overtures of other children. Their poor social skills make it more likely that they will be rejected or ignored by their peers. Being rejected again and again leads them to expect that they will always be rejected. They are on the lookout for every minor expression or gesture that could mean other kids don't like them. If a classmate doesn't greet them, most kids think, *I guess she didn't see me,* but Shy Children assume, *She must not like me.* Because they anticipate negative responses, Shy Children feel even

Figure 5.1

THE CYCLE OF SHYNESS

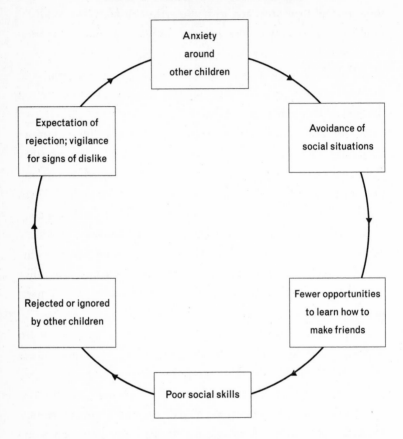

more anxious around other kids, bringing them back to the beginning of the cycle.

The Cycle of Shyness shows why the sink-or-swim method of just thrusting Shy Children into social situations and hoping they do okay rarely works. Shy Children need help with each point in the cycle. They need to learn how to manage their feelings of anxiety and how to approach other children. They need to learn to recognize and respond appropriately to friendly overtures. They need to gradually build up their confidence in social situations. Telling them that there is no reason to be afraid only adds to their self-doubt. It makes them think, *I shouldn't feel this way.* Forcing Shy Children into social interactions without giving them the tools to cope will only make them feel embarrassed and cause them to withdraw more.

Our society puts tremendous pressure on Shy Children. We tell our kids, "Get out there and WIN!" We want them to be popular and outgoing. We place such high value on being gregarious that we imply there is something wrong with someone who tends to be reserved or contemplative. Not all cultures feel this way. In some countries, "Hey, look at me!" self-promotion is considered boorish. As the parent of a Shy Child, you need to make an effort to see (and to help your child see) the value of a more cautious and gentle approach to life. At the same time, you don't want your child to be limited by fears — to think, *I want to, but I can't.* Shy Children deserve to be who they really want to be and to do what they really want to do.

ON THE POSITIVE SIDE

Shy Children often have a rich inner life. They may be thoughtful, creative, even artistic. Their ability to concentrate and to work independently can serve them well throughout life.

Because they warm up slowly to other people, Shy Children generally prefer to have a small number of close relationships rather than a large number of acquaintances. Their tendency to proceed with caution gives them a chance to notice more about others. They can be very perceptive. They are often excellent listeners. Once they get past their initial reserve, Shy Children are very loyal and giving friends.

SO, WHAT CAN WE DO?

Shy Children need help to build up their sense of comfort and security. They need to learn the Unwritten Rules about joining with others so that they can gradually gain confidence in social situations. The goal isn't to remake every Shy Child into an effervescent social butterfly. Instead, the goal is to build on their unique strengths and to provide the tools for handling fears so that Shy Children can feel more comfortable with others *and* with themselves. If your child's shy behavior is extreme or pervasive, or if he or she is unresponsive to your help, you may need to consult a mental health professional.

In this chapter, we talk about Michael, who becomes flustered when approached by a potential playmate, and Emma, who stands apart from her classmates, feeling miserable because she doesn't know how to join the group.

Michael: Not Knowing What to Say

Michael couldn't wait to meet the kids in his new neighborhood. For weeks before the move to the new house, he'd been thinking and talking about nothing else: "Do you think there will be kids my age? When can I meet them? What are their names?"

On the day that his family moved in, Michael planted himself on the front steps. He looked around eagerly, waiting for the kids to come. Finally, a boy rode by on his bicycle. "Hey, are you the new kid?" he called.

Michael felt his heart lurch in his chest. His throat tightened. He couldn't think of what to say. He looked away, then looked at his shoes. Finally, he mumbled something unintelligible and started plucking at a loose thread on his sneakers.

The other boy watched him for a moment, then rode away.

*   *   *

Michael was so eager to make new friends, but when he finally met his new neighbor, he froze. Instead of thinking, *Great! Here's someone to play with,* Michael panicked and thought, *Yikes! I don't know what to say!*

Shy Children can't enjoy being around other kids because they are too busy worrying about what to do and what everyone thinks of them. They are so afraid of doing the wrong thing socially that they often do nothing. Like ostriches hiding their heads in the sand, they avoid even looking at other people. Unfortunately, this can make them come across as uninterested, aloof, or even snobbish. Because they are preoccupied with their own fear of being rejected, Shy Children have no idea that other kids interpret their reticence as rejection.

The following Unwritten Rules are guidelines for starting a relationship with another child. Going over these rules and doing the corresponding activities can help your child feel more comfortable meeting and greeting a potential playmate.

THE UNWRITTEN RULES

- Greet people you know (or want to know).
- Not responding makes you seem snobbish.
- Looking away says "I'm not interested."
- You have to show kids you like them — no one can read your mind.
- Giving an honest compliment is like giving a gift.
- Kids like kids who are willing to do things with them.

ACTIVITIES FOR LEARNING
THE UNWRITTEN RULES

1. Greeting Others

Because a lot of Shy Children's worries center around starting relationships, they have an especially hard time greeting people. If you
are not shy yourself, you may wonder, *What's the big deal? They
should just say hi.* The problem is that for Shy Children there is no
"just" about saying hi. They feel stupid and awkward doing it, and
frankly, because they are so anxious, they often do it badly. They
rarely initiate a greeting. If someone greets them, they usually say
nothing, or like Michael, they mumble and look away.

Greetings are important because they are the first contact with
another person and can form the basis for a first impression. Most
Shy Children don't realize that almost every social encounter starts
with a greeting. Encourage your child to notice the way other kids
greet one another when they arrive at school and throughout the day.
Spell out the components of greeting people.

Components of Greeting
1. Look the person you are greeting in the eye.
2. Smile.
3. Say "hi" or "hello."
4. Say the person's name if you know it.

All four components are important. Looking people in the eye
and smiling are necessary because otherwise the greeting seems reluctant. A small, relaxed smile is fine. Saying the person's name is important because it makes the greeting personal. Studies show that people
enjoy hearing their own names. So, help your child remember and
use people's names.

Have your child practice greeting people. We have found that role-play is a great way to learn new behaviors. If your child complains that it feels weird, you can explain that new things often feel weird but that they become more comfortable over time. Keep practicing until your child's greetings sound and feel natural.

We are big believers in "method acting." Method acting is a drama technique in which people try to become the character they are playing. Your child may want to pretend that he or she is someone else while practicing greetings. Help your child choose an especially outgoing child (*not* a sibling). Then have him or her pretend to be that child. Ask, "How would John act if he saw someone he knew? How would he stand? What would his face look like? What would he say? How loudly would he say it?" Don't let your child wait until he or she feels friendly to start acting friendly. It works the other way around: after your child starts acting friendly, he or she will begin to feel like a friendly person.

Once your child has rehearsed enough at home, it's time to take the show on the road. Help your child decide which people outside the family he or she wants to practice greeting. It could be the kids at school, either in the morning, waiting to go in, or during the day, passing in the hall. It could be the kids at soccer practice or even your adult friends. Start with the people or circumstances that seem easiest but be sure that, at some point, your child tries greeting kids at school.

2. Giving Compliments

Giving compliments is a great way to be friendly. We all like to be around people who make us feel good about ourselves. Compliments can even work as a greeting. Children usually compliment one another's actions, possessions, or appearance. Have your child practice saying the following compliments with a smile and a friendly voice.

Compliments
"Nice shot."
"Good save."
"Cool backpack."
"Wow! That's a cool bike!"

After practicing these general compliments, it's time to turn to specifics. Which classmate would your child like to compliment? What does your child like or admire about that person? How could your child say this? Have your child try it and tell him or her to pay attention to how the other person responds. Remind your child to give only honest compliments. You may need to tell your child not to overdo it. One compliment is nice; a list of compliments ("I like your shirt. I like your pants. I like your shoes.") seems insincere.

You may also need to talk to your child about the importance of avoiding negative comments. If your child can't think of an honest compliment, a neutral statement can express interest and communicate "I care enough to notice." If your child can't honestly say to a classmate, "Your haircut looks great!" saying, "You got a haircut," is fine. Saying, "Your new haircut makes your ears stick out," is not okay, even if it's true.

3. Finding Shared Interests

Finding shared interests is the basis for most friendships. To do this, your child first has to have a sense of his or her own self. Help your child make a Things I Like Collage. Cut out photos from old magazines or catalogs, draw pictures, or just write down what he or she likes using colorful markers. Be sure to include "Things I Like to Eat," "Things I Like to Do," and "Places I Like to Go." You can also describe favorite colors, books, TV shows, music, and sports teams. Make a comparable collage for yourself. You may want to do this with all family members. Once you've come up with nice full collages, look for similarities and differences. Mark the overlapping items and explain to your child that these are shared interests.

Have your child select someone at school that he or she wants to get to know better. Look over your child's Things I Like Collage and talk about which interests the other child might share. Is he a Mets fan or a Cowboys fan? Does she like going to McDonalds? How could your child find out? How could your child let that classmate know that he or she also shares that interest? Asking interested questions and agreeing with a classmate's comments are good strategies. Your child could also try bringing something to school that shows a shared interest (e.g., part of a collection). If necessary, caution your child against bragging ("I'm the best . . ."; "I have the biggest . . ."). Some children believe that bragging will impress others, but it rarely does. It's more likely to irritate people.

Trying to learn about other people forces Shy Children to act interested in others. It pulls them out of their self-consciousness by making them focus on someone else. Before they know it, they are no longer just acting interested — they truly are interested in others.

4. Doing Things Together

Kids make friends by doing things together. The quickest and easiest way to connect with another child is to do the same thing. In Michael's case, when he saw the other boy riding a bike, he should have gotten his own bike out. This is an ideal strategy for Shy Children because they are usually very observant, so they pick up on what other kids are doing. Also, doing things together often means they don't have to say anything or feel tongue-tied. If your child sees a kid collecting leaves, he or she can start a pile nearby. If the other child is practicing cartwheels, your child should too. The key is not only to copy the other child but to do it in close enough proximity that the other child realizes it. If your child does cartwheels on the opposite side of the playground, the other child won't even notice. Doing the same thing nearby is a compliment. It's a way of saying "Good idea! That looks like fun."

Another good strategy for becoming friendly with another child is to invite him or her to go on an outing. Having a clear agenda from the start helps minimize your child's agonizing worries about what to do in social situations. Try inviting a potential friend to go ice-skating, bowling, or out for ice cream.

Having activity-based play dates with a variety of classmates, one at a time, can go a long way toward helping your child feel more comfortable at school. However, since being around unfamiliar people is a strain for your Shy Child, keep play dates short at first. It's better to have a brief play date that ends on a high note, with both children wishing for more time together, than to have a prolonged visit that has too many awkward moments.

Ideally, your child can ask the other child some questions before a play date to figure out shared interests. Otherwise, board games or two-player video games are good choices for Shy Children because the rules provide structure. Physical activities, such as riding bikes, playing catch, or shooting baskets, can also work well because they don't require much talking. Discourage your child from watching TV or videos on a play date. These activities prevent interaction.

Try to anticipate rough spots. You may need to rehearse with your child how to suggest possible activities. Be ready to offer a snack to give your child a little break or to fill in an uncomfortable lull. Remind your child not to wander away and leave the guest alone. If your child has to use the bathroom while a friend is over, he or she should say, "I'll be right back," and make it a quick trip.

5. Learning Telephone Etiquette

Using the telephone can be torture for Shy Children. Talking to a disembodied voice is even harder for them than talking to someone face-to-face. Although young children might be able to get away with avoiding the phone, by third or fourth grade, children will need to be able to talk to their classmates on the phone.

Your child will be more comfortable making and receiving calls if he or she knows what to say. The start and end of telephone conversations are like little rituals — they are pretty much the same every time. You probably do them without even thinking, but your child needs the steps spelled out. A nice thing about being on the phone is that it's easy to use crib notes.

Start by deciding how you want your home telephone to be answered. Write out the words and post them where they can easily be seen when your child needs them. Have your child practice with you, using either a cordless phone that is turned off or an unplugged phone, until your child is able to say the words smoothly. Make it your child's job to answer the phone for the next week. Be sure to keep paper and pen near the phone, in case your child needs to take a message. Children who are too young to take a message are probably too young to answer the phone.

Once your child is comfortable answering the phone, write up notes for calling a friend. Explain how to start and how to end the conversation. It's important to use a transition statement, like "See you tomorrow" or "Thanks for the homework assignment," before saying good-bye. Otherwise it seems like your child is hanging up abruptly.

Anticipate various scenarios. What if your child calls and the friend answers the phone? What if someone else answers? What if the friend isn't home? What if your child gets an answering machine instead of a real person? Many children are intimidated by answering machines. As adults, we leave messages so often that it's easy to forget that children aren't born knowing this procedure. Tell your child to (1) wait for the beep, (2) speak clearly, and (3) leave a short message, greeting the friend and stating your child's name and phone number.

Practice all of these scenarios, then have your child try calling a classmate with a specific question, such as "What was the math assignment?" You might want to have your child call one different classmate a night for a week. If your child feels up to it, he or she can even try calling a friend to set up a play date. Although they still need to consult parents, elementary school children usually take a bigger role in initiating play dates as they get older by making the call to set up the date and time and by planning activities.

Once your child is comfortable with the mechanics of short calls, work up to having full telephone conversations. Pick a warm and friendly relative to call (e.g., Grandma). Help your child make a list beforehand of things to tell and things to ask. Your child may want you to stay in the room during the call so you can give prompts or reminders if necessary. Afterward, praise your child's efforts lavishly.

In addition to teaching your child what to do on the phone, you may need to explain what *not* to do. Children sometimes cope with feeling scared by acting silly. Here are some guidelines about unacceptable behavior on the phone: It is never appropriate to make obnoxious noises on the phone. Staying silent on the phone is also rude. When someone asks, "Who is this, please?" never say, "Guess," or "Not telling." Never claim that you are someone else. Never hang up on someone. If the caller asks, "Is your mother there?" that means the caller wants to speak to your mother. Don't say, "Yes, she's here," and just stand there. Say, "Just a moment, please," then go get her. After the person the caller requested picks up the phone, hang up the extension. Don't listen in on someone else's conversation. If someone can't come to the phone, just say, "She can't come to the phone right now. May I take a message?" Do not say, "My mother isn't home," or "She's on the toilet." Unless it's an emergency, most people don't want to be called before 9:00 A.M. or after 9:00 P.M.

Increasingly, elementary school children are using the Internet to communicate. In many ways, this is a boon for Shy Children. They often find it easier to write an e-mail than to talk to someone in person or on the phone. Also, interacting with classmates on-line helps children to be "in the loop" about what's going on at school. However, be careful that your child doesn't substitute virtual relationships for real ones. Communicating on-line is a limited way of relating. It doesn't have the same immediacy as talking face-to-face, seeing each other's expressions, hearing each other's tone of voice, and actually doing things together. The goal for Shy Children is to make real relationships with real kids. Interacting on-line can be a great way to start, but it's not enough.

Emma: Hiding from the Group

Emma's mother drove into the school parking lot with the lunch her daughter had left on the kitchen table. Out of the corner of her eye, she noticed several girls from Emma's class playing hopscotch on the blacktop. She looked around for her daughter. Scanning the playground, she spotted her standing alone in the shadow of the building. Emma was staring longingly at the group of girls, but she made no move to join them. Emma's mother sighed. Their family had moved to this town three months ago, but her daughter still hadn't managed to make any friends. Just last week, the teacher called to say that Emma was spending a lot of time in the bathroom and at the nurse's office, especially during recess. Suddenly, Emma saw her mother. She hurried over and said tearfully, "Mommy, nobody wants to play with me. Please take me home. I hate it here."

Emma desperately wishes she could join the group of girls playing hopscotch, but she hangs back and does nothing. Maybe she feels it's easier to be miserably alone than to try to join and risk being rejected. Maybe she just doesn't know how to join the group.

Shy Children often feel like outsiders. They hold themselves apart from other children, acting like observers instead of participants. They wish they could be part of the group, but the distance between them and the other children seems like an impassable gulf. If a parent or teacher urges them to join in the group's activities, they refuse and shrink away. They react as if the adult had said, "Go ahead, honey, just leap over the Grand Canyon." Usually, kids playing in a group are too busy enjoying themselves to notice anyone who isn't playing, but even if another child invites them to join the group, Shy Children just shake their heads. The risk of failing seems too great.

Shy Children worry endlessly about everything that could go wrong and about all the ways they could humiliate themselves. They are certain that everyone is watching them and waiting for them to make a mistake. A group of children seems like a critical audience rather than a bunch of potential playmates.

If your child is intimidated by groups, you need to explain how to join a group and how to cope with the anxiety that holds him or her back. The Unwritten Rules and the following activities can help.

THE UNWRITTEN RULES

- You have to be where the action is to be included.
- Don't wait for an invitation.
- Standing on the fringes keeps you outside the group.
- To join a group, observe then blend.
- The thoughts running through your head affect how you act and feel.
- You can't succeed unless you try.
- Everyone makes mistakes.
- People are more worried about how they appear than how you appear.
- Your mistakes seem bigger to you than they do to anyone else.

ACTIVITIES FOR LEARNING
THE UNWRITTEN RULES

1. Joining a Group

Shy Children often stay on the fringes of groups because they don't know how to join in. They stand around waiting and wishing for an invitation that never comes.

Going up to a group of children and saying, "Can I play?" is a bad idea. It gives the mean or mischievous children a chance to say, "No, go away." Observations of children on playgrounds show that those who successfully join existing groups *don't* call attention to themselves. When they see a group of kids that they'd like to join, they first *observe,* to understand what the kids are doing, then they *blend* in to the ongoing action.

Explain this "observe then blend" sequence to your child. Shy Children are already good observers; they need to focus on the blending part. Your child may be relieved to learn that joining a group doesn't involve having all the other kids stop what they are doing and stare at your child. The goal is to join without interrupting the ongoing action. You may want to sit in the car with your child at a playground and see if you can spot some children actually doing the "observe then blend" sequence.

Point out that to join a group, your child needs to put him- or herself physically close enough to the other kids to be *inside* the perimeter of the group. Standing at the edges doesn't help. It practically guarantees being closed out.

Also explain that if the group is playing a sport, your child should try to join the losing side. The losing team is likely to welcome some extra help, even if your child is not a great athlete.

2. Starting a Group

Shy Children sometimes find it easier to start their own group than to join an existing one. This way they don't have to approach anyone — the other kids come to them.

Have your child bring a cool toy to the park. Make sure it is something that requires more than one person to play and that your child won't mind sharing. Good possibilities include a large ball, Kadima paddles, or walkie-talkies. A kite or a glider can also work. A Game Boy is not the best choice because it encourages playing alone. Rehearse with your child what to say when other kids approach. Have your child practice smiling and saying, "Wanna play?" or "Wanna try it?"

3. Coping with Negative Self-Talk

Often, what keeps Shy Children from approaching others is their negative self-talk. Explain to your child that we all have a little voice inside our heads that talks about how we are doing and what's going on around us. If that voice is saying negative things, it nibbles away at our confidence. The trick to feeling less scared is to learn to reassure that inner voice. Point out that your child's inner voice tends to be loudest and most negative in social situations. Help your child make a list of the things this voice says that make him or her feel anxious. You may want to use some of the examples below to get things started.

Explain to your child that the reason it's so important to counter negative self-talk is that it affects how we act and how we come across to other people. If that inner voice is yelling *I'm going to mess up!* we probably will. If it keeps saying *Nobody likes me,* other people will sense that we expect rejection, and they will reject us. It's a self-fulfilling prophecy. Our inner voice affects our behavior in subtle or not so subtle ways and brings about the reactions we are looking for. Negative self-talk leads to negative reactions from others. Learning to

Negative Self-Talk	Possible Counter Statement
"Everyone is staring at me."	"So what?"
"They think I'm weird."	"I know I'm not."
"I'm going to mess up."	"I'm going to do my best."
"I don't know what I'm doing."	"I probably know as much as most of the other kids."
"They're all going to laugh at me."	"Probably not."
"Nobody likes me."	"The people who know me well like me."
"I know they'll say they don't want to play with me."	"I won't know unless I try."

temper negative self-talk enables children to lift an anchor that could drag them down.

Once you have a list of negative self-statements, have your child read them aloud into a tape recorder. Then rewind the tape and play it back. Stop the tape after each statement to give your child a chance to counter the negative self-talk. What could your child say to reassure that inner voice? If your child can't think of a specific reassurance, he or she can just say something general like "So what?"; "I can handle it"; or "That's not true." Practice this several times, over several days, until your child can deflect negative self-talk quickly and easily. Once your child is good at countering the inner voice's negative statements aloud, he or she can say the same coping statements silently in social situations.

Keep in mind that reassurances *your child* comes up with are much more powerful than anything you suggest. Almost every parent of a

Shy Child has tried saying something like "Don't worry, kiddo. You're going to do great! Everyone will love you!" Although these comments are sincere efforts to help, they rarely work because they come from the parent's voice, not the child's. The goal in countering negative self-talk is not necessarily to substitute positive statements but to temper the negative ones. Help your child come up with statements that are believable and meaningful *to him or her*.

Practice identifying and countering negative self-talk for the first time when your child is feeling calm. After that, when you see your child feeling shy, wait for a private moment, then talk about what the inner voice was saying that made your child feel anxious. You may need to add these new negative self-statements to the tape and have your child work on answering them. With practice, reassuring the inner voice will become more automatic.

4. Planning for the Worst-Case Scenario

When your child is apprehensive about a new situation and is worrying frantically about all sorts of possible disasters, it can help to actually plan for these potential but unlikely events. Bringing fears out into the open can take away their power to control us. Label one column on a paper "Worst-Case Scenario." In that column, make a list with your child of everything he or she can imagine going wrong in the anxiety-provoking situation. Let your child list any worry, no matter how far-fetched. Label a second column "Plan." Help your child come up with a plan of action for each scenario. If your child comes up with new worries, encourage him or her to write them down on the list and come up with appropriate plans. If your child brings up a worry that is already on the list, say, "I don't think that will happen, but if it does, you'll know what to do." Here's an example of worst-case-scenario planning for a music recital.

Worst-Case Scenario	Plan
What if I drop my music?	I'll pick it up calmly.
What if I drop my music again?	I'll pick it up again.
What if I play the wrong notes?	I'll just keep playing. The audience won't notice or won't care.
What if everyone stares and laughs at me because I make a mistake?	I'll look for someone in the audience who cares about me.
What if I'm so scared that I forget what I'm supposed to play?	I'll take a deep breath to calm down. I'll keep a list of the pieces on a card in my pocket.
What if I get stuck in the middle of a song?	I'll repeat the part I remember.
What if I can't remember any of it?	I'll pretend it's the end of the piece or just skip that piece.
What if my pants fall down?	I'll pull them up and pretend nothing happened.

5. Visualizing Success

Visualization is a technique that athletes often use to help them perform better. They vividly imagine themselves playing well, and it helps them to actually do it. The same technique can help Shy Children before a social event. Often, Shy Children are so used to cowering and feeling painfully self-conscious around other people that they see this behavior as inevitable. It's hard for them to imagine acting any other way. Visualization gives them a positive alternate image of themselves. It's a way of mentally rehearsing success. Vividly picturing themselves feeling comfortable and confident around others makes it seem possible to do just that. In our experience, visualization can have almost magical affects. "I can see myself doing this" often precedes "I can actually do this!"

Older children may be able to visualize on their own, but younger children will need a parent's participation. As your child lies in bed at night before going to sleep (prime worry time!), have him or her imagine the steps leading up to the big event, as well as the actual event, in as much detail as possible and with the best possible outcome. Suppose your child is feeling scared about going to a birthday party. He or she can imagine

getting dressed
being driven to the party
standing on the doorstep and hearing the talking and laughter
ringing the doorbell
warmly greeting the birthday child and handing him or her the present
smiling and joining a group of other kids
listening with interest to the conversation
asking a relevant question
laughing at a joke
eagerly participating in party games
winning a prize
confidently sitting next to someone nice when it's time to eat
relishing the cake and ice cream

The more details your child can incorporate into the visualization, the better. You want your child to have a clear picture of things going well to counterbalance his or her tendency to focus on everything that can go wrong.

6. Acknowledging Success and Coping with Failure

Shy Children routinely beat themselves up mentally for their mistakes and discount their successes. If your child has a setback, help him or her to see this as an expected and probably necessary part of learning. Explain that the mistake looms much larger in your child's mind than in anybody else's. Most people are too preoccupied with their own concerns to notice, let alone dwell on, other people's mistakes.

Make sure your child takes credit for his or her triumphs. When your child manages to greet someone or join a group, he or she is likely to say or to think, "It was just luck," or "They didn't really like me," or "It's no big deal." As your child's chief cheerleader, it's your job to help him or her recognize progress. Point out accomplishments. Help your child see improvement. Make sure your child understands how his or her new friendly behavior led to positive responses from others. Help your child take credit for his or her victories.

Looking at old photos can be a fun way to help your child see how much he or she has grown and learned. Telling your child cute baby stories about his or her first words or first steps usually brings delighted giggles. You may even want to make a "Birthday Album" for your child, with just one or two photos from each birthday party. The change from year to year is remarkable. Interrupt your child's constant focus on his or her failings and inadequacies by showing how far he or she has come. Tell your child how proud you are of who he or she is right now.

Looking at photos can also be an opportunity to project into the future. Point out to your child that learning most things (e.g., walking, talking, eating with a fork, riding a bike) takes time and practice. What other changes do you imagine your child will accomplish in the next year or so? What would your child like to accomplish?

One of the best ways to help your child acknowledge his or her successes is to take appropriate credit for your own accomplishments. This doesn't mean being a braggart. It does mean being self-assured and legitimately proud of your efforts. Whether it involves your job, volunteer work, or a hobby, let your child hear you say, "I worked really hard on that. I'm pleased with how it turned out." If someone gives you a compliment, make sure your child hears you say, "Thank you," rather than "Oh, that's nothing. It isn't really very good. Anyone could have done it."

THE HOME-SCHOOL CONNECTION

Your child's teacher can be an enormous help in encouraging, but not forcing, your Shy Child to spread his or her wings. If your child's shyness is severe, you should talk with the teacher privately at the beginning of the year to explain which situations are difficult for your child and to ask the teacher for help.

Encouraging Friendships: Having even one buddy in the classroom makes Shy Children much more comfortable than if they have to face everything alone. Ask your child's teacher to give you some ideas of potential friends for your child, then invite them over for play dates. The teacher may also be able to help your child get over initial social hurdles by encouraging promising pairings. The teacher may be able to assign your child to work with someone who is socially comfortable, patient, and not overwhelming. Participating in one-on-one activities is less daunting for Shy Children than dealing with the whole group.

If the teacher is around at recess, a wonderful technique to break the ice socially is to start a game with the Shy Child and then back out. For instance, the teacher could bring a ball out on the playground and begin playing catch with your child. Other children will gravitate toward the teacher, and they can be included in the game. If necessary, the teacher can even prompt your child to throw the ball to another child, or prompt the other child to throw it to your child. Before long, your child is involved in a group game, and the teacher can slip away.

Respecting Differences: Class assignments that are fun for some children can be nightmares for others. If it would be unbearable for your child to stand in front of the class in a costume and give a book report, you need to let the teacher know this. Not all assignments can be modified, but when possible, it's a good idea if the teacher can give students some choices about how to do an assignment. Most children benefit from having choices, but it's especially helpful for Shy Children because it gives them some sense of control and allows them to build confidence gradually. For instance, if the assignment involves public speaking, could your child choose to do a written report instead? Could your child do the presentation with a partner? Could he or she choose to give the report sitting down at a desk instead of standing in front of the class? The goal is to find a middle ground that allows your child to grow but doesn't set him or her up for failure. Wrapping Shy Children in cotton and protecting them so much that they never have to do anything difficult restricts their world. On the other hand, forcing Shy Children into terrifying situations that they truly can't handle will only compound their fears.

You may also want to ask the teacher not to call on your child unless he or she raises a hand. Many Shy Children live in terror of being called on. When the spotlight is suddenly and unexpectedly on them, their minds empty, and they are mortified. The teacher could instead say, "I'd like to hear from someone who hasn't answered in a while," a general prompt that offers your child a choice.

Building Confidence: The teacher can help build your child's confidence by giving him or her the opportunity to shine. If your child is good at math or reading, the teacher may be able to assign your child to help a classmate who is having trouble. Or maybe your child could read to younger children during story time. If your child has a hobby that involves a special expertise, such as collecting rocks, insects, or stamps, tell the teacher about it. The teacher can express interest in front of the other students and maybe even invite your child to bring in the collection.

Shy Children may seem self-contained, but they are actually desperate for their teachers to notice and like them. This means that a teacher's words have enormous impact on Shy Children. You may need to suggest that the teacher *not* praise your Shy Child for being quiet. When the other kids are chattering noisily and poking one another, teachers understandably appreciate that your Shy Child is sitting calmly. However, praising Shy Children for being quiet could shut them down even more. For the child who is eager to please, it can unintentionally give the message that you want them to be even quieter. The teacher should definitely praise your Shy Child (without drawing too much attention) if he or she manages to speak up or to give an opinion. But in the meantime, ask the teacher to praise your child for behaviors unrelated to quietness, such as being creative, doing something helpful or kind, or excelling in some area.

IF YOU TOO . . .

If you are also shy, you can understand the paralyzing fear that your child experiences in social situations. This gives you a special compassion for your Shy Child, but be careful that you aren't so sympathetic that you prevent your child from dealing with these fears. Because you love your child and hate to see him or her suffer, you may hold your child back from going to social events or trying new activities. You may just accept it when your child says, "I don't want to. It's too hard." By doing so, you could unintentionally be telling your child, "Yes, this is a truly dangerous situation that you can't handle." You are accepting the limits that your child has placed on his or her world. But, as we described in our discussion of the Cycle of Shyness, avoiding social situations just makes matters worse. It prevents your child from learning how to relate to other people and how to manage fears. Your child needs to build confidence by gradually facing more and more social situations. This will undoubtedly involve some short-term anxiety. Watching your child suffer may be harder on you than participating is on your child, but you need to show your child that you believe in his or her ability to cope.

It's also important to remember that even though you are both shy, your child doesn't necessarily have the exact same fears you do. Don't restrict your child's activities because of your own fears. Don't assume that situations that are terrifying for you are also terrifying for your child. Shyness can take many forms. Your child may be able to handle playing in the school orchestra or calling someone for a play date or joining the soccer team, even if you couldn't do it at that age. Moreover, your child deserves a chance to try.

The best thing you can do for your Shy Child is to begin to face some of your own fears. When you feel anxious about an activity and do it anyway, you inspire your child to do the same. As your confidence grows, you show your child that it's possible to overcome fears.

SUMMARY

Shy Children are usually perceptive, caring, and loyal, so once they get over their initial reticence, they have a lot to offer as friends. They need to learn how to manage their anxiety and how to initiate friendships.

They need to gradually gain confidence in social situations. There is no need to try to remake them into outgoing children. Shy Children simply need the right tools to build on their strengths so that they can do what *they* want to do instead of being limited by their fears.

You Will Also Want to Read:
    Chapter 2, "The Vulnerable Child"
    Chapter 6, "The Short-Fused Child"
    Chapter 8, "The Sensitive Soul"
    Chapter 10, "The Pessimistic Child"

THE UNWRITTEN RULES FOR THE SHY CHILD AT A GLANCE

- Greet people you know (or want to know).
- Not responding makes you seem snobbish.
- Looking away says "I'm not interested."
- You have to show kids you like them — no one can read your mind.
- Giving an honest compliment is like giving a gift.
- Kids like kids who are willing to do things with them.
- You have to be where the action is to be included.
- Don't wait for an invitation.
- Standing on the fringes keeps you outside the group.
- To join a group, observe then blend.
- The thoughts running through your head affect how you act and feel.
- You can't succeed unless you try.
- Everyone makes mistakes.
- People are more worried about how they appear than how you appear.
- Your mistakes seem bigger to you than they do to anyone else.

CHAPTER 6

The Short-Fused Child

Does your child . . .

have a hot temper?

overreact to things that other children take in stride?

seem to be coping well and then suddenly explode over a minor frustration?

get so worked up that you can't reason with him or her?

often insist that other children deliberately did something to provoke him or her?

rarely take responsibility for his or her angry outbursts because it's always the other kid's fault?

frequently "lose it" in front of others?

get worrisome reports from the teacher about having poor self-control?

frequently get chastised at school for getting into arguments or fights?

act like the weight of the world is on his or her shoulders?

Do you . . .

feel embarrassed by your child's excessive outbursts?

feel exasperated that your child hasn't outgrown tantrums yet?

worry that stress at home or at school is causing your child's outbursts?

suspect that your child's explosive temper is the reason that he or
she has so few friends?

sense that other children are just a little afraid of your child?

dread play dates because minor disagreements often turn into
heated arguments for your child?

wonder if your child is developing a reputation for being a hothead?

Short-Fused Children are like simmering volcanoes. One minute
everything seems quiet, but the next minute their fiery rage explodes,
raining down on anyone around them.

Once Short-Fused Children become enraged, they can't think
straight. Their automatic reaction takes the place of reason. They see
the world through a red haze. They are likely to act impulsively and
even to lash out aggressively. However, unlike Intimidating Children
(chapter 3), their aggression isn't planned or targeted. Instead of sys-
tematically picking on weaker children, they fight with anyone about
anything that frustrates them — without thinking of the consequences. In fact, Short-Fused Children are often the victims of bullying because other children know that a little bit of taunting will get a
big reaction from them. (If your child is being bullied, see chapter 2,
"The Vulnerable Child.")

By elementary school, teachers and classmates expect a degree of
maturity and self-control. When Short-Fused Children violate these
expectations with their angry outbursts, teachers tend to see them as
"problem" children, and other kids think they are weird. Some classmates are scared of Short-Fused Children's blowups and actively
avoid them. Other classmates are entertained by the fireworks and go
out of their way to provoke them.

In many ways, Short-Fused Children themselves are the ones who are hurt the most by their explosive tempers. They know that their rages set them apart from other kids. Once they have a chance to cool down, they are often embarrassed about losing it in front of everyone. They may even feel frightened by how out of control they were. They often feel helpless to prevent another outburst.

Short-Fused Children may appear to be strong, but inside they feel vulnerable. These children are extremely sensitive. They often believe that the whole world is against them. Because they feel threatened, they respond angrily, instinctively fighting to protect themselves. In their minds, their rages are a matter of self-defense. The keys to helping Short-Fused Children are lessening their sense of threat and providing them with other, more adaptive, options for dealing with frustration.

ON THE POSITIVE SIDE

Short-Fused Children are passionate. They have strong beliefs, and they have the courage to stand up for themselves. These children are not pushovers. With proper guidance, they can learn to express their convictions appropriately and to channel their "fighting spirit" in positive directions.

Once Short-Fused Children are able to manage their anger appropriately, they can develop their natural capacity for friendship and connection. When less of their energy goes toward protecting themselves from perceived threats, Short-Fused Children have more opportunities to relax, enjoy life, respond warmly to others, and cultivate their own true potential.

SO, WHAT CAN WE DO?

Some parents believe that yelling and fighting are beneficial ways of "letting off steam." This is *not* true. Children don't feel better after acting out in angry ways; they usually feel frightened or ashamed.

Short-Fused Children need to learn the Unwritten Rules about managing anger. They need to understand clearly the social costs of an unrestrained temper and to develop ways of avoiding and resolving conflicts. The exercises in this chapter can help you teach your child to refrain from acting impulsively when angry, to interpret social situations in benign ways, and to minimize stress-related tantrums.

Anger-related problems are some of the most common difficulties we see, but they can also be some of the hardest to change. These problems rarely get better on their own. Developing anger-management skills takes considerable time and effort from both you and your child, but this effort is worthwhile because knowing constructive ways to handle feelings can free your child from being driven blindly by his or her temper and allow your child to make and keep friends.

Frequent furious or violent reactions may be more than just a sign of poor coping skills or a lack of understanding of how to relate to others appropriately. They may be symptoms of serious difficulties, such as a mood disorder. If the exercises in this chapter and the supplemental books we recommend are not enough to teach your child better ways of relating, you should seek the help of a mental health professional.

In this chapter, we describe three examples of Short-Fused Children. You may recognize your child in one or all of them. Gregory shows poor sportsmanship and resorts to threatening and yelling to solve a minor disagreement. Lorena has trouble understanding social situations. She overreacts when she wrongly interprets an accident as a deliberate provocation. Malcolm has a stress-related outburst. His angry reaction is a sign that his coping abilities are swamped — he just can't take it anymore.

Gregory: Acting Like a Poor Sport

"You lie! You lie!" Gregory screamed, clutching the basketball. "I did not foul him! I was only guarding him! He slipped and fell!"

"You can't push someone down and snatch the ball, Gregory! That's not fair!" Will argued.

"I didn't! That ball was loose, and the basket I made counts!"

"No way!" Peter insisted. "That basket doesn't count, and we get a free throw."

"You guys are such cheaters!" Gregory yelled.

"Come on! It's almost dark," Carlos said. "Let's just play. How about if we don't count either the foul or the basket and just start over with a jump ball?" Carlos reached for the ball.

"No deal!" Gregory yelled, elbowing Carlos out of the way. "It's my basketball, so what I say goes! I'm not gonna play if you're gonna cheat! I'm taking my ball home."

"Oh, who cares!" David snapped. "Give the baby the two points. Let's just get on with the game!"

Gregory used a variety of strategies to get his way: he yelled, he argued, he called the other boys names, he threatened to take the ball away. Ultimately, these strategies worked. The other boys gave in, and his basket counted. But at what cost? Gregory's outrage is disruptive and tiresome. The other boys certainly won't seek out his company. They may not even let Gregory play next time.

When disagreements occur, Short-Fused Children automatically resort to aggressive strategies without thinking of any alternatives. In fact, they don't even realize that they have a choice in how they respond to others. They are completely focused on the terrible offense that the other person committed. They even see that offense as the cause of their own actions. "He made me kick him because he took my pencil."

Short-Fused Children believe that arguing or fighting will get them what they want. Like Gregory, they focus on the short-term victory and don't realize they will incur a long-term loss. They don't understand that nobody wants to be around a hothead. It's not fun to be hit, screamed at, or insulted. Other kids might give in temporarily in response to a fit of anger, but after that, they will go out of their way to avoid Short-Fused Children and to seek out friends who are easier to play with. Relatives might tolerate your child's outbursts, but other kids, especially those who don't know your child well, just won't stick around if there's constant conflict.

Many children like Gregory have problems relating to family members as well as peers. Short-Fused Children and their parents sometimes become caught in an escalation trap in which screaming, fighting, whining, nagging, and being nasty to one another is more the norm than the exception. This pattern was first described by Dr. Gerald Patterson and is based on observations of mothers and children. Neither parents nor children enjoy this way of relating, but they often don't know how to break out of the pattern.

In Stage One of the escalation trap, parent and child work each other up into a rage (see figure 6.1). It starts with some minor provocation, like the child being told "No" or "Stop that." This leads the child to respond angrily. The parent reciprocates this anger, causing the child to react with even more hostility. By now the parent is furious. The parent yells, threatens, and demands respect. This is like throwing gasoline on a fire. The child erupts. The parent finally gives in because he or she can't stand the child's horrible behavior. Sometimes it's one parent who both gets into battles with the child and then ultimately gives in. Sometimes parents share the work in this cycle: one parent battles with the child and spurs him or her into a frenzy, and the other parent, unable to stand the fighting, gives in.

Figure 6.1

THE ESCALATION TRAP

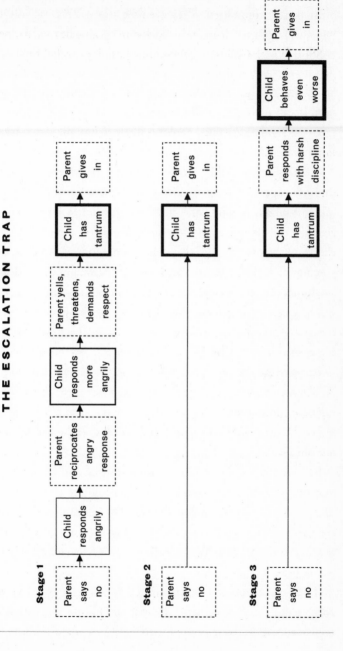

After many of these interactions, Stage Two of the escalation trap sets in. By now, the child has learned that getting his or her way will require more than a little obnoxious behavior; the child has realized that it will take a full-blown explosion to get what he or she wants. So the child skips the preliminaries and goes straight to the explosion. Because every little thing seems to set off a huge argument, the exhausted and exasperated parent is likely to give in, just to try to get some peace. Unfortunately, giving in sustains the pattern.

Although the child's overreaction to provocation is learned through experience, the resulting tantrums are not part of a well-thought-out plan. The child does *not* respond to a parental no by gleefully calculating, *Aha! I know just how to get them to give in!* The child's outbursts, by this stage, are automatic reactions. A simple parental no is no longer simple. It carries the weight of the dozens of battles that have come before it. The child hears no and reacts to the whole long, terrible power struggle. He or she becomes instantly enraged. And once the child reaches an extreme level of anger, he or she can't think straight. Dr. Daniel Goleman, author of *Emotional Intelligence*, refers to this phenomenon as "emotional flooding." While in this state, the child is physiologically incapable of processing new information, seeing another person's point of view, or thinking of the consequences of his or her actions. So the child just lashes out blindly.

In Stage Three, the parent becomes worried and frustrated about how out of control the child is and periodically responds with harsh discipline when the child throws a fit. The child reacts by behaving even worse. The parent feels helpless and gives in, and the pattern continues with an even higher level of hostile behavior from the child (see figure 6.1).

If our discussion of the escalation trap strikes a chord with you, you are not alone. It is extremely easy to fall into this trap without even realizing it. Your Short-Fused Child is probably more easily frustrated, less flexible, and more intense than most children. It's understandable that there are times when you are so fed up with his or her angry outbursts that you decide to give in just to avoid another tirade. However, once you recognize this pattern, you can see that it won't get better unless you make some changes in how you deal with your child.

We described the escalation trap in terms of parent-child interactions, but sibling conflicts can work the same way, training children to respond to provocation with intense anger. A certain amount of sibling squabbling is normal. Teasing, put-downs, and name-calling are typical ways that kids socialize at this age. This kind of behavior usually peaks around the fourth, fifth, and sixth grades. But just because it's typical doesn't mean you have to put up with it. Often, siblings argue because they are bored, so a bit of distraction can help. You also need to make it clear that you won't tolerate disrespectful behavior. Elizabeth Crary's book *Help! The Kids Are at It Again* offers additional suggestions for minimizing bickering between siblings. If you find that your children's sparring often escalates into intense fighting, you definitely need to step in. Children who fight a lot with their siblings also tend to fight a lot at school. If you are concerned about your children's arguments, the exercises about managing sibling conflict in chapter 3, "The Intimidating Child," might help.

The following activities offer some suggestions for breaking out of the escalation trap and for helping your child learn positive ways to handle angry feelings. Minimizing blowups requires prevention and early intervention. Your child needs to be able to recognize when he or she is starting to feel angry and immediately take steps to calm down before he or she reaches a full-blown rage or does something impulsive. Learning the Unwritten Rules and practicing the following exercises can help your child (and you) keep cool when provoked.

THE UNWRITTEN RULES

- Don't "lose it" in public.
- It's better to walk away from a bad situation than to do something you'll regret later.
- It takes courage to stay calm under fire.
- New relationships won't survive conflict.
- Angry outbursts might win an argument, but they can result in the loss of a friend.
- Forcing someone to give in to your wishes creates hard feelings.

ACTIVITIES FOR LEARNING THE UNWRITTEN RULES

1. Understanding the Consequences of Acting Out of Control

The biggest problem in changing the behavior of Short-Fused Children is that their angry outbursts often work — at least in the short term. Short-Fused Children are focused on getting what they want at that moment, so they just don't see the social cost of their tirades. They have no motivation to act differently.

You need to find a gentle and compassionate way to show your child the link between his or her aggressive behavior and others' withdrawal. If your child is feeling satisfied after managing to impose his or her will on someone through angry words or actions, you may want to bring up the concept of winning the battle and losing the war. Spell out the consequences for your child: "Yelling at Patrick made him agree to play the game you wanted, but did you see his expression? He didn't give in happily, and he seemed annoyed for the rest of the play date."

Sometimes it's easier for children to get the "aggression doesn't pay" message when it's presented in terms of someone else's misbehavior.

A good way to do this is to read a book together about the consequences of angry behavior. For children nine and under, we recommend *How to Be a Friend* by Laurie K. Brown and Marc T. Brown. Nine- to eleven-year-olds might benefit from *The Very Angry Day that Amy Didn't Have* by Dr. Lawrence E. Shapiro. Both books describe social difficulties arising from uncontrolled tempers, and they also explain positive alternatives to acting out.

For older children, you can use the actions of friends, relatives, celebrities, TV characters, or even irate strangers at the grocery store as examples of appropriate or inappropriate ways of handling angry feelings. Talk about your admiration for someone who was able to keep cool in a stressful situation. Remark or speculate about the negative consequences for someone who lost it in public. Comment on how foolish that person seems. Point out that angry actions tend to elicit angry responses. Discuss with your child how the person could have handled the situation better.

2. Playing the Relationship Points Card Game

Children who are old enough to add and subtract can learn about building relationships by playing the Relationship Points Card Game. Explain to your child that the way we treat people can either build or destroy relationships. Copy each of the phrases in the box below onto an index card. You may also want to use additional cards (both positive and negative) referring to your child's specific difficulties. Shuffle the deck and take turns drawing cards and keeping track of relationship points. The person with the most points when all the cards have been drawn, wins. As a follow-up, you can also try discussing the negative cards. Why do those actions lose relationship points? How do they make the other person feel? What's a better response? You may also want to tell your child that new relationships are especially at risk when there is conflict because there hasn't been any opportunity to build up positive points to counterbalance it.

RELATIONSHIP POINTS CARD GAME

Points	Behavior
+10 points	Greet someone with a smile and a cheerful voice.
+15 points	Offer to let someone go in front of you in line.
+20 points	Tell someone, "Nice play!" when they do something well in a game.
+50 points	Say, "Okay, no big deal," and drop the matter when someone apologizes to you.
+50 points	Say, "I'm too mad to talk about this right now," and walk away, rather than screaming at someone.
+15 points	Ask someone, "What would you like to play?"
–20 points	Call someone a cheater or a liar.
–20 points	Hit or shove someone in anger.
–15 points	Yell at someone.
–15 points	Tell someone they had better do what you want "or else."
–15 points	Say, "I quit. I'm not playing anymore!" when a game isn't going your way.
–20 points	Break something that belongs to someone else because he or she is being mean to you.

3. Recognizing Early Warning Signs of Building Tension

Bodily signs of building tension are a warning bell that an angry outburst could be coming. Your child needs to learn to tune in to this warning. Have your child lie down on a large piece of paper and trace his or her body. Now have your child draw what it feels like inside when he or she *starts* to feel angry. Common signs include a racing heart, a tight or fluttery stomach, tense muscles, and a hot face. You want your child to be aware of these early warning signals because it's easier to calm down while the bodily tension is still at a low level.

You may be able to help your child recognize early warning signs during ordinary day-to-day activities. When you see your child becoming tense, annoyed, or frustrated, comment on this and ask your child to describe what it feels like in his or her body. Explain that whenever your child has these angry feelings, he or she should do something to calm down.

4. Learning to Calm Down

Help your child learn some unobtrusive ways to calm down in social situations. These techniques can help your child feel more in control, making it less likely that he or she will act out angrily without thinking. The following list includes a variety of calming techniques. Pick the ones that appeal to your child.

Explain to your child that it's much easier to use these techniques *before* he or she becomes utterly furious, but better late than never. Once people are enraged, it typically takes them twenty minutes or more to cool off.

Walking Away: One of the simplest and best possible responses when your child notices a buildup of angry feelings during a stressful interaction is to walk away. If your child is at school, he or she can get a drink, go to the bathroom, or walk to the other side of the playground. At home, your child can go to his or her room or go outside.

Sometimes kids are reluctant to walk away from an argument because they think they are letting the other person win. Explain to your child that it takes courage to be able to step away from a bad situation. The person who gets furious and acts out is the real loser of an argument. Walking away can prevent your child from doing or saying something he or she will regret later. You may want to role-play with your child how to walk away calmly from an argument. Storming away doesn't work. Sometimes it helps to use an exit statement, which can be said either silently or aloud before leaving. Possible exit statements include "I need a break," "I need time to cool off," or "I'm too mad to deal with this now." If necessary, your child can come back to the issue later, when he or she can handle it with a cool head.

Counting: Another tried-and-true calming technique is counting. Counting helps put some time between feeling and reacting so your child won't lash out without thinking. Experiment to find out the number your child feels comfortable using. For some children, just counting up to five is adequate.

Using Calming Statements: Some children like to have a phrase that they repeat to themselves when they start to feel riled up. Have your child choose one of the following calming statements or come up with some other phrase that is meaningful to him or her, to use when needed.

"I'm not going to let this get to me."
"It's not worth getting upset over this."
"It's my choice how I respond to this."
"I can handle this."
"This is their problem, not mine."

Using Imagery: Imagery is a powerful technique for coping with negative feelings. Mental pictures can sometimes connect directly with emotional experience in a way that words can't. One of our favorite images for children who are prone to take offense is a giant umbrella. Have your child imagine holding the umbrella over his or her head while insults and aggravations hit the umbrella and slide off like rainwater without touching your child. For fun, and to make the image especially vivid, you may even want to try acting this out. Go outside on a warm day and give your child a big umbrella to hold. Gently spray a hose on top of the umbrella. Comment on how your child is managing to stay dry and unperturbed despite a shower of offenses.

Imagery can also help reduce tension. Some children like to close their eyes and imagine a warm golden light gradually spreading over their bodies. It starts at the top of their head and flows downward, smoothing away their tension.

Using Slow Breathing: Help your child practice breathing slowly: in through the nose for two counts, and out through the mouth for four counts. Concentrating on breathing pulls your child's attention away from what is bothering him or her, and also helps relax your child's whole body. If your child is using the slow breathing technique around other children, it's important to do it quietly so that others don't notice.

Practicing Muscle Relaxation: To teach your child muscle relaxation, have your child sit on a comfortable chair or couch. Tell your child to imagine all of the tension flowing out his or her fingers and toes. Lift your child's arm by the wrist, then drop it. It should flop down with no hesitation or resistance. Check the other arm and both legs. If there is any tension remaining, tell your child to relax even further, then check again.

Muscle relaxation is a skill. The more your child practices it, the more likely he or she will be able to use it when stressed. You can make relaxation part of your family's daily life by incorporating it as an after-dinner activity or as part of the bedtime ritual.

5. Being a Good Sport

No one is born knowing how to be a good sport. We all have to learn it. We start learning it in preschool when we see that other children shriek if we snatch their toys. We continue to use and cultivate our sportsmanship skills throughout adulthood — when we congratulate a coworker on a promotion we wish we had gotten or share household chores with a spouse or thank fellow volunteers for their help with a fundraising effort even if we did most of the work. Being a good sport is a basic part of getting along with others. It means being able to act for the greater good and to acknowledge other people's needs and wishes, not just our own.

Ask your child to think of three classmates who are well liked. Have your child think about how these children act during gym, after school, or on the playground; then have him or her rate these children on the Good Sport Checklist. Highlight the behaviors that all three children have in common. Talk about why people like being around someone who is a good sport.

GOOD SPORT CHECKLIST

Do they . . .

Yes	No	follow the rules of the game?
Yes	No	try their best?
Yes	No	listen to the adult in charge without arguing?
Yes	No	smile and talk to people in a friendly voice?
Yes	No	say only positive things about other players?
Yes	No	never accuse others of cheating?
Yes	No	listen to others' ideas?
Yes	No	let others have a turn?
Yes	No	give in gracefully when things don't go their way (i.e., no whining)?

Yes	No	act like a team players — doing what's best for the team, even if it's not what they want?
Yes	No	apologize sincerely when they've done something wrong?
Yes	No	keep cool when losing a game?
Yes	No	never quit in the middle of a game because they are losing?
Yes	No	congratulate the winners, without sulking, when they lose?
Yes	No	thank the losers for playing, without gloating, when they win?

Once your child understands what good sportsmanship is, consider having him or her join a team to practice these skills. Teammates and the coach can help teach appropriate behavior, and the camaraderie of a team is great for a child who often feels at odds with the world. As you cheer for your child, be careful not to give a "winning is everything" message. Sure, it's fun to win, but let your child see that you are more concerned about whether he or she is having fun, developing team skills, and being a good sport.

Another way of promoting good sportsmanship is by playing board games with your child. Don't allow your child to cheat or change the rules of the game, because other children won't put up with this. Don't deliberately play badly to let your child win, because your Short-Fused Child needs practice taking losing in stride. By nine years of age, your child should be able to win or lose graciously. Teach your child to tell the other player cheerfully, "Good game!" regardless of the outcome.

If your child is having a play date, it's a good idea to anticipate possible sportsmanship trouble spots. You may want to role-play with your child some good and bad ways of handling typical situations, such as those in the following list. Sometimes children don't even realize that their behavior is rude or obnoxious. Being on the receiving end of some of the Bad Sport examples can help your child become aware of the impact of this behavior on others. If you and your child ham it up, the Bad Sport examples can also provide some comic relief. The Good Sport examples show your child how to handle the situations appropriately.

POSSIBLE PLAY DATE TROUBLE SPOTS

Choosing What to Play

Bad Sport:	"No way! That's a stupid game!"
	"It's my house, so you have to do what I say!"
Good Sport:	"Okay. Why don't we play your game first; then we'll try my game."
	"You're the guest. You get to choose."

Negotiating Rules

Bad Sport:	"It's my house, so I get to decide the rules, and I say that point counts!"
	"No fair! You can't do that! You're cheating!"
Good Sport:	"How about if, from now on, . . ."
	"I usually play that that point counts, but we can do it your way, if you want."

Changing Activities

Bad Sport:	"This is a stupid game! I'm not playing anymore!"
	Walks away from the game without saying anything.

| Good Sport: | "I'm getting tired of this game. How about if we do one more round and then play something else?" |
| | "You're winning. Do you want to finish the game, or do you want to go get a snack now?" |

Losing

Bad Sport:	"This is a stupid game!" (Disrupts game board.)
	"No fair! You cheated!"
Good Sport:	"Good game."
	"Would you like to play again, or do you want to do something else?"

Winning

Bad Sport:	"YES!!! I won! I won! I won! I'm the best! I'm the champion!"
	"I win. You lose. Ha-ha! You stink! I bet even my baby sister could beat you!"
Good Sport:	"Good game."
	"Would you like to play again, or do you want to do something else?"

6. Breaking Out of the Escalation Trap

If your child has learned, over an extended period of time, to respond to provocation with extreme anger, the two of you may be caught in the escalation trap described earlier. Unfortunately, it's much easier to fall into this trap than it is to break out of it. If possible, choose a time in your life when you and your family are not feeling unusually stressed and can make the following activities your top priority. You should expect things to get worse before they get better. Your child is not going to be able to change this behavior quickly or easily. He or she may not even know or remember any other way of relating.

The following paragraphs outline the main strategies for ending the escalation trap. For more detailed discussions of how to defuse anger and minimize power struggles, see *Kids, Parents, and Power Struggles* by Mary S. Kurcinka; *The Secret of Parenting* by Dr. Anthony E. Wolf; and, for more severe difficulties, *The Explosive Child* by Dr. Ross W. Greene. If the conflict between you and your child is very intense or long-lasting, we suggest that you consult a mental health professional.

Catching Your Child Being Good: Too often, when a parent and child are caught in an escalation trap, it takes over their whole relationship. Somehow, just about every interaction ends in a yelling match. To change this pattern, you need to deliberately create positive interactions. Don't make the excuse that you'll start being nicer when your child starts behaving better. It's your job to get the ball rolling. Be on the lookout for anything your child does that is kind, helpful, capable, or pleasant and offer a brief but sincere compliment or thank-you: "Thanks for helping me carry the groceries"; "You really worked hard on that science project"; " It was nice of you to tie your brother's shoe." Don't spoil your compliments by adding a sarcastic comment like "For once in your life!" or "It's about time!" Focus on describing good things your child did ("I like how you got ready for school so quickly this morning!") rather than bad things your child didn't do ("I like how you didn't have a screaming tantrum this morning!"). Praise that describes specific behavior ("Nice job putting away your clothes!") is more meaningful than global praise ("You're great!").

Every day, or at least every week, try to have some low-key positive time with your child. Research on close relationships shows that the ordinary, little connections of day-to-day life are more important for building and maintaining a sense of closeness than the big events are. With your spouse, the "How was your day?" and "Would you mind picking up the dry cleaning?" conversations have a bigger impact on your relationship than an elaborate night on the town. Special events are a great way of celebrating a relationship, but these alone can't sustain a relationship. In fact, it would be hard to enjoy a fancy dinner with your spouse if the two of you spent most of your time together bickering. Similarly, showing interest in your child's hobbies or having a calm and cozy bedtime routine is more important than taking him or her to Disney World. Elaborate vacations and excursions can provide wonderful family experiences, but these alone won't enable you to form a good relationship with your child. Moreover, big outings, planned with the best intentions, sometimes end in tears, exhaustion, and disappointment. You may find that simpler events, which carry smaller expectations from both you and your child, are more likely to be successful.

Look for ways of turning everyday activities into opportunities for connecting. Try joining your child on the floor for fifteen minutes to help build a Lego tower (and be sure to follow your child's lead rather than impose your ideas). Let your child help you cook dinner. Invite your child to come along on a quick trip to the hardware store, just the two of you.

Planning Ahead: Planning can help minimize conflict. First of all, pick your battles. You can't deal with everything at once, so just pick one or two of your child's behaviors that are really bothering you, stay firm and consistent in how you respond to them, and let everything else slide — for now. Be sure to take into consideration what your child is realistically capable of doing. Start small to build on success. Second, plan how to approach the situation in a positive way. Instead of just reacting to misbehavior, think about how you can encourage good behavior. You already know that screaming and threatening doesn't work with your child. It just riles him or her up. You need to think of ways to encourage cooperation. Emphasize what your child *can* do rather than what he or she can't do. Ask your child for suggestions. Offer choices. Do chores together, and then do something fun afterward. Third, plan so that you don't overreact to misbehavior. If you give your child a consequence for doing something wrong, you should make sure that the punishment fits the crime rather than your level of anger. Also, you'll have fewer arguments if your child already knows the rules.

Trying Not to Take It Personally: When a child regularly has angry outbursts, it's easy for a parent to take this as a sign of disrespect and to want to show the child who's boss. In our experience with elementary school children, true disrespect is rarely an issue. Your child already knows that you are the boss. Your child really does want to please you. He or she is simply stuck in a destructive pattern of relating and lacks the skills necessary to moderate and express feelings appropriately.

More than anything, your child needs to know that you are on his or her side. Instead of letting yourself get sucked into another battle, mentally take a giant step backward. Acknowledge your child's feelings. Honestly try to see the situation from your child's perspective. Ask yourself, *What can I do to help my child calm down and behave appropriately, either now or in the future?* Keep in mind that as horrible as your child's tantrums are for you, they are even worse for your child. Many Short-Fused Children are frightened or ashamed of their out-of-control rages. Your child doesn't consciously choose to behave this way. He or she needs your help to learn better ways of relating.

Focusing on Teaching Coping and Relating Skills: One of your main jobs as a parent is to teach your child how to get along with others. The lessons you teach your child, directly and indirectly, about how to behave when angry will carry through to other relationships outside the family. Show your child how to express feelings respectfully and to look for ways to compromise.

When your child loses it, think about what led up to the tantrum. What was the initial trigger? Was there anything else going on that made it extra hard for your child to cope (e.g., was he or she tired, hungry, in a noisy or crowded environment, handling too many frustrations at once)? Did your responses make the situation better or worse? Don't try to teach your child anything while he or she is in the midst of a blowup. Your child is emotionally flooded at that point and is incapable of learning or even thinking clearly. Later, when you and your child are both feeling calm, you can talk about how the situation could be handled differently next time.

7. Working Toward Conflict Resolution

Often, what perpetuates Short-Fused Children's angry outbursts is that they don't know any other way to respond to provocation. In their calmer moments, they may realize that they shouldn't fly off the handle, but they don't know what else to do. Research shows that when children learn how to resolve conflicts peacefully, they are less likely to resort to aggression.

Explain to your child that disagreements, disappointments, misunderstandings, and arguments are inevitable in relationships. How we handle these problems determines whether a relationship ends or grows stronger. When conflicts come up, instead of trying to win or to get even, your child needs to focus on explaining, understanding, and compromising. Most of the time, it's possible to work things out and move on.

The National Liberty Museum, America's Home for Heroes in Philadelphia, Pennsylvania, has a wonderful exhibit on brotherhood that features an inspiring list of peaceful conflict resolution strategies. Go over this list with your child and see if he or she can explain why each strategy solves problems and helps people get along with one another. Have your child decorate the list and then post it on your refrigerator. Consult it often. Pull it out when your child is feeling angry with someone at home or at school and talk about which of the strategies seem most relevant for your child's particular situation. Plan or rehearse how to carry out these strategies. Help your child understand that we are each responsible for spreading peace in the world.

Ten Ways to Resolve Conflicts
© 2000 National Liberty Museum

1. **Listen more. Talk less.**
   It helps you understand the other person's point of view.
2. **Ask when you want something.**
   Making demands only makes things worse.
3. **Focus on the problem, not the person.**
   It's the only way to solve a disagreement.
4. **Always deal with the problem at hand.**
   Never bring up old issues.
5. **Take responsibility for your part in the conflict.**
   Your view may not be completely right either.
6. **Express your feelings without blaming the other person.**
   Blame never solves anything.
7. **Always talk things out.**
   Never use physical force to express your anger.
8. **Choose your words carefully.**
   Once a word is spoken, it cannot be taken back.
9. **Look for a solution that is agreeable to both parties.**
   If one person isn't satisfied, the problem isn't solved.
10. **Step back and put the problem in perspective.**
    A problem you have today may not seem so bad tomorrow.

Lorena: Assuming Malicious Intent

"How was school today, Lorena?" her mother asked.

"Terrible!" Lorena snarled. "Casey dumped a whole can of soda into my backpack! I had to clean up that whole mess, and it ruined all my stuff, and she wasn't even sorry!"

"Well, did she do it on purpose?"

"Of course she did!" Lorena snapped. "How do you do a thing like that by accident? My backpack was on the floor, and she put her soda right on the edge of the table. What did she think was going to happen?"

"Well, honey, she probably didn't realize your backpack was there."

"Yes, she did," Lorena insisted. "It was right there. How could she not see it? I started yelling at her and telling her she had to clean up the mess. And then, Mr. Beck, the lunch aide, came over and yelled at me! I got so mad that I knocked a chair over. Then I got sent to the principal's office, even though Casey was the one who started the whole thing. She should have been the one who got in trouble. It's not fair. I hate her."

Where other people see an accident, Short-Fused Children see a deliberate offense. In the story above, Casey used poor judgment in leaving her drink on the edge of the table, but it's unlikely that she put the soda there because she planned to dump it into Lorena's backpack. Instead of giving Casey the benefit of the doubt, Lorena immediately assumed that Casey's intentions were malicious. Lorena wasn't just upset about the mess, she was outraged by what she saw as a deliberate attack.

Short-Fused Children put a negative spin on most things they see — even positive behaviors. When a peer gives them a compliment, they are more likely than other children to respond with surprise and hostility. They are also less able to recognize a friendly overture or to remember the details of a peer's kind action. So, even if Casey looked concerned after dumping the soda, apologized profusely, and tried to help clean up, Lorena probably either missed it or discounted it. Moreover, Casey's attempts to help were probably short-lived in the face of Lorena's shouting and chair-throwing.

Ironically, Short-Fused Children's worries about other people "doing them wrong" can actually produce the social outcomes that they fear. Figure 6.2 shows how this happens. Because Short-Fused

Figure 6.2

THE SHORT-FUSED CYCLE

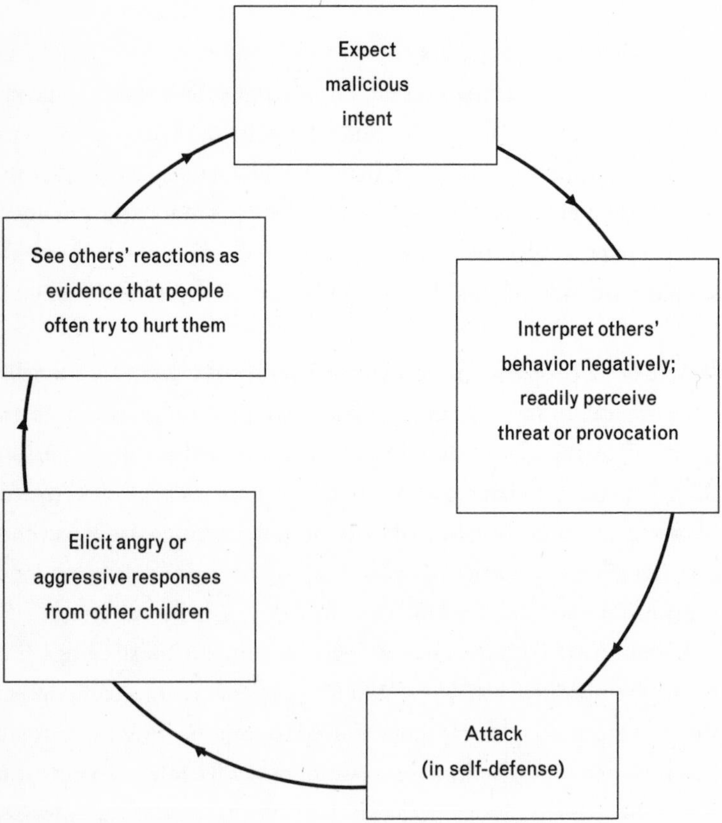

Expect
malicious
intent

See others' reactions as
evidence that people
often try to hurt them

Interpret others'
behavior negatively;
readily perceive
threat or provocation

Elicit angry or
aggressive responses
from other children

Attack
(in self-defense)

Children expect malicious intent, they are on the lookout for offenses or provocation. This causes them to interpret other people's actions in a biased way and to perceive threats even when none is intended. They bristle at the tiniest slight. Their hair-trigger temper comes from being poised to attack in what they see as self-defense. When they respond angrily or aggressively, other children reciprocate. This then confirms Short-Fused Children's belief that their peers often deliberately try to hurt them.

Short-Fused Children not only take offense easily but also have a hard time letting go of grievances. They don't just hold on to grudges; they cling to them and relive them and sharpen them as if their lives depended on not allowing their resentment to recede even slightly. A year from now, Lorena will still remember how Casey dumped soda in her backpack, and she will be as angry as if it had just happened. Because Short-Fused Children are constantly either anticipating or remembering how others have hurt them, they spend a lot of time feeling miserable.

If your child's feelings are too easily hurt, learning the Unwritten Rules and doing the following exercises can help your child gain some perspective and control his or her automatic angry response. It's also important to teach your child to tune in to benign explanations of misdeeds, to notice positive actions, and to forgive others' mistakes. (If your child is prone to overreacting to perceived slights, you may also want to look at the exercises in chapter 8, "The Sensitive Soul." If your child misjudges teasing, see the exercises in chapter 2, "The Vulnerable Child.")

THE UNWRITTEN RULES

- It's better to overlook misdeeds than to wrongly accuse someone.
- Don't assume malicious intent. Accidents happen, and everyone makes mistakes.

- If you are looking for insults, you will find them.
- You can't control what other people do; you can only control how you respond to them.
- Holding on to grudges hurts you, not the other person.

ACTIVITIES FOR LEARNING
THE UNWRITTEN RULES

1. Arguing for the Defense

Short-Fused Children go through life thinking like prosecuting attorneys. They are ready and eager to convict wrongdoers and make them pay for their crimes. They are willing to fight to make sure people don't get away with anything.

Give your child a chance to play a different role: defense attorney. The next time your child is indignant about something someone did to him or her, compliment your child on how well he or she presented the prosecution's case. Then challenge your child to present an equally compelling case for the defense. For inspiration, you can provide your child with a description of the main kinds of arguments defense lawyers make.

Arguments for the Defense

Lack of intent: It was an accident. They didn't mean to do it.

Negligence (lack of foresight): They didn't realize that what they did would have harmful consequences.

Mitigating circumstances: There was some legitimate reason for why they did it.

Diminished capacity: That's the best they could manage.

Self-defense: They felt someone was trying to harm them.

Having to vehemently argue the other side can help your child gain a more balanced view of the situation. You may even want to take notes on your child's defense arguments. The two of you can then go over the arguments and talk about how plausible or convincing they are. You could also talk about the consequences for your child of choosing either the prosecutor's or the defense attorney's position. Seeing the event as a deliberate assault is infuriating; seeing it as an accident makes forgiveness possible. You may also want to tell your child that in a democracy people are presumed innocent and explain why this is a good idea.

2. Recognizing Kindness and Sincerity

Because Short-Fused Children are anticipating threats, they often misinterpret or just don't know how to respond to other children's friendly behaviors. If another child says, "Nice jacket!" they are apt to respond, "What's it to you?" because they fear some veiled insult. When someone says, "I'm sorry," they might snarl back, "No, you're not! You did it on purpose!" because they don't pick up on the sincerity of the apology. If another child says, "Hi, what's your name?" they might snap, "It's none of your business!" or they might just stand there in wary silence, unsure of the other child's intent. Short-Fused Children are primed to lash out at an offense, so they mistrust and are baffled by kindness.

Role-playing can help your child learn to identify friendly overtures. Have your child stand in front of a mirror and act out insincere and sincere statements, using the following scenarios. Talk about which verbal and nonverbal cues indicate sincerity. Sincere remarks are more likely to be said in a warm tone of voice, with direct eye contact and relaxed body posture. Sometimes it's hard to tell whether someone is being sincere. For instance, some people look guilty when they are not, simply because they are nervous. Feeling the difference between saying sincere and insincere remarks can help your child pick up on the relevant cues when listening to others so that he or she can interpret their comments correctly.

DISTINGUISHING BETWEEN INSINCERE AND SINCERE REMARKS

Insincere Compliment

A kid in your class thinks she is such a great athlete, but she really isn't. Now she just made a foul that could cost your team the game. What would your face and voice be like if you told her sarcastically, "Great job!"?

Sincere Compliment

Your friend just threw an amazing shot that won the basketball game for your team in gym. How would you tell your friend, "Great job!"?

Insincere Apology

Suppose you deliberately knocked someone's papers on the floor because he was annoying you and you think he is a jerk. The teacher catches you and forces you to apologize, but you are not one bit sorry. How would you say it?

Sincere Apology

Suppose you accidentally break something that belongs to someone else. How would you apologize to him or her to show that you didn't do it on purpose and that you really feel bad about breaking it?

Insincere Question

A really nerdy kid in your class is wearing a gymnastics T-shirt. You think gymnastics is for babies, and you feel like making fun of this kid. How would you ask, "Do you do gymnastics?"

Sincere Question

You notice that a kid in your class, whom you don't know very well, is wearing a gymnastics T-shirt. This kid seems nice. You love gymnastics, and you wonder if this kid does too. How would you ask, "Do you do gymnastics?"

You can help your child further hone these interpretation skills by talking about the sincerity of remarks made by people on television or in daily life. Ask your child about the intentions of different characters: "Does he really mean this or is he just saying it to be polite?"; "Is she being genuine or sarcastic when she says that?"; "How do you know he means what he is saying?" Help your child tune in to the specific verbal and nonverbal cues that show sincerity.

3. Response Chaining

Short-Fused Children are quick to perceive how other people hurt or insult them, but they tend to be oblivious to how their own angry actions contribute to problems. If your child is fuming about something that another child did, it might help to actually write down what happened as a chain of events. Choose two sheets of paper, each a different color, and cut them into strips. Use one set of colored strips to write down what the other person did; use the other set to write down how your child responded. Put the strips together sequentially, making a paper chain with links of alternating colors. Making the chain shows your child that you are taking this distressing event seriously and that you understand exactly how put-upon he or she was. Your child will probably focus exclusively on what the other person did, but you should be sure to ask about and include your child's actions. It's fine to comment on how horrible the other person's actions were, but avoid judging your child's actions. Once you have completed the chain, ask your child at what point he or she could have done something differently to end the anger chain. Your child will probably come back with "Well, he shouldn't have . . . ," or "It's not fair that she . . ." Agree with your child. Say, "You're right. That was a terrible thing he / she did. The problem is, we can't do anything about what someone else does. We can only work with how you respond to it. Your responses can either continue the chain or end it." You may want to make a special silver link out of aluminum foil to represent any action your child takes to end an anger chain. Silver Link Actions could include compromising, apologizing, or walking away.

4. Learning to Listen During Family Arguments: Using a Peace Stick

Family arguments, whether between you and your child or between your child and a sibling, are great opportunities to practice peaceful conflict resolution and to see how angry feelings often dissipate when we really understand the other person's point of view. Find a stick and designate it the Peace Stick for your family. You may even want to decorate it. When a disagreement comes up, have one person hold the Peace Stick and state his or her concerns, while the other person just listens. No yelling, insulting, or name-calling allowed. Instead, say, "I think . . . ," "I feel . . . ," or "I want . . ." The goal is to create understanding rather than to hurt each other. When the speaker finishes, both partners hold opposite ends of the Peace Stick, and the listener paraphrases the speaker's thoughts and feelings. The speaker then has a chance to say whether this summary was accurate and to clarify any misperceptions. Once the speaker agrees that his or her view has been correctly paraphrased, partners swap roles. The other person now gets sole possession of the Peace Stick, and it's his or her turn to talk, while the original speaker listens. This technique may seem awkward at first, but we've found that the physical reminder of the Peace Stick helps people to just listen without arguing or thinking of a rebuttal. This can be very helpful in keeping the focus on really hearing and understanding the other person's perspective.

5. Learning to Forgive

Short-Fused Children hold on to grudges because they fear that if they forget an offense, the other person has "won" somehow. They believe that they are paying the other person back by keeping their anger burning bright. The other person probably doesn't realize that they are still upset about what happened. While Short-Fused Children mentally rehearse their resentment, the other person has most likely moved on and may not even remember the event.

Short-Fused Children need to understand that they only hurt themselves by clinging to the hurt of past offenses. They need to see that they have a choice: they can stew in their resentment indefinitely, feeling bitter, angry, and miserable, or they can let it go and get on with more important and more satisfying things in their lives.

Research shows that forgiveness can be powerfully healing. It gives us a chance to exchange bitterness for freedom, injury for self-respect. Forgiving someone who hurt them helps people to feel less anxious and depressed and to like themselves more. There's some evidence that forgiveness can even enhance physical health.

Explain to your child that forgiving someone doesn't mean forgetting what happened or becoming that person's best friend. It does mean accepting that we're all human and that we all make mistakes, and then letting go of the hurt, anger, and disappointment. Forgiveness is not a wimpy response. It takes courage to acknowledge a slight and decide, "I can move past this." Tell your child that forgiveness isn't a one-shot deal. Being in a relationship requires that we forgive one another again and again and again.

We've found that some kind of symbolic action is helpful in letting go of grudges. Have your child make a list of all the grudges he or she is currently carrying. Cut out each grudge and tape it onto a heavy object, such as a rock, a brick, or even a big book. Put all of the objects in a bag. Have your child hold the bag to feel how it weighs him or her down. One by one, remove the objects from the bag. Read the grudge, then tear off the paper and throw it away. As the bag gets lighter, so will your child's heart.

Malcolm: Falling Apart in Public

"I was shocked when you called me and told me that Malcolm screamed and threw things in the classroom today. That's just not like him!" Mrs. Epstein said.

"Well, I was shocked too," Mrs. Connolly, the third-grade teacher agreed. "I have to say, however, that it's not the first time he's acted this way. When it happened before, I thought Malcolm was just having an off day, but this is the third occurence, and his outbursts are getting more volatile. I'm very concerned."

"What actually happened today?" Mrs. Epstein asked.

"We were going over math story problems from last night's homework, and I called on Malcolm to put his answers on the board. The next thing I knew, he was screaming that this was a stupid assignment, that it made no sense, and that he hated school. Then he threw his notebook on the floor and ran out of the room."

"I don't know what to say," Mrs. Epstein replied worriedly.

"Malcolm is a bright little boy, and normally he is not a behavior problem," said Mrs. Connolly. "These explosions seem to come out of the blue, but they have to stop. I can't have him disrupting the class or running off unsupervised. Plus, the other children are starting to avoid him. I thought maybe you could shed some light on why he is acting this way."

Stress-related outbursts occur when children are overwhelmed. In Malcolm's case, maybe he didn't know how to do the assignment or how to ask for help. Maybe he was embarrassed because he hadn't done the homework. Or maybe Malcolm was worried about something completely unrelated to school, and being called on in class was just the final spark that set him off.

Parents of children with stress-related outbursts often say things like "I don't know why he's acting this way — it's so unlike him!" or "She used to be pretty easygoing, but now everything I say seems to set her off!" Unlike the other children we've described in this chapter, these children usually don't have general problems negotiating with others or interpreting social situations. Instead, their intense reactions are a sign that their coping abilities are overloaded — they just can't take it anymore. However, the social consequences of their volatile behavior are the same as for any other Short-Fused Child.

In the midst of a blowup, children are beyond caring if anyone sees them screaming or crying. They will probably feel mortified afterward, but during the explosion, they are unable to think of anything except how angry they feel. Unfortunately, if they act out of control too often in front of their classmates, it can be very damaging to their social relationships. Other elementary school children are likely to find their unpredictable behavior alarming and definitely off-putting.

Your goal is to offer both empathy and guidance. Your child needs you to understand that he or she is feeling stretched to the breaking point. Your child also needs help coming up with some concrete ways to improve the situation or at least to make it more bearable. Even with completely uncontrollable problems, there is always something that can be done to help your child feel better. You may not be able to prevent the divorce, but maybe you can spend some extra time playing catch with your child. You may not be able to cure the illness, but maybe you can encourage your child to take up painting or writing in a journal. You may not be able to solve a learning difficulty by yourself, but you can get your child the help he or she needs to cope with it. The Unwritten Rules and the following activities emphasize the importance of asking for help and of getting to the root of the problem.

THE UNWRITTEN RULES

- It's easier to manage feelings before they build up.
- Before you get to the breaking point, ask for help.
- If you want help, you have to ask for it directly — no one can read your mind.
- Talking about your troubles with someone who cares makes you feel better.
- There is almost always something that can be done to make a difficult situation better.

ACTIVITIES FOR LEARNING THE UNWRITTEN RULES

1. Getting to the Root of the Problem

Children often have trouble articulating what is bothering them. They know they feel bad, but they don't always know why. Stressed children are apt to lash out at any convenient target. Or they may overreact to some minor event because for them it feels like just too much to deal with on top of all their other concerns.

You may have to do some detective work to figure out what the main problem is. Children who have stress-related outbursts often feel like their tantrums suddenly descend upon them from nowhere. But, if you look closely, you can usually see a pattern in when and where blowups occur. You may want to keep a diary of what is happening just before each episode to see what sorts of situations set your child off. You should also talk with your child and your child's teacher to get their impressions of what is behind the eruptions. Once you identify the triggers, it's easier to know how to prevent these reactions.

Talk with your child privately about his or her behavior, and be gentle with your questions. Your child is likely to feel ashamed of either the outbursts, or the underlying problem, or both. We've found that children are often more willing to talk when their hands are busy, so try going out for ice cream or working on a big jigsaw puzzle together, then saying casually, "I've noticed you've been getting mad a lot lately. Is there something you're worried or upset about?"

Many different kinds of stress can lead to outbursts. Events that seem small to adults can loom large in children's minds. In the following paragraphs, we list some of the most common triggers of stress-related outbursts. If you have trouble identifying the source of your child's distress or if the problems are enduring, we recommend that you get professional help for your child.

Academic Stress: Children who are extremely frustrated at school because of unidentified learning difficulties often have problems managing their tempers. They see that they have trouble picking up on things that their classmates grasp easily, and they conclude that they must be stupid. They act out in class because they'd rather be seen as "bad" than as "dumb." A learning evaluation can help detect a specific learning disability. Tutoring can help boost confidence and skills.

Perfectionist children can also experience academic stress from trying to keep up with the demands that they place on themselves. These children are extremely capable, but they tend to push themselves too hard. They are harsh and unforgiving with themselves when they feel they don't measure up. They can become more and more agitated, worrying about failure, until finally some minor event sets off an explosion. These children need help managing their expectations of themselves and learning how to relax and have fun. Some of the exercises in chapter 7, "The Little Adult," might help.

Family Stress: When children are experiencing serious difficulties at home, such as illness, financial problems, or parental conflict, they sometimes act out at school. They feel like their world is falling apart, so they fall apart. It's very important to reassure your child that family difficulties are not his or her fault. Your child doesn't have to know all the gory details of what is going on, but you need to give your child a chance to ask questions and to provide enough information so that he or she doesn't imagine that things are worse than they truly are. Do what you can to keep your child's life peaceful and predictable in the face of family stress.

Bullying: Sometimes stress-related outbursts are a sign that your child is being bullied. The sense of shame and helplessness that comes from being victimized can cause children to lash out at other people, in other situations. Do a little behind-the-scenes investigating. Talking to one of your child's friends at snack time might be very revealing. Many parents have learned things about their child by quietly listening while carpooling. Sometimes the bullying might be coming from an overly stern teacher or a playground aide. Be open to all possibilities. Chapter 2, "The Vulnerable Child," has suggestions for helping children who are bullied.

Overload: Sometimes it's not any one thing that sets a child off but rather a cumulative sense that they have too much to deal with. Look carefully at how fully packed your child's schedule is. All children need some downtime, and your child's comfortable activity level may be lower than your own. The anticipation and frantic preparation before a big event, such as a holiday, party, or performance, can also sometimes trigger blowups. For some Shy Children, just the ongoing strain of being around people they don't know well can precipitate an outburst. Other children have trouble dealing with crowds. They feel bombarded by all the sights, sounds, and smells, and eventually they erupt. Talk with your child about the importance of recognizing when he or she is starting to feel overwhelmed and come up with some adaptive ways that he or she can tell you "enough is enough."

THE HOME-SCHOOL CONNECTION

A child who has angry outbursts makes a teacher's job much harder. So be prepared for the fact that your child's teacher might be feeling quite frustrated with him or her. Your best bet is to try to create a collaborative spirit with the teacher (i.e., we're all working together toward the same goal). Acknowledge the problem. Agree that your child needs to work on self-control. Explain that your child doesn't enjoy these outbursts either and really wants to change. If possible, describe what strategies you are working on at home to decrease the intensity and frequency of these reactions. You may also want to share with the teacher any unusual stressors that your family is experiencing.

Identifying Triggers: Ask for the teacher's ideas on what might be triggering your child's distress. The teacher can help you decide whether a learning evaluation is necessary. The teacher may also be able to tell you about the kinds of social situations that might be setting off your child. Sometimes arranging to keep your child away from a particular classmate helps prevent trouble.

Rewarding Self-Control: Brief notes from the teacher, sent home on a regular basis, could help you praise your child for good sportsmanship or role-play better ways of handling a situation that went awry. Alternatively, the teacher may want to discreetly reward your child in class for staying cool when frustrated, asking for help appropriately, or solving a disagreement peacefully.

IF YOU TOO . . .

If you also tend to be short-fused, your interactions with your child present both risk and opportunity. The risk is that the two of you will work each other up so that every little conflict becomes a full raging battle. The opportunity comes when your child sees you actively working on managing your temper. Teaching by example is probably the single most powerful way of helping your child. When you tell your child, "I'm going to my room now because I'm starting to feel really mad and I don't want to do something I'll regret," you not only demonstrate a useful technique but also convey the importance of keeping your cool. Even when you make a mistake and yell at your child, your willingness to keep trying and to do things differently next time sends a powerful message.

Take a close look at the different kinds of Short-Fused Children we've described in this chapter and think about how their difficulties might be relevant for you. Do you automatically respond to provocation with anger? What could you do instead? Do you often view your child's misbehavior as a deliberate attempt to annoy you? Try giving your child the benefit of the doubt. Are you feeling overwhelmed by something that is going on in your life? Most parents make sure that their children get enough food, rest, and relaxation, but too often, parents expect themselves to run on empty. You will have more energy to tackle problems and be better able to keep things in perspective if you take care of yourself and give yourself some time off for fun.

SUMMARY

Short-Fused Children easily feel threatened and respond aggressively in what they see as self-defense. Sometimes the threat comes from being frustrated or provoked and not knowing any other way to respond. Sometimes the threat has to do with misperceiving other people's actions or intentions as malicious. Sometimes the threat has to do with overwhelming academic, social, or family circumstances. Regardless of the specific causes of their distress, Short-Fused Children need to learn to recognize their building tension and to calm themselves down *before* they act out impulsively. They also need to learn constructive ways of dealing with stressful situations so they can resist the urge to automatically lash out. Once they learn to manage their tempers, Short-Fused Children can let their guard down. They have an easier time connecting with others, and they feel better about themselves.

You Will Also Want to Read:
Chapter 2, "The Vulnerable Child"
Chapter 3, "The Intimidating Child"
Chapter 7, "The Little Adult"
Chapter 8, "The Sensitive Soul"
Chapter 9, "The Born Leader"

THE UNWRITTEN RULES FOR THE SHORT-FUSED CHILD AT A GLANCE

- Don't "lose it" in public.
- It's better to walk away from a bad situation than to do something you'll regret later.
- It takes courage to stay calm under fire.

- New relationships won't survive conflict.
- Angry outbursts might win an argument, but they can result in the loss of a friend.
- Forcing someone to give in to your wishes creates hard feelings.
- It's better to overlook misdeeds than to wrongly accuse someone.
- Don't assume malicious intent. Accidents happen, and everyone makes mistakes.
- If you are looking for insults, you will find them.
- You can't control what other people do; you can only control how you respond to them.
- Holding on to grudges hurts you, not the other person.
- It's easier to manage feelings before they build up.
- Before you get to the breaking point, ask for help.
- If you want help, you have to ask for it directly — no one can read your mind.
- Talking about your troubles with someone who cares makes you feel better.
- There is almost always something that can be done to make a difficult situation better.

CHAPTER 7

The Little Adult

Does your child . . .

relate better to adults than to other children?

seem indifferent or oblivious when his or her classmates are excited about a new toy or collectible?

express disdain for common childhood interests?

try to impress other kids but end up pushing them away?

speak more formally than other children his or her age?

use words that most kids don't understand?

refuse to do any activities in which he or she doesn't excel?

feel lonely because he or she just doesn't fit in with other children?

Do you . . .

feel proud of your child's unique interests and extensive vocabulary but worry because he or she has no friends?

wish other kids liked your child as much as your adult friends do?

fear that your child gets picked on for being a nerd?

feel irritated when your child acts like a know-it-all?

wish your child weren't such a perfectionist?

worry that your child will never learn to get along with peers?

Little Adults are the children that parents describe as "eight going on forty-eight." They are poised and articulate around adults, but they have trouble relating to other children. They often express uninterest in common childhood activities. They set themselves apart from their peers by acting very serious, superior, or just too old for their years.

In many cases, Little Adults have received a lot of praise from parents and teachers for their intellect, talents, or achievements. This is wonderful because it encourages them to pursue their interests and cultivate their unique strengths. But sometimes children take this praise too much to heart. Little Adults tend to define themselves entirely in terms of their accomplishments and to believe that people will only like them if they are successful. This is a very narrow and fragile sense of self.

Little Adults assume that they need to prove their worth to their peers. Instead of relaxing, enjoying the company of other children, and blending in with a group, they show off their knowledge, trying to impress other kids the same way they impress adults. Unfortunately, this comes across as bragging and leads other kids to ridicule or avoid them. Little Adults then feel like social failures, so they focus even harder on their achievements, chasing an elusive sense of self-worth. A secret part of them hopes that if they try hard enough, perform perfectly, and accumulate enough awards, they can make people like them. Relaxing their standards and doing a merely adequate job is unthinkable to them because this would mean abandoning the only way they know to gain positive recognition. However, awards are cold company, and these children are often terribly lonely.

Little Adults need help learning to be regular kids. Of course, their special talents need to be cultivated, but these children also need to realize that there is more to life, and more to *them,* than achievement.

Performing perfectly is irrelevant to friendship. Little Adults have to understand that being "the best" won't help them make friends, whereas having fun and caring about other people will. These children need to learn that they can relate to others without taking on the role of "the Expert." They need to see that they can be less than perfect and still enjoy themselves. When we nurture their capacity to be kind or silly or playful, we help Little Adults not only to fit in with other kids but also to understand that they are worth more than the sum of their successes.

ON THE POSITIVE SIDE

Little Adults tend to have a mature outlook on life. They are usually responsible and trustworthy, and generally show good judgment. They can be hardworking and persistent. They are often bright.

Their passion for their unique interests is delightful. When these children find a topic or activity that captivates them, they pursue it with zeal. They aren't satisfied with a cursory overview of a favorite subject; they want to plumb its depths. Their enthusiasm for their hobbies can bring Little Adults an inner sense of satisfaction and mastery.

Little Adults are independent thinkers. These children are unlikely to give in to peer pressure to do something dangerous. They usually have the courage to stand up for their convictions, and they are often very idealistic. Because they aren't preoccupied with needing to be like everyone else, they are more open to trying new and fascinating activities. They are often creative and imaginative. With guidance, Little Adults can transform their independent streak into a strong sense of self that allows them to connect with others.

SO, WHAT CAN WE DO?

As Little Adults get older, some of the behaviors that set them apart from their elementary school peers will become more commonplace, and they may have an easier time fitting in. However, it's not very comforting to say to a lonely child, "Don't worry. By the time you are thirty, you probably won't seem so different from everyone else." Moreover, if a child constantly feels that there's an enormous gulf separating him or her from other people, that distance isn't suddenly going to disappear when the child gets older. Too often, Little Adults withdraw into their own intellectualism, giving up on making friends because it seems impossibly difficult.

It's worth doing what we can *now* to help Little Adults so that they can feel happier in the present and the future. The same skills that help them get along with their classmates will serve them well with coworkers and friends throughout their lives. Once they understand how to relate to their peers, they can develop friendships and gain a more balanced view of themselves.

Little Adults need to understand the Unwritten Rules for fitting in. They need to learn to speak the language of their peers and to develop some interests that they can share with other children. They need to have fun with their classmates instead of feeling obligated to inform and educate them. They need to learn to pick up on group opinions and flexibly adjust their behavior to fit the social situation. They need to understand when and how it's appropriate to share their knowledge, and when it's best to just listen to others.

The three Little Adults described in this chapter have a "superior" style of relating that creates distance between them and their peers. Margaret acts like a walking encyclopedia, regaling her classmates with facts instead of joining in the fun. Simon acts disdainful of the other boys' collections. Nathan refuses to participate in sports because he doesn't perform perfectly.

Margaret: Playing "the Expert"

"Cool!" Ethan exclaimed. "Look at that huge spider!"

"I've never seen a spider that big!" Kyle said enthusiastically.

"Actually," Margaret said, "that's not a spider; it's a daddy longlegs. Daddy longlegs aren't considered true spiders because they don't have a thorax, they have only two eyes, and their legs are unusually long."

The other children ignored her.

"Let's try to catch it," Sarah suggested. "My mom says daddy long-legs spiders don't bite."

"Yeah!" Kyle said.

"Here's my yogurt cup," Sarah said. "See if you can get it to walk in."

"Maybe I'll put some leaves in first, to give it some food," Ethan said.

"To my knowledge, daddy longlegs are not inclined to consume vegetation," Margaret said. "Their preferred food is live or dead insects, although they do sometimes eat carrion."

"Oh, shut up, Margaret," Kyle said.

"I caught it!" Ethan yelled. Sarah and Kyle eagerly moved closer to look in the cup. Margaret remained standing a few feet away.

"Recess is almost over," Sarah noted. "How are we going to get it into class?"

"I don't think Ms. Meyers will appreciate having an arachnid in the classroom," Margaret pronounced.

Margaret's knowledge of insects is remarkable, and her vocabulary is exquisite — but her ability to relate to other children is seriously lacking. Margaret tried to impress the other kids with her expertise. She didn't just offer her knowledge — she flaunted it. She used it to try to set herself above everyone else. This strategy of displaying her superior intellect might earn Margaret glowing approval from adults, but it earned the disdain of her peers. She came across as an overbearing spoilsport. The other children weren't looking for an entomology lesson; they just wanted to catch a big spider.

Margaret truly was not trying to be obnoxious. Although children like Margaret sound poised and mature, they are just kids, and they want to be liked. Little Adults desperately want friends, but they feel awkward around other children. The more insecure they feel, the harder they try to impress other kids, a tactic that leaves them less able to become part of the group. Children like Margaret are painfully aware that other kids don't like them, but they usually don't understand how their own behavior contributes to their isolation.

Margaret's very formal speech sets her apart from the other children. She needs to learn to speak the language of her peers so that she can blend in. Her statement about daddy longlegs' disinclination to consume vegetation elicited scorn from her classmates. She could have said, "They like to eat dead bugs. Let's go see if we can find some." This statement conveys the same information in a friendly way that classmates can easily understand. It could have resulted in the whole group, including Margaret, running off together to look for dead bugs.

Does this mean your child has to act dumb to fit in? Absolutely not. It does mean that children, like adults, need to be able to adapt their communication style to fit the situation. Think about how you would speak if you were (1) having lunch with your best friend, (2) meeting your spouse's boss for the first time, or (3) giving a formal presentation on the budget at work. In each situation the content and tone of your communication would be different. This isn't being fake; it's behaving appropriately for the circumstances.

Little Adults tend to use a single communication style — formal lecturing — that is off-putting in casual situations. Learning to speak in a more conversational manner is an important goal for them. It's a skill that will be useful throughout their lives. It will help them relate better to other elementary school kids now and to friends and coworkers when they grow up. Some of the greatest scientists and theoreticians are those who not only understand complex ideas but also can explain them clearly to others.

The Unwritten Rules and the following activities can help your child learn to relate to others in a casual, friendly way. They are designed to provide your child with alternatives to playing "the Expert." If your child insists on imposing his or her views on others, you may also want to read chapter 9, "The Born Leader."

THE UNWRITTEN RULES

- The goal is connecting with other kids, not impressing them with your knowledge.
- Nobody likes to listen to bragging or lecturing.
- It's not your job to report other children's misbehavior.
- You don't have to share everything you know; sometimes it's better to listen.
- You make friends by showing other people that you like and respect them, not by telling them how good you are.
- It's okay just to have fun and enjoy yourself.

ACTIVITIES FOR LEARNING
THE UNWRITTEN RULES

1. Learning the Language of One's Peers

If your child wants to fit in with the kids at school, he or she needs to know how to speak their language. Little Adults often have extensive vocabularies, but they don't know or use the current slang words. You may need to make a deliberate effort to become familiar with the current slang and teach it to your child. Learning slang doesn't erase your child's advanced vocabulary; it adds to it. Think of it as helping your child to become multilingual: Little Adults already know formal English and can use it in written work or during intellectual discussions, but they need to learn the language of the playground.

Start a slang dictionary (to be kept at home). Make it a family project. Explain to your child that slang is a casual way of speaking that conveys group membership. Different groups, based on age, interests, or geographical location, use different slang words. Telling your child some of the slang words from when you were growing up often gets a giggle. Your slang dictionary should include all the common phrases that you hear your child's classmates using. You might want to elicit help from another parent with school-age children who could fill you in on the latest slang over a cup of coffee. Practice using these terms with your child. You can even make a game of it by seeing which family member can use the most slang words during dinner.

2. Recognizing Different Communication Styles: Nonsense-Word Charades

Little Adults typically use a manner of speaking that comes across as stiff, preachy, or pedantic in casual settings. They need to learn to match their behavior to the situation. We've developed a game called

Nonsense-Word Charades that helps children identify the nonverbal cues that make up different communication styles. You can play this game with the whole family, using teams, or you can play it with just you and your child and either switch sides or use props to represent additional actors.

Write each of the following communication scenarios (and any other relevant ones you can think of) on a scrap of paper. Fold up the papers, place them in a box, and mix them up. Take turns choosing a paper and acting out the scenario. You go first, to show your child how to do it. Actors are not allowed to say any words, but they can pantomime and use the nonsense word *lumma* to convey information about the situation with the tone of their voice. For example, actors might say, "Lumma-lumma? Lumma! Lumma, lumma, lumma-lumma." The other player or players try to guess the relationship between the people in the scenario. Are they peers or is one person an authority figure? How can they tell? If your child has difficulty guessing, you can provide a list of all the communication scenarios so that this exercise is like a multiple-choice test.

Communication Scenarios

- Two best friends are whispering about a funny secret.
- A teacher is lecturing a classroom about math.
- Two teammates are congratulating each other on winning the game.
- A parent is scolding a child for tracking mud into the house.
- One kid comes up to another kid to ask about and admire a cool toy.
- An older sibling is bossing around a younger sibling.

Once your child is good at this game, you can mention that it's important to talk to other children as peers. Approaching classmates as an authority figure says "I think I'm better than you," and it pushes kids away.

3. Knowing the Difference Between Telling and Tattling

Some Little Adults run into trouble with both adults and children because they tattle. They see someone doing something wrong, and they feel compelled to speak up, simply because they know that's not how things *should* be done. They are baffled when people respond with resentment rather than appreciation. Their intention was to impart knowledge. They don't realize that their remarks make them seem critical and inappropriately superior.

It's okay to tell on someone when safety is at stake, but in general, Little Adults will get along better with others if they don't tattle. You may want to read Joy W. Berry's picture book *A Children's Book About Tattling* with your child. This book explains the difference between tattling and telling in a simple and appealing way.

Before reporting another child's behavior to an adult, Little Adults should ask themselves several questions:

- Am I trying to help, or am I trying to get the other person in trouble?
- Am I trying to solve a problem, or am I trying to prove I'm better than the other kids?
- Have I done everything I can on my own to try to solve the problem before involving an adult?

What distinguishes tattling from telling is the motivation behind the behavior. When Little Adults report another child's actions to get that child in trouble or to make themselves look good or just because they don't want to try to solve the problem any other way, they are *tattling*. When they alert an adult because they are honestly concerned about a dangerous situation, or because they truly can't deal with it on their own, they are using good judgment by *telling*.

Discuss with your child the situations in the Telling or Tattling Quiz. Use the motivation questions listed previously to decide whether or not it's appropriate to inform an adult about the behavior. If the two of you decide that reporting the behavior is *not* the right thing to do (i.e., it would be tattling), talk about other possible ways of dealing with the situation. You may need to remind your Little Adult that if it's just a minor misbehavior, ignoring it is usually the best option.

TELLING OR TATTLING QUIZ

Decide whether reporting each of these behaviors to an adult would be telling or tattling.

- You see your little brother playing with matches. (Telling)
- Your sister borrowed your sweater without asking. (Tattling)
- Your classmate didn't throw away his garbage. (Tattling)
- Your friend is bragging to everyone that she got 100 percent on a math test. You know that's not true. (Tattling)
- Some big kids keep picking on an unpopular kid in your class and stealing his money. (Telling)
- Your friend tells the teacher that he forgot his homework at home. You know he didn't do it. (Tattling)
- Your brother tells your parents that he fell and ripped his pants. You know he got beaten up by the big kids who are always picking on him. (Telling)
- Your sister stole some earrings from a store. (Telling)
- Your friend tells her mother that she ate the carrots in her lunch, but you saw her throw them out. (Tattling)

4. Cultivating Silliness and Seeing Humor in Mistakes

Little Adults are exemplary workers, but they need help learning how to play and be silly. Make a point of regularly seeking out activities that give everyone in the family a chance to make a fool of him- or herself and have a great time doing it. Let your child see you perform badly and laugh it off. Go roller-blading — especially if you don't know how. Rent a video about learning to belly dance and have Dad participate in the lesson. Play Clay to Win, a charades-style game in which players make things out of Play-Doh, and laugh about your unrecognizable sculptures.

Try some of the ideas in the book *Simple Fun for Busy People* by Gary Krane. Choose the suggestions that are completely undignified. For instance, you could have two family members start at opposite corners of a king-size bed and see who can pull the other's socks off first. Or, you could try having one family member be the comedian, while the other family members have their mouths full of water and try not to laugh. The person who spits out first is the next comedian. (Obviously, you should do this outside on a warm day.) A less moist alternative is to make it a family ritual that everyone has to tell a joke at dinnertime. Get some joke books from the library for inspiration. Keep in mind that you are trying to cultivate juvenile humor: think slapstick and knock-knock jokes rather than political satire.

5. Building Individual Friendships

Building individual friendships can help Little Adults feel more comfortable with their peers. Little Adults often behave in an aloof or arrogant manner when they are with groups of children but are much more relaxed and approachable in one-on-one situations. Because they are so intense, most Little Adults prefer close individual friendships to casual group membership. If they can find a buddy or two, Little Adults won't feel lonely, even if they are not part of the "in" group at school.

Have your child identify several classmates who could be friends. Invite each of these children over, one at a time, for activity-based play dates. Tell your child that the job of the host is to make sure that the guest has a good time. Planning activities beforehand helps your child know what to do when the classmate arrives and makes it less likely that your child will wander off alone, get flustered and start lecturing, or select an activity that is boring or incomprehensible to the other child. Activities that will probably appeal to both your child and the guest include

baking cookies
putting on a play with costumes
building with Legos
collecting bugs
going to a children's program at a nature center
going for a hike
driving remote-control cars
flying kites
making birdhouses, using hammers, nails, and paint
playing board games
riding bikes
playing Frisbee

Before the play date, you may need to caution your child that trying to impress the other child isn't necessary or helpful. Little Adults sometimes brag about their knowledge, possessions, or abilities because they want other people to like them. They secretly hope that their peers will respond by saying, "Wow! That's amazing! I sure want to be your friend!" This never happens. Kids usually react by belittling them ("So what?" or "You think you're so great, but you're not!") or just rolling their eyes and walking away. Bragging comes across as a put-down because saying, "I'm great!" implies, "You're not!" Classmates will respond better if your child just acts friendly or offers them a sincere compliment. The point of a play date is simply to spend time together doing a pleasant activity. Enjoying each other's company is the basis for most friendships. (If your child has trouble knowing what is or isn't bragging, see the exercise on avoiding bragging in chapter 4, "The Different Drummer.")

Simon: Belittling Peers' Interests

As usual, after the Scout meeting, all of the boys except Simon pulled out their trading cards. "I just got three of the new ones!" Kevin announced.

"Oh, you are so lucky! Cool! Let me see!" the other boys exclaimed as they gathered around him. Simon just sat there, staring off into space, looking bored.

"I'm still trying to finish the Blue Series," Josh said. "Does anybody have some of those they want to trade?"

"Here, these are my doubles," Nick said, offering some cards. "See if you need any of these."

While Josh looked through the pile of cards, Nick turned to Simon and asked, "Hey, Simon, how come you never bring your trading cards?"

"I'm not interested in trading cards," Simon answered. "I mean, if you think about it, they're just little pictures. My dad says if you add up the cost of the cardboard and the ink, they are really worth less than a penny each, but the packs cost several dollars and some really stupid people pay lots of money to get the rare ones. How dumb is that? It's just advertisers trying to get you to spend your money."

Technically, Simon is correct. Trading cards are silly, commercial, and intrinsically worthless. They are also fun for a lot of kids. The other boys were having a great time comparing and swapping cards. Simon's disdain for their hobby makes him come across like a wet blanket.

There are always fads among kids. Whether it's trading cards, stuffed animals, gadgets, or plastic toys, there is always something that kids are eagerly trying to collect. Children like Simon are not interested and often openly scornful of these hot trends.

As adults, we know that fads come and go, so what does it matter if some children choose not to participate? The problem is that this makes them "the odd men out." Instead of joining in their classmates' activities, they sit on the sidelines. They don't even understand what the other kids are saying because they don't know the collectors' vocabulary. Children who are already well-liked can get away with a bit of eccentricity, but children who are having trouble relating to other kids further isolate themselves by not knowing about or participating in the latest activity. When 90 percent of the kids in the lunchroom are playing with or talking about the current collectible, it's easier for your child if he or she can do so too.

To relate to other kids, your child must cultivate some interests in common with them. This doesn't mean your child has to become a cookie-cutter copy of everyone else; it does mean your child needs to participate in some popular activities. Little Adults often have unique interests that make them fascinating individuals. Parents and teachers may be charmed by their unusually mature hobbies, but other kids don't know what they are talking about. You should certainly support your child's special passions. It's wonderful when a child becomes intrigued by a topic and enthusiastically masters a body of knowledge. Prize your child's uniqueness, but don't let your Little Adult cut him- or herself off from ordinary childhood activities.

Sometimes Little Adults don't participate in the latest trend because their parents discourage it. Be careful about doing this. If some fad is completely against your family values, of course your child should not be involved in it. Being true to one's principles, even if they are unpopular, is an important lesson for children. But the more you do to make your child different from other kids, the more hurdles your child has to overcome to fit in.

Try to find ways for your child to participate in popular activities (or similar alternatives) that fit with your values. For instance, if you truly cannot, in good conscience, let your daughter collect Barbies because you object to the unrealistic body image they foster, can you live with having her collect Barbie's little sister, Kelly, who has a child-shaped body? If you feel the latest trading cards promote violence, could you get your child started on a baseball card collection instead? How about a marble collection? If you find that your family values are making a lot of common activities off-limits, you owe it to your child to find other families with children who share these values so that your child doesn't always feel left out.

Sometimes parents forbid their children to participate in a trendy activity not because of some deeply held conviction but because they (the adults) think it's silly. Of course it's silly. It's not supposed to appeal to adults; it's aimed at kids. If this is your only objection to the latest fad, we suggest that you grit your teeth and encourage your child's participation anyway. You can take comfort in the fact that the current popular interest won't last long. Your child's classmates will either outgrow it or get bored with it, and another "in" thing will take its place.

What if your child is completely uninterested in popular activities? You may need to lead the way. The Unwritten Rules and the following activities explain how to do this.

THE UNWRITTEN RULES

- You can usually find something to like about a popular interest.
- Asking someone for help or advice shows you respect him or her.
- You can't join a group by disagreeing — you have to look for common ground.
- Some opinions are best kept to yourself.

ACTIVITIES FOR LEARNING
THE UNWRITTEN RULES

1. Getting Involved with the Current Hot Collectible

Elementary school children love collecting things. One of the quickest and easiest ways for your child to have something in common with other kids is to become involved with the current "in" thing. If you are not sure what's "in," ask other parents or your child's teacher.

Although Little Adults want to impress everyone, they will make more friends by showing that they are impressed by other kids. Little Adults need practice letting someone else be the expert. You may want to arrange for a child with an established collection to explain it and help your child start one of his or her own. Your child could even invite this experienced collector to come along as a consultant on a shopping trip to buy the first items in your child's collection. Encourage your child to ask classmates questions and make appreciative comments about their collections. Have your child ask other kids for advice on building a collection. This indicates that your child is interested in their ideas and respects their opinions, and it's a promising way to begin a friendship.

Buy your child enough items to start the collection, as well as a nice way of storing the items (e.g., an album or a divided box). Don't go overboard and buy your child the best collection in town. This is not necessary, and it could backfire. Remember, your goal is to help your child fit in, not to give your child more ammunition for trying to impress people. Also, make sure that your child doesn't give away the collection out of indifference or in an effort to win other children's friendship — doing this defeats the purpose, and it will come across as odd rather than generous.

Try to build up your child's enthusiasm for this new interest. Talk about it at the dinner table. See if you can find an aspect of the collection that is especially appealing to your child. For instance, if it's Barbies, maybe you can get your child interested in the history of Barbie or in the Barbies that wear the traditional costumes of many nations. If the new interest involves cartoon characters, try getting your child a book on cartoon drawing to see if he or she can learn to draw the characters. If possible, take your child to a collectors' trade show. The excitement at these shows can be contagious.

You may need to help your child realize when a fad has cooled off. Once Little Adults have experienced some social success through their interest in a collectible, they may have a tendency to cling to this interest long after their classmates have dropped it. If most of the other kids are no longer talking about a collectible, your child needs to move on to the next thing too. Your child can still play with the old collection at home, but around other kids, he or she should concentrate on learning about the new "in" collectible.

2. Looking for Ways to Agree

One of the reasons that Simon's comments were so jarring is that they flagrantly disagreed with the general opinion of the group. The other kids were excited about the cards, while Simon was disdainful. Little Adults often state their opinions officiously, without considering other people's reactions. It probably didn't even occur to Simon that his remarks were insulting and irritating to the other kids. That's what he thought, so that's what he said. Little Adults' tendency to disregard group opinion makes it hard for them to blend in with their peers.

Help your child learn to pick up on the general tone of a group and to look for ways of agreeing with group members. If all the other kids are complaining about a huge school assignment, your child should complain too. For instance, your child could say, "Yeah, it took me forever to do the definitions." Saying, "Oh, it was easy. I already finished the whole thing," won't impress the other children — it will annoy them, and it will prevent your child from being part of the group. If all the other kids are excited about the upcoming school carnival, your child should mention something that he or she likes about the carnival too. Saying, "I hate large crowds," doesn't contribute to the conversation or win your child any friends — even if it's true.

The point here is not to tell your child to be insincere but to help your child focus on finding things in common with peers. Your child needs to learn to make comments that fit with the group consensus and to refrain from mentioning contrary ideas when speaking to people he or she doesn't know well. Not every thought or opinion should be shared with others. When your child says something that disagrees with the opinion of everyone in a group, he or she might as well get a bullhorn and announce, "I don't belong here!" The other children will pull away. But when your child finds a sincere way to agree with the group opinion, it builds a connection and allows your child to blend in with the others.

Explain to your child the importance of looking for ways to agree with others. You should emphasize both honesty and discretion. Use role-play to help your child practice picking up on group opinion and adding to the discussion appropriately. You can pretend to be two children having a discussion (alternate making comments as one child and responding as the other child), while your child tries to blend in by making a remark that fits with the previous comments. Act out a variety of scenarios, involving both positive and negative group opinions, such as

- complaining about a test
- being excited about an upcoming sporting event
- complaining about how strict parents are
- being worried about finishing a long-term assignment by the deadline

You may also want to reverse roles and have your child play the two kids having a discussion, while you try to join in by either agreeing or disagreeing. This allows your child to experience firsthand how jolting it is for group members when someone barges in with an unsolicited dissenting point of view.

3. Dressing to Fit In

Sometimes Little Adults announce that they are not part of a group without even opening their mouths: their clothes speak for them. They may dress too formally; they may wear clothes that are out of style or just not what most kids at school are wearing. If your child's surface appearance is off-putting, other kids are not going to make the effort to get to know what a wonderful person your child really is.

When you pick up your child at school, take a mental survey of what the other kids are wearing. Are the majority of kids wearing sweatpants, jeans, or chinos? Are they wearing shirts with collars or T-shirts? Are the clothes baggy, skintight, or in-between? How many of the girls are wearing dresses? What colors are "in"? How are the kids wearing their hair? Share the results of your survey with your child. Talk about how clothes are a signal that tell people either "I'm like you" or "I'm different from you." If your child wants to be accepted by the kids at school, he or she needs to look the part. You don't have to buy your child expensive clothes, just clothes that blend in with everyone else's.

Nathan: Needing to Be Perfect

"I'm never playing baseball again," Nathan announced to his father as they drove home from the game.

"It's the first game of the season," Nathan's father said. "I'm sure you'll improve."

"I'm not doing it," Nathan insisted.

"You weren't the only kid who struck out," Nathan's father reminded him.

"I was the only kid who struck out three times and missed two ground balls."

"Well, it takes time and practice to get good at a sport. Just stick with it. Besides, you don't want to let your teammates down."

"I'd be doing them a favor by quitting," Nathan grumbled.

Sports are wonderful for any child, but they are especially helpful for Little Adults, who need to learn to be team players. However, many Little Adults resist participating in sports because they are not good at them or because they are not the best player on the team.

Being in a situation in which they don't excel is torture for Little Adults. They want to be instantly brilliant and perfect at an activity, or they don't want to do it. Because they believe that they can only earn other people's approval through achievement, they lack the confidence to be mediocre. They don't know how to play just for fun.

If your child is truly terrible at a sport, it doesn't make sense to force him or her to be the subject of ridicule. However, don't immediately accept your child's judgment that he or she is athletically hopeless. Athletics is a big part of socializing for both boys and girls, so it is worth trying to find some way that your child can participate.

The Unwritten Rules and the following activities describe ways of helping your child get involved in sports and other team-related activities.

THE UNWRITTEN RULES

- You don't have to be good at something to enjoy it.
- You can contribute to a team without being a star.
- Mistakes are part of learning.
- It feels good to be part of a team.

ACTIVITIES FOR LEARNING
THE UNWRITTEN RULES

1. Finding the Right Sport and Building Athletic Confidence
Sometimes, getting your child involved in athletics is just a matter of finding the right sport. You may need to have your child try several different sports before you find the one that is right for him or her. Soccer is very popular, but if your child doesn't like to be crowded, tennis or gymnastics might be better options. If your child suffers from bad allergies, indoor sports, such as basketball or ice-skating, might be good choices. If your child lacks hand-eye coordination, try a sport that doesn't involve a ball, such as swimming, running, or martial arts. For some children, dance classes are an appealing alternative to sports, allowing them to be part of a group, practice skills, and increase physical fitness.

Often, Little Adults are reluctant to try any sport because they are afraid of making fools of themselves. A little extra coaching before they start can go a long way toward building their confidence. You may want to arrange for an older child to be an athletic mentor for your child by providing some one-on-one instruction. If your child can walk into the activity already knowing the rules and the basic moves, he or she won't feel completely at a loss.

Your child may be more willing to try a sport if it involves a short-term commitment and emphasizes *learning* rather than *competing*. Regular team sports usually involve two or more practices per week, plus a game on the weekend in front of an audience of parents. This is a huge and scary commitment for a child who is reluctant to play a sport. Your local YMCA or YWCA probably offers a less intense experience with sports that involves only an hour or so, one day a week, learning the fundamentals and playing on randomly divided teams, without an audience. Attending a two-week sports camp over the summer is another good way to try out a sport. Even if your child never moves beyond these activities to a real team, at least he or she will understand how to play the game and know what other kids are talking about when they discuss sports.

What if your child is on a team and really hates it? Should you let your child quit before the end of the season, or should you insist that he or she stick it out? Try to find out what is making your child so upset. Remind your child that signing up for a team means making a commitment for the season and do what you can to help your child solve the problem. Quitting too quickly could make your child feel like he or she has failed. If your child is getting picked on by the other kids, you may want to look at the activities for dealing with teasing in chapter 8, "The Sensitive Soul." If your child is having trouble because he or she isn't the star of the team, it may help to explain that the definition of a team is "everyone working together." Talk about how each player contributes in his or her own way. Maybe your child is not the best player, but he or she could be the most enthusiastic player or the player who tries the hardest. Additional coaching and practice could help improve your child's skills. If your child makes an error during a crucial play and causes the team to lose the game, you may want to take the whole team out for ice cream or pizza to help your child save face. If the problem involves the coach, use your judgment. It's good for kids to learn to deal with a variety of people, but if the situation is truly intolerable, it's okay to pull your child out.

2. Following Professional Sports

Becoming a sports fan is a way for even nonathletes to participate in sports. It gives your child something to talk about with other kids. Watch games on TV with your child and explain the rules. Sharing a nice snack while you watch will make it more appealing for your child to sit through the game. Help your child get to know the players so he or she can feel some personal connection to the action. Teach your child about the sports page in the newspaper. Check out fiction and nonfiction books about sports from the library. Subscribe to *Sports Illustrated for Kids*. Get your child interested in the history of the game. Some Little Adults love memorizing sports statistics. You may even want to take a family trip to a sports museum. Every major sport has one: the National Baseball Hall of Fame and Museum is in Cooperstown, New York; the Pro Football Hall of Fame is in Canton, Ohio; the Basketball Hall of Fame is in Springfield, Massachusetts; and the Hockey Hall of Fame is in Toronto, Canada.

Take your child and a classmate to a game. If you can't make it to a professional sporting event, a minor league, college, or even high school event is fine, just as long as there is an enthusiastic crowd. Buy the kids mementos (e.g., flags, caps) and snacks, and help them get caught up in the excitement. Cheer wildly. Join in the wave. Talk up the anticipation and the tension of the big moments. Going to a game is a big deal for elementary school kids, and it could be a special shared experience on which your child and the classmate can build a friendship.

3. Seeking Out Other Team Experiences

If you absolutely cannot get your child involved in sports, seek out other kinds of team experiences that can help your child learn to be part of a group. A well-led Scout troop can help your child develop a circle of friends. Singing in a choir is another activity that involves working together with group members. Many Little Adults enjoy drama-related activities. Acting gives them a chance to step out of the narrow role they've made for themselves, and it also lets them interact in a cooperative way with other kids. Your child might also be interested in academic teams, such as Destination ImagiNation,

ThinkQuest, or Junior Scientists, but be careful not to let your child limit him- or herself to only intellectual activities.

4. Encouraging Cooperation

Cooperating isn't easy for Little Adults. They are extremely independent, and they are often very competitive. Because they believe they have to prove their worth, they have a strong drive to be the best. Encouraging cooperation can help your Little Adult learn a kinder, less self-focused way of relating.

Try to notice your child cooperating and comment on it. You could say, "I really liked the way you and your brother cooperated to pick up the toys," or "You really helped me by setting the table. Now dinner is ready faster. That's great cooperation!"

Playing cooperative games is a fun way to encourage family members to work together. When no one loses, there are fewer tears, and younger siblings especially enjoy being on equal footing with older family members. Most ordinary games can be adapted to be played in a cooperative way. For example, with race-around-the-board games, you can take turns moving a single piece around the board. Or you can play so that whoever reaches the end first helps the other player or players until everyone wins. The finished player continues to take turns rolling the dice but now moves whichever piece is farthest behind. With other games, you can work together to accomplish a goal, such as finding all the pairs (make one pile for everyone) or building one big tower that is larger than the previous one you and your child built together. Games designed for a single player can often be played by a group.

You can also play games that were specifically created to be cooperative. *Everybody Wins!*, a book by Cynthia MacGregor, describes 150 noncompetitive games for children, and Family Pastimes has a catalog of cooperative games for ages three to adult. (To order a

catalog from Family Pastimes, call 1-888-267-4414 or visit www.
familypastimes.com.)

THE HOME-SCHOOL CONNECTION

Because Little Adults are generally eager learners and responsible students, teachers usually enjoy having them in their classes. Your child's
teacher is likely to be very open to helping him or her learn to get
along better with peers.

Knowing What's "In": Teachers always know what's "in." Your child's
teacher is likely to be a gold mine of information about popular kid
culture. He or she can offer suggestions about which activities or collections your child could take up in order to share classmates' interests.
The teacher may also be willing to help with the slang dictionary (see
activity 1, on page 186).

Avoiding Distancing Behaviors: Because the teacher sees your child in
action around other kids, he or she may have some important observations about things your child does that push people away. For
instance, some Little Adults read books during recess. They do this
because they feel awkward around other kids, but the message they
communicate is "Don't come near me! I'm not interested in playing
with you! I'm above your silly little games!" It may help to ask the
teacher to have a private talk with your child and give some gentle
pointers about getting along. The teacher may be willing to come up
with a subtle signal to remind your child not to do certain off-putting
behaviors, such as lecturing or being disdainful of others' ideas.

Cultivating Individual Friendships: The teacher might also have some
suggestions about which classmates are potential friends for your
child. Invite these children to your home for individual play dates

with your child. If possible, the teacher could use class assignments to partner your child with compatible classmates. Although most Little Adults do better with one-on-one pairings, group projects can help your child learn to be part of a team.

IF YOU TOO . . .

If you were a Little Adult, you probably understand how important it is for your child to gain a well-rounded sense of self and to learn to build relationships with peers. Be sure to practice what you preach. If your own life seems to be "all work and no play," it will be hard for you to persuade your child to relax and enjoy social activities. Invite other families over to your home for a barbecue. Have a Halloween party with costumes. Go out for dinner with friends. Let your child see you chatting with the neighbors. Join a bowling league, book club, or local softball team. Volunteer at school or in the community. Talk with your child about what you do to build and maintain friendships.

Your own experiences affect how you view your child's problems. Be careful not to either minimize or worry excessively about your child's social difficulties.

If you feel comfortable socially now, you may have a tendency to dismiss the importance of your child's problems, thinking, *I was the same way, and I survived. Things turned out okay eventually. Besides, not being part of a crowd builds character.* However, the problems that *you* found bearable might be making *your child* truly miserable. No matter how bright or talented a child is, it is always painful to be rejected by other kids. You managed to learn to get along with others on your own, but your child may need some extra help. Don't let your Little Adult endure unnecessary suffering. Why wait for things to work out eventually if you can help your child now? Just as you encourage your child's intellectual development, you should also do what you can to encourage his or her social development. The lessons that your child learns now about relating to peers will be valuable throughout life, both personally and professionally. It is possible to nurture your child's unique talents and to foster independent thinking while also teaching your child to value joy and friendship. Let your child see that you love him or her for more than accomplishments. Spend time together doing fun things that have no redeeming educational value. Show your child that it's okay to be just a regular kid.

If you have vivid, painful memories of feeling like an outsider as a child, you may have a tendency to put too much pressure on your child to be sociable. If your child picks up on your anxiety about his or her ability to relate to others, he or she might withdraw from peers even more, thinking, *If my parents are so worried, I must be really bad at this. I'm not even going to try.* As much as you can, try to have an attitude of relaxed confidence as you go over the Unwritten Rules and the exercises in this chapter. If you feel like you are working harder than your child to solve your child's social difficulties, it may be a sign that you are pushing too hard. You may need to slow down or take a break and offer your child some reassurances of your love and acceptance. As you help your child learn to relate to peers, you also need to support your child's talents, independence, and unique interests, because these are part of who he or she is. Try not to worry about whether your child is popular. He or she doesn't have to be the best-liked kid in school to be content. If your child has one or two good buddies, that may be enough.

SUMMARY

Little Adults tend to be bright, responsible, independent, and imaginative, but they need help fitting in with other kids. They need to find some interests that they can share with their peers, and they need to learn to relate in a relaxed, casual manner instead of trying to impress people with their knowledge. When Little Adults are able to cultivate their capacity for joy, fun, and frivolity, they learn not only to get along better with others but also to see that there is more to them than their achievements.

You Will Also Want to Read:

Chapter 2, "The Vulnerable Child"

Chapter 4, "The Different Drummer"

Chapter 8, "The Sensitive Soul"

Chapter 9, "The Born Leader"

THE UNWRITTEN RULES FOR THE LITTLE ADULT AT A GLANCE

- The goal is connecting with other kids, not impressing them with your knowledge.
- Nobody likes to listen to bragging or lecturing.
- It's not your job to report other children's misbehavior.
- You don't have to share everything you know; sometimes it's better to listen.
- You make friends by showing other people that you like and respect them, not by telling them how good you are.
- It's okay just to have fun and enjoy yourself.
- You can usually find something to like about a popular interest.
- Asking someone for help or advice shows you respect them.
- You can't join a group by disagreeing — you have to look for common ground.
- Some opinions are best kept to yourself.
- You don't have to be good at something to enjoy it.
- You can contribute to a team without being a star.
- Mistakes are part of learning.
- It feels good to be part of a team.

CHAPTER 8

The Sensitive Soul

Does your child . . .
    cry easily?
    misunderstand friendly teasing?
    have his or her feelings easily hurt?
    perceive criticism where none was intended?
    interpret other people's mistakes as deliberate meanness?
    hold on to grudges and grievances?

Do you . . .
    vacillate between wanting to protect your child and wishing he or she would "toughen up"?
    find your sympathy waning as your child continues to rehash grievances over and over again?
    worry that your child will never make it through life's rough terrain?

*S*ensitive Souls are thin-skinned. They are easily bruised by the everyday bumps and scrapes of life. When a friend cancels a play date, instead of accepting the change of plans with mild disappointment and assuming that the friend must have had a good reason for canceling, they are devastated. If someone criticizes or rebuffs them, or if they just imagine that someone has slighted them, they can brood about it for days or even weeks. They get themselves all worked up over situations that most children would just shrug off.

Sensitive Souls have an inner sense of vulnerability that often causes them to misinterpret other people's actions. They quickly jump to the conclusion that others are trying to hurt or reject them — even when they are not. Sensitive Souls are often preoccupied with the "unfairness" of other people's actions. They take things too personally. When a classmate mistakenly takes their usual seat in the lunchroom, Sensitive Souls interpret this ordinary thoughtlessness as a deliberate attack. Instead of just sitting somewhere else or asking the other child to move over, they are likely to create a scene or march off in a huff. When a parent offers simple advice, Sensitive Souls take it as criticism, asking, "Why are you always picking on me?"

Sensitive Souls dwell on their grievances. They focus with tunnel vision on how upset they are and how they have been "wronged," so they have trouble seeing another person's point of view. An argument with a friend often ends the friendship for Sensitive Souls because they can't step away from their distress long enough to solve the problem. Instead, they nurse their resentments and wounded feelings, vowing, either privately or publicly, never to speak to the friend again.

Although some Sensitive Souls stew silently (and indefinitely) about unspoken hurts, many Sensitive Souls express their feelings vocally and inappropriately. Once they become agitated, they don't consider the situation, the audience, or the consequences of their response. They just react. They often burst into tears or sulk dramatically, even in front of people they don't know well. These kinds of overblown scenes shout a message to other children that says "I'm vulnerable! I'm different! Pick on me!" Their behavior leads other children to reject, avoid, and even ridicule them. One Sensitive Soul we know burst into tears in front of her entire fifth-grade class when her teacher told her to sit down after she misspelled a word in a spelling bee. She loudly protested, "But I *knew* that word; I just said it wrong!" She sat down grudgingly, amid the disdainful snickers of her classmates.

The overreactions of Sensitive Souls generally are *not* manipulative. Their sulks and tears aren't intended to get any particular response from other people. In fact, they aren't even thinking about other people once they get emotional (that's part of the problem!). They are simply blinded by their preoccupation with their own distress.

ON THE POSITIVE SIDE

When sensitive souls feel secure, they are capable of picking up on very subtle clues in social situations. With the right kind of help, their awareness of their own feelings can be broadened to provide them with a special understanding of other people's reactions and motivations. They could have the ability to care about and respond to people with great empathy, becoming wonderful friends. In addition, their capacity for intense feelings can easily lend itself to creative expression of many kinds. These sensitive children may well become artists, writers, or musicians one day.

SO WHAT CAN WE DO?

Sensitive Souls need to learn to interpret other people's actions in more reasonable ways so that they are less likely to overreact. They need to learn the Unwritten Rules about how to respond appropriately to everyday social dilemmas. They need to develop the ability to calm themselves down instead of working themselves up.

In the following sections, we describe three different Sensitive Souls who overreact to common social situations. Jonathan is deeply hurt by ordinary teasing. Claudia perceives personal criticism where none was intended. Lauren nurses a grudge about an event that she mistakenly interprets as a personal rejection. In each section, we describe the causes of the overreaction and offer practical suggestions for help.

Jonathan: Overresponding to Teasing

Jonathan's dad had signed him up for Boy Scouts, hoping it would help Jonathan make friends. But, based on today's events, it didn't seem to be working. After dropping his son off at the troop leader's home, Jonathan's dad saw one of the other boys in the troop playfully punch Jonathan in the arm and say, "Hey, butthead, did you borrow that shirt from your sister?" The other boys all laughed.

"Leave me alone," Jonathan said in a trembling voice.

Another boy taunted, "Do you have a skirt to match?"

At that point, Jonathan covered his face and wailed loudly, "You're hurting my feelings!" The other boys rolled their eyes and walked into the house together, leaving Jonathan alone, just as he had requested.

Teasing is part of the normal give-and-take of children's interactions. At some point, just about every child has to face being teased or called names. Sometimes teasing is friendly. The insults are untrue or exaggerated, and are meant to be silly rather than hurtful. But, even if teasing is intended as a taunt, children are better off dealing with the teasing in a matter-of-fact or friendly way. (If your child is dealing with teasing that has crossed the line to become *bullying,* if he or she feels frightened or threatened rather than merely embarrassed, or if he or she is being physically hurt by another child, see chapter 2, "The Vulnerable Child.")

If Jonathan had taken the teasing in stride — if he had laughed along or responded with a friendly retort such as, "No, I don't have a skirt to match. Can I borrow yours?" — the whole incident would have ended amicably. Jonathan would have seemed like "one of the guys." Instead, Jonathan's overreaction separates him from the group and turns a potentially minor incident into a major scene. The other boys lose respect for him, and he becomes a target for more unpleasant teasing in the future. How can the other boys resist teasing him again, when they know they can get such a big reaction with just a few comments?

Because he is a Sensitive Soul, Jonathan may never really enjoy any kind of teasing. However, instead of focusing on how wounded he feels when someone teases him, Jonathan needs to learn to see teasing as an annoying but ordinary part of life — like spelling tests. Most children don't enjoy taking spelling tests, but they can endure them with the proper preparation.

Jonathan also needs to understand when and how to express his feelings. At home, we encourage our children to talk about their feelings. We tell them it's okay to cry if they're upset. But Jonathan was expressing vulnerability to people who don't know him well and don't really care about him. Jonathan needs to learn that there is a time and a place to express hurt feelings. Sometimes it's just prudent to keep your wounded thoughts to yourself. Revealing them to the wrong people at the wrong time is asking for trouble.

If your child overreacts to teasing, explain the following Unwritten Rules to him or her. You can use some or all of the following activities to help your child understand how to put the rules into action.

THE UNWRITTEN RULES

- Teasing is an ordinary and sometimes friendly way that children relate to each other.

- Don't express your innermost feelings to everyone — not everyone cares about you.
- Try not to cry in front of other children.
- Avoid reacting emotionally to teasing.

ACTIVITIES FOR LEARNING
THE UNWRITTEN RULES

1. Distinguishing Between Friendly and Unfriendly Teasing
Explain to your child that teasing can be either friendly or unfriendly. Say the following phrases to your child in both a friendly and an unfriendly way, changing your tone of voice. Have your child guess your intent. Then have your child try saying the phrases both ways.

"Hey, sleepyhead, get out of bed!"
"I've never seen that outfit before!"
"Hello."
"Okay."

Most emotional communication is nonverbal. This means that to understand other people, your child has to pay attention not only to what they say but also to how they say it. Even a neutral word like *hello* can carry kind or unkind overtones, depending on how someone says it. Talk with your child about how to judge the intent behind people's words, focusing on the nonverbal side of communication. The following chart lists some key signs of friendly and unfriendly teasing.

SIGNS OF FRIENDLY AND UNFRIENDLY TEASING

Unfriendly Teasing	*Friendly Teasing*
Hostile facial expression	Smiling facial expression
Scornful tone of voice	Joking tone of voice
Threatening body posture	Open, relaxed body posture
Fists, hands on hips	Hands open and at sides
Looming, "in your face"	Friendly punch or push
Standing facing or behind the child being teased	Standing next to the child being teased

---

2. Learning to Ignore Teasing

Dr. Lawrence Shapiro developed a wonderful game that helps children learn to ignore teasing and that seems especially useful for Sensitive Souls. The following is our adapted version of this game.

Have your child play Pick-Up Sticks. While your child is concentrating on the game, you (or better yet, a sibling) should do whatever you can think of to try to distract him or her *except* talking or touching. You can make sounds but no words. You can make animal noises; you can make silly faces; you can stick out your tongue; you can blow on your child; you can flap your arms or dance around . . . Your child gets one point for not reacting to the teasing and two points for ignoring the teasing *and* retrieving a stick without moving any others. This game not only lets your child practice not reacting to provocation but also helps him or her to enjoy the fun, silly side of teasing.

3. Giving Strong Retorts to Teasing

Encourage your child to tell you the specific statements that other children are saying when they tease him or her. Use the following list of retorts, or your own suggestions, to help your child learn good responses to these statements. Have your child rehearse the retorts until he or she feels comfortable using them.

Pay attention to your child's nonverbal communication while practicing. Have your child look into a full-length mirror, or video-tape him or her, so your child can see how he or she comes across to others. Make sure your child looks the teaser in the eye; stands tall, with shoulders back; and speaks in a calm tone of voice. Point out to your child that a strong retort doesn't mean an aggressive retort but one that creates the impression of being confident, secure, and unflappable.

Be sure to watch your own expectations with this exercise. You want to work *with* your child's temperament, helping your child to gain new skills and confidence but also recognizing who he or she is. The point of this exercise is to give your child some ready-to-use, well-practiced retorts to say so that he or she can avoid falling apart emotionally. Your Sensitive Soul is not likely to turn into a master of witty repartee. Make sure your child knows that it's okay to say just one thing, or even to say nothing, and then walk away. Even if your child only thinks about a favorite retort to teasing and never says it out loud, it can help him or her hold it together and not become a target for future unfriendly teasing.

RESPONSES TO TEASING

Indifference:

Look teaser in the eye with a bored expression, then look away.

Walk away slowly.

Challenge:

"So, what's your point?"

"Tell me when you get to the funny part."

Disgust:

"Grow up!" or "Get a life!"

"Tell someone who cares."

Roll your eyes.

Humor:

"Why, thank you for noticing! I'm especially proud of . . ."

Assertiveness:

"Cut it out. I don't like it when you . . ."

(This response is best used when other friends are around as backup, or when there is some friendship with the teaser.)

4. Knowing What Not to Say in Response to Mean Teasing

Help your child understand why it is never a good idea to make the remarks listed below when being teased. Comments like these usually escalate unfriendly teasing.

Never Say to a Teaser:

"You hurt my feelings."

"I'm telling."

"I'm going to tell my mom."

"You're going to get in trouble."

"That's not nice."

5. Avoiding Crying in Front of Other Kids

Talk with your child about when it is and isn't appropriate to cry. In general, your child should only express vulnerable feelings with people who care about him or her. It's okay to cry at home, but grade school children generally don't cry in front of their peers. Acknowledge that everyone feels like crying sometimes but help your child come up with some strategies for what to do when he or she feels like crying in an inappropriate situation. The following list offers some ideas.

What to Do When You Are in Public and You Feel Like Crying

- Take deep breaths. Breathe in through the nose for one count and out through the mouth for four counts.
- Count to 10 or 100.
- Think of something else — a favorite activity, the contents of your lunchbox, the color of your shoes, what you're doing after school — anything but what's upsetting you.
- Go to the bathroom.
- Get a drink of water.
- Walk away calmly.

Claudia: Overreacting to Criticism

"Mrs. Jordan hates me," Claudia informed her mother between bites of cookie.

"Oh, honey, I'm sure she doesn't hate you."

"Yes, she does. She tells me I'm calling out, and when I raise my hand and don't call out, she never calls on me."

"Well, there are twenty-three children in your class, sweetie. I bet if you talked to Mrs. Jordan about how you're feeling . . ."

"I told you: she hates me. I can't talk to her. She's not fair. She likes everybody else in the class except me. It's awful. I can't stand it. I don't want to go to school anymore."

Claudia was unnecessarily hurt by an ordinary event — not being called on in class. She also interpreted her teacher's insistence that she raise her hand as a sign of personal dislike. Based on this flimsy evidence, she jumps to the conclusion that the teacher hates her. Claudia doesn't grasp that criticism isn't necessarily a sign of dislike. In fact, it's part of a teacher's job to give constructive criticism so children can learn. Teachers correct children when they give the wrong answer to a math problem so that they can get it right the next time. Teachers also correct children when they don't follow the classroom rules so that they can learn to behave appropriately. There is nothing personal or malicious about it.

Claudia overreacts to the teacher's criticism because of the skewed way she thinks about the situation: she interprets it as a terrible injustice, an unbearable personal attack. She tells herself, *This is awful. I can't stand it.* This kind of thinking is paralyzing because it makes even small problems seem insurmountable. Claudia needs to learn how to talk herself down rather than work herself up when she starts to feel upset. She also needs to gain some perspective so that she can accurately decide whether a situation is truly unbearable or merely unpleasant.

Claudia also overreacts because she focuses on her own distress. Claudia's strong emotional reactions grab her attention. But focusing inward, on how miserable she is feeling, intensifies her distress. This escalating cycle of distress → self-focus → more distress → more self-focus, etc., makes it hard for Claudia to shift her attention so that she can understand other people's points of view. It also impedes her ability to react constructively to her situation. Claudia is so preoccupied with her perception of events that she completely ignores her mother's attempt to explain the teacher's perspective. Her self-focus also prevents her from seeing obvious solutions to her problem, such as discussing the situation with the teacher or just raising her hand often so that sometimes she will be called on. Instead, she comes up with an extreme and childish alternative (avoiding school) that's aimed at reducing her distress but does nothing to solve the problem directly.

If your Sensitive Soul overreacts to criticism or minor problems, go over the Unwritten Rules with him or her. Pick from the following exercises to help your child vividly understand the relevant rules.

THE UNWRITTEN RULES

- Criticism doesn't mean dislike.
- The teacher's job is to help you learn.
- Give people the benefit of the doubt — true malice is rare.
- There are at least two sides to every story.
- Not all problems have the same weight.

ACTIVITIES FOR LEARNING
THE UNWRITTEN RULES

1. Seeing Another Person's Perspective

One strategy that can help Sensitive Souls to stop focusing on their own distress is to imagine exchanging roles with someone else, in order to gain another perspective. Too often, Sensitive Souls assume that hurtful actions are deliberate. If your child is upset with someone, make a list together of possible reasons for the other person's behavior. Include both benign and malicious possibilities on your list and then talk about the likelihood of each one.

Claudia and her mom might come up with a list like this:

"Why didn't Mrs. Jordan call on me?"

> She hates me.
> She is trying to make me miserable.
> She thinks I'm stupid and isn't interested in what I have to say.
> She didn't see my hand.
> She needs to give all the kids a chance to answer.
> She already knows I know the answer, so she wants to see what
>   other kids know.

Talk with your child about the consequences of assuming kind or mean intent. Giving another person the benefit of the doubt makes it possible to continue a relationship and resolve problems. Putting a negative spin on actions makes both parties feel bitter and hurt, and can ultimately end relationships.

A variation on this exercise is to use role-play to help your Sensitive Soul understand another person's point of view. Discuss the problem, with you taking your child's role and your child taking the role of the other person. Pretending to be the other person can help your child come up with reasonable and plausible explanations for that person's actions. If your child tries to portray the other person as deliberately cruel and malicious, play along. Exaggerate your own comments and reactions ("Mrs. Jordan, do you stay up late every single night thinking of ways to make your students suffer?"). Pretty soon, the role-playing is likely to dissolve into giggles, and the interpretations will seem silly and implausible. Encourage your child to role-play again, this time trying to portray what the other person might be thinking and feeling in a realistic way. Role-playing another person's perspective can cultivate Sensitive Souls' special capacity for empathy.

2. Judging the Size of a Problem

Sensitive Souls tend to react as if all problems are life-threatening calamities. But problems come in different sizes, and it's counterproductive to have a big reaction to a little problem. Divide a piece of paper into three vertical columns. Label these columns "Tragedy," "Moderate Problem," and "Minor Nuisance." Help your child come up with definitions for these three types of problems. For instance, you might define a *tragedy* as "a terrible and uncontrollable event that permanently changes your life in a bad way." A *moderate problem* could be defined as "a problem that will take some effort to solve." A *minor nuisance* could be "a little problem that can be ignored." Have your child come up with real or imagined examples of each type of problem. If your child can't think of any, you can mention some difficulties that occurred in the last week. How would your child categorize these? Does the magnitude of your child's reaction fit the size of the problem? When new problems come up, help your child judge their size by deciding which of the three labels best describes each problem. He or she may decide that the problems aren't so bad after all.

3. Countering Inflammatory Self-Talk

One very important way to help Sensitive Souls learn not to overreact is to teach them to become aware of how they talk to themselves about their problems. Inflammatory self-talk focuses on how terrible a problem is and gets your child worked up emotionally. Calming self-talk puts things in perspective and helps him or her cope.

Figure 8.1

INFLAMMATORY SPIRAL

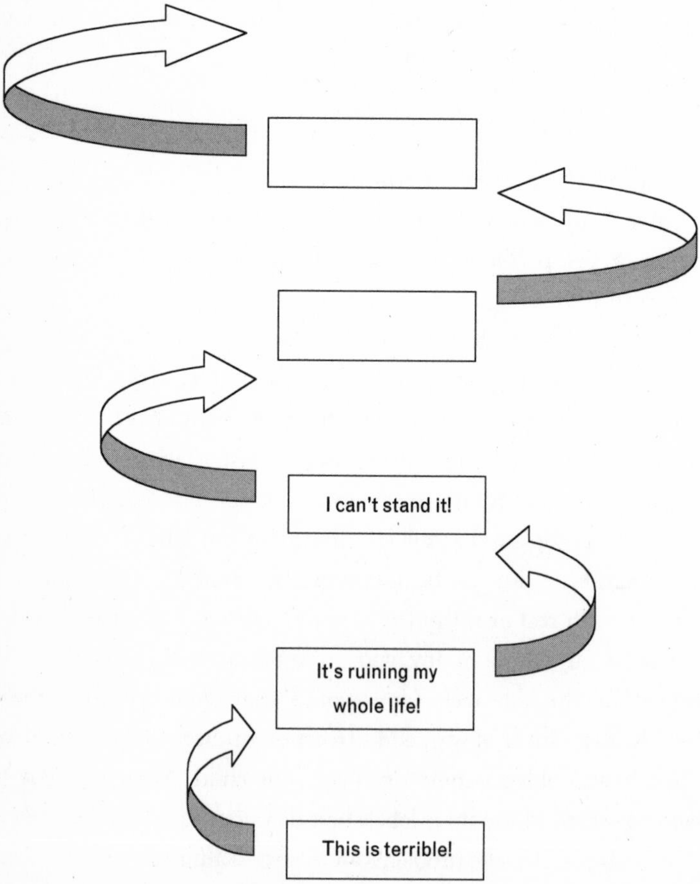

I can't stand it!

It's ruining my whole life!

This is terrible!

Figure 8.2

CALMING SPIRAL

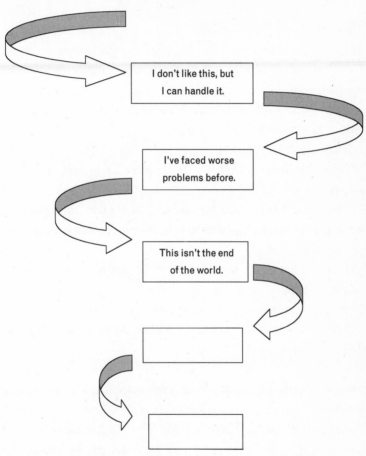

I don't like this, but
I can handle it.

I've faced worse
problems before.

This isn't the end
of the world.

Copy the preceding diagrams. Use them to explain to your child the effects of different kinds of self-talk. Have your child come up with his or her own examples of inflammatory and calming statements. Write them in the blank rectangles on the appropriate spiral. Stick the diagrams up on your refrigerator. When your child overreacts to a problem, refer to the diagrams to help your child use more adaptive self-talk.

Lauren: Holding On to Grudges

"Hey, Lauren," Ann called, "do you want to come over to my house this afternoon? You, me, and Kathleen can make posters for the Pumpkin Festival."

"No way," Lauren answered. "I'm never speaking to Kathleen again as long as I live!"

"How come?"

"She didn't invite me to her birthday party last month, and I hate her guts."

"Well, she didn't invite me, either," Ann said. "She was only allowed to invite three girls to the slumber party, and one of them had to be her cousin."

"I invited her to my bowling party last year, so she should have invited me back."

"But that's different . . . ," Ann began.

"I don't care. I don't want to have anything to do with her ever again," Lauren insisted.

Lauren has been stewing about not being invited to Kathleen's party for a month, and what's more, she plans to continue to hang on to this resentment for the rest of her life. What Lauren doesn't understand is that at this point, she only hurts herself by keeping the grudge alive. Kathleen, the person who committed the "crime," has most likely forgotten the offense.

One reason that Lauren was so upset about not being invited to Kathleen's party is that she has very rigid ideas about how a friend *should* act. Unfortunately, since no one is perfect, no one is likely to live up to her lofty standards. Unless she learns to adjust her expectations and cut other people some slack, Lauren is destined to be constantly disappointed in others and to leave a string of broken friendships behind her.

Lauren also shows a ruminative coping style. *Rumination* means focusing passively and repetitively on one's misery. Because Sensitive Souls have strong emotional reactions, they are prone to rumination. Numerous studies show that rumination intensifies and prolongs distress. When people sit around thinking about how bad they feel and about all the things that make them feel that way, they make themselves feel worse. They are more likely to see everything in a negative light, with little possibility for change. Lauren's rumination keeps her pain alive. The party took place a month ago, but because Lauren continues to dwell on not being invited, she is still as upset about it as she was when it first happened — maybe even more so. As she continues to brood about how terrible it was that Kathleen didn't invite her, how unfair it was, how hurt she is, how she will never forgive Kathleen, etc., she breathes new life into the old problem and prevents herself from moving past it.

There are two alternatives to rumination that help decrease negative feelings: active problem-solving and distraction. *Active problem-solving* means thinking in a practical way about what one can do to make a stressful situation better. Unlike rumination, which involves passive brooding, active problem-solving involves coming up with solutions and carrying them out.

The other alternative to rumination is distraction. *Distraction* means using pleasant and engrossing activities to take one's mind off troubles. For instance, Lauren could try riding her bike, working on a hobby, doing something with friends, or even just finishing up her homework (if it's not too hard and it would make her feel good to have it out of the way). It may seem as though distraction just means avoiding distress, but research shows that people who use pleasant activities to lift their mood are *more* likely to follow up with active problem-solving than people who ruminate are. Amazingly, only a few minutes of distraction can be enough to pull people out of a funk and make them more willing to do something about their dilemmas. Taking a break from a pressing problem can reenergize people as well as help them put difficulties in perspective.

If your Sensitive Soul holds on to grudges indefinitely, talk about the following Unwritten Rules to help your child understand the importance of not getting bogged down with grudges and rigid thinking. Follow up with some or all of the exercises to make sure your child learns how to act on these rules.

THE UNWRITTEN RULES

- There is no such thing as a perfect friend.
- We can't control what other people do, but we can choose how we respond to their actions.
- Dwelling on bad feelings makes them worse.
- Holding grudges mainly hurts the person holding the grudge.
- The definition of a good relationship is "working things out."

ACTIVITIES FOR LEARNING THE UNWRITTEN RULES

1. Recognizing and Toning Down Rigid Thinking

When your child complains about how someone has "done him or her wrong," use it as an opportunity to teach your child to recognize and tone down rigid beliefs. Sensitive Souls are prone to righteous indignation. This not only gets them very upset about ordinary problems, it also makes them hard to live with. No one can possibly measure up to their extremely high standards of how people ought to behave.

Rigid beliefs set a child up for one disappointment after another.

They are black-and-white judgments. They focus on how things should or must be. Realistic beliefs are more accepting. They acknowledge that things don't always work out the way we want but that life goes on. Rigid beliefs make disappointments seem unbearable, whereas realistic beliefs help us to accept disappointment and go on from there.

When you hear your child saying, "It's *not fair* that . . ." or "He *should* have . . ." or "She *has to* . . ." or "I *can't possibly* . . . ," write these comments down on one side of a piece of paper. Point out the phrases that indicate rigid thinking. Use the other half of the paper to help your child come up with realistic alternatives. Have your child read the two lists out loud. Ask your child how saying these statements makes him or her feel.

Here are the lists that Lauren and her father might have come up with about not being invited to Kathleen's birthday party.

Rigid Belief	*Realistic Belief*
Kathleen *should have* invited me to her party.	I would have liked to go to Kathleen's party, but whom she invites is her choice.
It's *not fair* to not invite someone who invited you.	It's nice to be invited to a party, but it's not the end of the world if I miss some parties. I can't expect to be invited to every event.
I *can't possibly* be friends with someone who didn't invite me to her birthday party.	There are lots of different kinds of friends. Some are closer than others. I can have close friends and casual friends.
She *has to* apologize if she wants to stay my friend.	I have a choice about whether I let one disappointment end my friendship with Kathleen.

2. Letting Go of Grudges

If your Sensitive Soul has been clinging to some grievance, talk to him or her about the costs of continuing to hold on to that grudge. If your child agrees that it's time to move on, a symbolic action may help him or her to do so. Have your child write the grudge on a piece of paper, rip the paper up into tiny pieces or crumple it into a tight ball, and throw it away with a flourish. If your child mentions the grudge again, remind him or her about the decision to let it go.

3. Knowing How to Self-Soothe

Help your child recognize how actions affect feelings. Ask your child to imagine that he or she is upset over an argument with a friend. What could your child do to make him- or herself feel *worse*? Possibilities include sulking alone in his or her room, remembering and complaining about all the rotten things the friend ever did, or picking a fight with a sibling. What could your child do to feel better (even if it doesn't solve the problem)? Many Sensitive Souls find repetitive physical motion soothing, so going for a walk, swinging, and riding a bike are good possibilities. Calling another friend and talking about fun things (*not* the argument) might also help. A favorite hobby can also be calming. Help your child come up with a list of soothing activities. Post this list in your child's bedroom, where it can be consulted when needed.

4. Using Active Problem-Solving

Before trying to help your Sensitive Soul learn problem-solving skills, make sure that he or she is in a calm enough frame of mind to think clearly. Maybe your child needs to do some relaxing or distracting activities first. Let your child be the judge of this. Review with your child the following steps for problem-solving. See if he or she can apply them to a relatively minor dilemma. Let your child come up with possible solutions; you shouldn't provide all the answers.

The point of this exercise is to help your child practice thinking of alternatives and choosing responses so that he or she can avoid impulsively acting on intense feelings.

Steps for Problem-Solving
1. Define the problem.
2. Brainstorm possible actions. (List any possibilities that come to mind, without censoring or critiquing.)
3. Evaluate the likely consequences of each alternative and choose the best one(s).
4. Follow through with the chosen strategies.
5. Afterward, assess how well the chosen strategy worked.

Lauren and her dad might define the problem as "Lauren is mad at Kathleen for not inviting her to the birthday party." Possible responses include (1) never speaking to Kathleen again, (2) confronting Kathleen about not being invited, (3) having a third friend tell Kathleen that Lauren is mad, (4) working to become closer friends with Kathleen so that Lauren will be invited next year, (5) forgiving Kathleen. Lauren and her father could go over these alternatives and talk about the likely consequences of each one. Once Lauren picks her favorite alternative, she should act on it, then evaluate the outcome.

THE HOME-SCHOOL CONNECTION

If your Sensitive Soul overreacts to ordinary social setbacks at school, it's very important to get the teacher's support in helping your child. The teacher may have important information for you about what sorts of situations cause difficulties for your child. You should describe the strategies you are using at home to help your child calm down and discuss which strategies your child can use at school without interrupting the class.

The following are some specific and easy-to-use activities that the teacher can do either with your child or with the whole class. Tread lightly when suggesting that the teacher try these activities. You need the teacher's assistance; therefore, you don't want the teacher to feel criticized or overburdened.

Using a Secret Signal: With your child's help, the teacher can devise a secret signal to let your child know when he or she is overreacting and needs to calm down. This might be pulling on an ear or placing an object on your child's desk — something simple and subtle that can serve as a gentle reminder for your child. Kids love secret codes.

Having a Peer Helper: The teacher may be able to assign another child as a peer helper for your child. Ideally, the peer helper would be an easygoing child who could temper your Sensitive Soul's tendency to overreact and who could also be a potential friend.

Recognizing and Rewarding Improvement: During regular class time, the teacher can help by noticing and praising your child when he or she manages *not* to overreact. The teacher should also praise your child when he or she starts to overreact but then manages to calm down — this is a big step in the right direction.

A regular conference with the teacher, you, and your child can be useful for setting goals, planning coping strategies, and discussing progress. If the teacher's schedule permits, an occasional lunch date between the teacher and your child to celebrate improvement is a wonderful way of motivating further changes. Providing a picnic for your child and the teacher on the day of their lunch date will make the event special for both of them.

Interpreting Tone of Voice Game: The teacher may be willing to involve the whole class in the Interpreting Tone of Voice Game. One child can say an ambiguous statement such as "Come over here" or "How are you?" and the other children can guess what feeling that child is trying to convey (e.g., anger, hurt, friendliness).

IF YOU TOO . . .

If you recognize some of the characteristics of a Sensitive Soul in yourself, you need to be aware of how your own sensitivity can interact with your child's. You may have a tendency to take your child's social struggles to heart. You may find yourself overreacting to your child's overreaction. You may notice that when you and your child talk about a problem, it starts out calmly but then you both get worked up about it.

Although your sensitivity can intensify your child's reactions, it can also provide you with special insight into your child's difficulties and a unique opportunity to show your child how to calm down. The next time you feel yourself getting upset, especially if it's about a situation that does *not* involve your child, try using some of the exercises in this chapter *in front of your child*. For instance, if you're having a problem at work, you could let your child see and hear you thinking up calming statements to counter inflammatory ones. If you're having trouble getting along with the neighbors, brainstorm aloud about possible reasonable explanations for their annoying behavior. If a friend cancels a social engagement, think aloud as you decide whether it's a tragedy, a moderate problem, or a minor nuisance. Talking with your child about your own struggles with sensitivity can also be wonderfully validating for your child. Too often, Sensitive Souls feel like they are suffering in a way that no one understands. It can be enormously reassuring for your child to hear that you know what he or she is going through and can relate to these struggles.

SUMMARY

Sensitive Souls have trouble getting along with other children because they overreact to ordinary events. They work themselves up over situations that most other children would shrug off. Their sensitivity often causes them to misinterpret social situations. They are especially apt to see criticism and rejection where none was intended.

The key issue for Sensitive Souls is learning to interpret other people's actions in more reasonable ways so that they are less likely to overreact emotionally. They need to learn the unwritten rules concerning how to manage common social dilemmas, when and how to express their feelings, and how to calm themselves down. If they can learn to step out of their preoccupation with their own grievances, their sensitivity can become an asset rather than a liability. It can be the basis for a special capacity for empathy and an intuitive understanding of people.

You Will Also Want to Read:
Chapter 2, "The Vulnerable Child"
Chapter 6, "The Short-Fused Child"
Chapter 10, "The Pessimistic Child"

THE UNWRITTEN RULES FOR THE SENSITIVE SOUL AT A GLANCE

- Teasing is an ordinary and sometimes friendly way that children relate to each other.
- Don't express your innermost feelings to everyone — not everyone cares about you.
- Try not to cry in front of other children.
- Avoid reacting emotionally to teasing.

- Criticism doesn't mean dislike.
- The teacher's job is to help you learn.
- Give people the benefit of the doubt — true malice is rare.
- There are at least two sides to every story.
- Not all problems have the same weight.
- There is no such thing as a perfect friend.
- We can't control what other people do, but we can choose how we respond to their actions.
- Dwelling on bad feelings makes them worse.
- Holding grudges mainly hurts the person holding the grudge.
- The definition of a good relationship is "working things out."

CHAPTER 9

The Born Leader

Does your child . . .

have strong ideas about the way things *should* be done?

frequently offer advice, opinions, and suggestions, even when other people don't want to hear them?

continue to push his or her ideas even after others have rejected them?

tend to dismiss other kids' ideas and act intolerant of children who aren't as "swift" as he or she is?

feel most comfortable around other kids when he or she is in charge?

have trouble seeing another person's point of view?

tend to override other people's feelings when pursuing his or her own goals?

often dominate younger or less outgoing children?

tend to be overly concerned with enforcing the rules?

feel hurt when other children revolt against his or her bossiness?

Do you . . .

feel proud of your child's leadership abilities but worry that he or she can be a bit overpowering around other kids?

often find yourself reminding your child not to be bossy?

fear that other kids don't really like your child because he or she comes on too strong?

worry that your child's good intentions are often misunderstood?

feel sad for your child because he or she has so much to offer but has so much trouble getting along with others?

$\mathcal{B}$orn Leaders are little dynamos. They are full of energy and initiative. They come across as confident and capable. They are extremely responsible. But sometimes they are just too much of a good thing. Other children can find them bossy, overbearing, or overwhelming.

Born Leaders have very definite ideas of how things ought to be. They are happiest when they are in charge of a group of people. Because they are frequently bright and dynamic, they often succeed in taking on leadership roles. These are the children who organize every club and head every committee. They like to be in control of things because they don't really trust others to do as good a job as they can. Born Leaders can't just sit back and let someone "less qualified" be in charge. They will try to find a way to take over.

Many Born Leaders are responsible oldest children who are used to being put in charge of their siblings. However, we have also known Born Leaders who are youngest children and who boss their peers the way their older siblings boss them. Sometimes Born Leaders are children who have grown up under difficult circumstances and compensate by working extra hard to make things the way they should be. They may have experienced scary, uncontrollable events, such as the divorce of their parents or the death of a loved one, and running the show gives them a sense of personal control.

Born Leaders are very social children. They seek out other kids and have a strong need to be appreciated and admired. It's not enough for them to carry out their good ideas on their own — they need to persuade others to go along with their plans. They need to feel needed. Born Leaders are secretly hoping that other kids will say, "What great ideas you have! You sure are a super organizer! We'd be lost without you!" Unfortunately, because they tend to be overpowering in their enthusiasm, Born Leaders are more likely to hear, "No way! You're not the boss of me!" This rejection stings. Born Leaders feel hurt and misunderstood. When others reject their ideas, Born Leaders feel like they themselves have been rejected.

Born Leaders are so focused on proving how "right" they are that they fail to recognize the impact of their behavior on others. They have a mental picture of the way things should be, and they pursue it with intense determination, regardless of anyone else's feelings. Instead of backing off when other children resist their efforts to impose their views, Born Leaders only work harder to prevail. When confronted with opposition, they act like relentless little steamrollers. While trying to promote their own ideas, Born Leaders are sometimes unkind and judgmental (e.g., "That's a dumb idea!" or "That makes no sense!"). Because of their unwavering persistence, Born Leaders can often get other kids to give in and let them have their way. They may even earn other children's reluctant respect because their ideas really are good. However, forced agreement comes at a high social cost. Born Leaders certainly won't earn anyone's friendship by dismissing others' ideas and always insisting on doing things their way. They may gain other children's compliance, but they also build their peers' resentment.

Born Leaders have such good intentions. Their vehemence comes from their conviction that they know what is best and from their belief that they must get others to see this. They don't think of themselves as coercing others; they are just trying to persuade them because they truly believe they are right. Born Leaders simply don't understand why other children balk at their directives. They are shocked to learn that others perceive them as pushy. They are baffled and wounded by the strong negative reactions they elicit from other children and sometimes from adults. More times than we can count, we've heard Born Leaders say in dismay, "I was only trying to help . . ."

Learning to let go and give up some control can be enormously freeing for Born Leaders. It's a heavy burden for children to be worrying constantly about what needs to be done and how it should be done, and to feel as if they can only rely on themselves. When they can drop some of the responsibility that they heap on their own shoulders, or share it with others, Born Leaders relate better to their peers and also feel happier. It's much more satisfying to have a friend than to have a follower.

ON THE POSITIVE SIDE

Born Leaders are full of energy and enthusiasm. It can be delightfully invigorating just to be around them because they live life with such zest. These children aren't the slightest bit wishy-washy. They have vision, conviction, and drive.

Born Leaders are our future lawyers, judges, teachers, entrepreneurs, and star salespeople. These children have the potential to persuade, motivate, and inspire others. They have a strong sense of justice and a desire to make things right. But coupled with their idealism, they also have a good dose of common sense. They tend to be quick-thinking, practical, and responsible. Others may complain about a situation or toss around ideas, but Born Leaders take action. They are positive risk-takers. They are willing to stick their necks out to make something happen. These children have the initiative and the determination to muster support for their ideas and to actually see them through.

SO, WHAT CAN WE DO?

Born Leaders appear outwardly confident, but because they have such a strong need for others' approval, they are easily bruised by criticism or rejection. This means that we need to be especially gentle and sensitive when working with them. We don't want to douse their fire. It would be a shame if these vivacious children, who are bursting with ideas, were to shut down completely. The goal with Born Leaders is to nurture their enthusiasm while helping them temper their habit of taking over.

Born Leaders need to learn to treat other kids as peers rather than subordinates. With guidance, these children can learn to present their wonderful ideas in a compelling, nondictatorial way. They can come to appreciate how getting other people's input can develop their ideas to an even higher level. They can experience how satisfying it is to be part of a team instead of always directing the action.

Born Leaders need to learn the unwritten rules about negotiation and compromise. They have to learn how to really listen to others. They must understand that they don't have to win every argument — sometimes it's okay to give in and go with the second-best idea, just to get along. These children also need to realize that it's not their job to enforce every rule or to correct other people's mistakes.

In this chapter we describe three Born Leaders whose take-charge attitudes alienate others. Samantha earns the resentment of her partners when she tries to direct the group project. Jack annoys the kids in the lunchroom by acting like the Rule Police. Francine irritates her coach and the umpire by arguing about their decisions.

Samantha: Running the Show

Jennifer and Carlie giggled as they used their pencils to swat a wadded-up piece of paper back and forth across their desks.

"Come on, you guys!" Samantha scolded. "This group project on dinosaurs is worth thirty percent of our grade! We can't fool around."

The other girls rolled their eyes at Samantha but stopped the game.

"I've already made an outline for us and divided up the work. Jennifer, you need to write two pages on the earliest dinosaurs. Carlie, you write about differences between carnivores and herbivores. I'll write about extinction and get some pictures from the Internet to put in the report."

"I don't want to do the early dinosaurs," Jennifer complained. "They're boring. I like the big ones."

"Yeah, and everybody knows about carnivores and herbivores. That's a dumb section," Carlie said. "I want to write about the first birds."

"I want to do how dinosaur bones were first discovered," Jennifer said.

"We only have three weeks to do this project," Samantha explained. "I'm just trying to be efficient. That's why I came up with the outline — so the work is divided fairly and so the sections fit together."

"Well, we don't like your sections," Carlie protested.

"Yeah, and how come you get to do the Internet pictures? That's the best part!" Jennifer said.

"If we all just follow the outline . . . ," Samantha began.

"Mrs. Halprin!" Carlie called. "Samantha is bossing us again."

"Samantha, remember what I said about everyone participating," Mrs. Halprin warned. Carlie smirked.

"I was just trying to help," Samantha protested, jumping up out of her chair and walking toward the front of the class. "See? I was telling them how if we just follow this outline I made, things will go very smoothly. We each have a different time period, so the three parts fit together. But they won't listen."

"You need to sit down, Samantha," Mrs. Halprin insisted. "This is a group project. You are not in charge. You have to listen to everybody's ideas."

"Well, they can still show their ideas on the topics I've picked . . . ," Samantha argued.

"That's enough, Samantha!" Mrs. Halprin said sharply. "I expect you to cooperate with the other group members."

Samantha walked back to her desk and sank into her chair, feeling defeated.

"I told you, Samantha," Carlie sneered. "You can't boss us around!"

Group projects often bring out the worst in Born Leaders. Lack of structure makes them uncomfortable, so they leap in and take over. However, as Samantha discovered, other children balk at commands from someone they consider a peer.

Samantha had the best intentions. She truly was trying to be helpful. She thought of a good way to organize the project and presented it to her partners, expecting their applause. She was baffled and hurt by their rebellion. When the other girls objected to her orders, Samantha kept insisting, certain that if she could just get them to try it her way, they would see the light. She even tried to argue her case to win the teacher's support. When the teacher also refused to consider her ideas, Samantha was crushed.

Because of their single-minded determination to get things done the "right" way, Born Leaders often tread on other people's feelings. They don't even realize that they are being pushy — they just know that they are right. They believe their peers don't understand things as clearly as they do, and they feel duty-bound to convince them of the correct course of action.

Born Leaders focus on efficiency: they are sure that things will work extremely well if everyone does exactly as they say. This is probably true. However, it's unlikely that their peers are going to completely and cheerfully acquiesce to their wishes, especially when they state them in such a domineering way. Most children like to have some say in what they do and how they do it. They want the opportunity to contribute their own thoughts, and they resent being pressured to comply with someone else's plans.

Samantha did have good ideas about organizing the group project, but her bossy presentation led her partners to automatically reject her plans. She probably would have had more success in persuading the other girls to follow her outline if she had asked for their input and offered her ideas as suggestions rather than orders. Her partners' feedback might even have helped her improve the original outline. (This probably never occurred to Samantha.)

The Unwritten Rules and the following exercises can help your Born Leader learn to be more of a team player.

THE UNWRITTEN RULES

- How you say it matters as much as what you say.
- There is always more than one path to the same goal.
- People find it easier to listen to you when they know you have heard and understood their point of view.
- Everyone needs to feel that his or her input is worthy.
- A good negotiation means everybody wins something.
- If you push people into doing something, they will resent you, even if you are right.
- You don't always have to come up with an answer — just listening is often enough.

- Getting along sometimes means giving in.
- It's usually better to lose an argument than to lose a friend.

> ### ACTIVITIES FOR LEARNING
> ### THE UNWRITTEN RULES

1. Changing a Bossy Tone of Voice

Often, it's not so much what Born Leaders say but how they say it that repels other children. Born Leaders come on too strong because they tend to use a bossy style of communicating. They speak loudly and forcefully, implying, "I'm in charge here!" Born Leaders don't realize that they are being domineering, but their bossy orders make other kids feel steamrollered. Other kids immediately want to disagree with them, regardless of what they really think. Even kids who are usually easygoing feel like rebelling against the Born Leaders' take-charge tone.

Go over the following list with your child so that he or she can recognize the specific characteristics that make a statement sound bossy, then review the strategies for expressing the same idea in a gentler manner. Bossy orders are direct commands said in an unyielding way. They demand immediate action without any explanation or acknowledgment of the other person's feelings. They may also involve threats or ridicule. In contrast, softer suggestions are more flexible and courteous. They ask questions or state opinions and have a more collaborative tone.

You may want to have your child read both the bossy orders and the softer suggestions into a tape recorder so that he or she can hear the difference in tone. You could also give your child an example of a bossy statement, such as "Gimme that!" or "This is how we're doing it," and have him or her try to fix it so that it sounds gentler. If you hear your child bossing younger siblings, pull him or her aside privately. Talk about how he or she could have said the same thing in a softer way. If possible, have your child try again.

Once Born Leaders learn the difference between bossy and respectful statements, they sometimes take it upon themselves to correct adults. This will get them into big trouble. You may need to explicitly tell your child that parents, teachers, coaches, and bosses are allowed to make bossy statements because they actually are in charge. However, children should not make bossy statements to other children, and they definitely shouldn't try to direct adults.

Bossy Orders	*Softer Suggestions*
"Do it!"	"Could you do it?"
"Do it now!"	"When you get a chance . . ."
"If you don't do it . . ."	"If you do this for me, I'll do that for you."
"This is how we're doing it!"	"I have an idea . . ."
"Get that for me!"	"It would really help me if . . ."
"Do it, butthead!"	"Could you please . . . ?"
"Let me give you some advice!"	"What do you think of . . . ?"
"Because I said so!"	"The reason I think so is . . ."
"This is the best idea!"	"How about if . . ."
"You have to!"	"I'd like . . ." or "We need to . . ."
"It's about time!"	"Thanks!"

2. Learning to Negotiate and Compromise

To help your child learn to negotiate with others, first lay some groundwork by explaining why it's important to compromise, then give some concrete examples of how to compromise.

Talk with your child about the social cost of imposing ideas on peers. With a younger child, you may want to read the picture book *Franklin Is Bossy* by Paulette Bourgeois. Acting bossy makes other children resentful — even if your child is right. If your child dismisses other children's opinions, they are likely to reciprocate by refusing to listen to anything your child says. Moreover, even if your child manages to get others to go along with his or her plans, this kind of short-term victory can sometimes create long-term problems. Kids may give in to the person who talks fastest, yells loudest, or persists longest, but they will dislike and avoid that person later.

When Born Leaders find themselves working strenuously to persuade someone, it's a sign that they need to take a deep breath, step back, and ask themselves, *Why am I pushing so hard? Is this worth the battle?* Sometimes Born Leaders just argue out of habit. They need to keep in mind that building or maintaining a friendship is more important than winning a trivial argument. Born Leaders are often so focused on promoting their viewpoints that they can trample over others' feelings without even realizing it. They treat their peers' opinions as obstacles rather than legitimate perspectives. To get along with others, your child needs to be open to compromise and to give in gracefully, sometimes, for the good of the team.

Born Leaders need to keep in mind that a successful negotiation means that everyone walks away winning something. They need to listen and understand the other person's viewpoint and then honestly consider it. As much as possible, they should focus on shared goals and points of agreement. They should ask themselves not just *What do I want?* but also *Where am I willing to give in?* They may choose to stick to their guns on issues that really matter to them, but they should also offer some meaningful concessions, or they will pay a social price.

The following list includes a number of argument scenarios. Explain to your child the importance of creating win-win situations. Help your child come up with several possible compromises for each scenario. Ask your child, "What could you do that would be fair to everyone?" Follow up in your day-to-day life by encouraging your child to find ways to compromise with you or with a sibling when disagreements occur.

FINDING WAYS TO COMPROMISE

- On a play date, you want to play Ping-Pong, but your friend wants to ride bikes.
- Your friend wants to use crayons to decorate the group project report, but you think markers would be faster and more eye-catching.
- You and your friend are at the movies. You can't wait to see the new monster movie, but your friend hates scary movies.
- During recess, you want to play with your best friend, but he / she wants to include another kid whom you don't like.
- Both you and your friend want to run for class president. If you both run, it will probably split the votes, and someone else will win.

3. Knowing When and How to Back Down

Born Leaders' take-charge style of relating can be very annoying to peers. But these determined children often either don't notice their peers' growing irritation, or they simply discount it. They honestly believe that if they keep talking and explaining and insisting, others will understand how right they are. Unfortunately, it rarely works this way. The harder they push, the more resistant or resentful their peers become. Even when Born Leaders do pick up on their peers' annoyance, they don't know how to respond to it appropriately. So they just continue to argue, digging themselves deeper and deeper into a social rut.

Many Born Leaders need help knowing when and how to back down gracefully. They need to recognize when they are trapped in an arguing rut. Moreover, they need to know what they can say to get out of that rut without losing face.

Talk with your child about the kinds of reactions that signal other children are feeling pushed. Help your child understand that these are warnings or "yield signs." They mean that your child needs to stop talking, at least temporarily, and listen to someone else's ideas. If your child continues to argue in the face of a yield sign, he or she risks antagonizing the other child. The following list includes a number of possible yield signs. You may want to act these out with your child to make sure he or she can recognize them.

Yield Signs

Indications that Other People Are Feeling Pushed
   Tense silence
   Rolling eyes
   Looking away
   Arms crossed over chest
   Not responding to anything you say
   Annoyed tone of voice
   Negative comments ("Shut up!"; "No way!"; "You're not the boss!")
   Surly agreement ("Fine!" or "Whatever!")

Once your child understands yield signs, you need to give him or her some specific strategies for backing down gracefully. Have your child try saying the following alternatives. Your child should select one or two of these statements, or variations that the two of you come up with, and then practice them until he or she feels comfortable and confident saying them. When your child notices yield signs, he or she should use one of these statements and then *stop talking* for a while.

You may need to reassure your child that he or she doesn't always have to give in to others. Some battles are worth fighting. However, sometimes ceasing arguments for a little while can end a deadlock and help people come up with a solution that works for everyone. The statements we describe for backing down gracefully offer a means of making a temporary retreat from an unnecessary or unproductive battle.

Ways of Backing Down Gracefully
"I guess I can't convince you. What do you think we should do?"
"I guess I've said enough."
"That's what I think, but you need to do what you think is right."
"I like that idea, but let's do something we all agree on."
"Well, if you guys really don't like that idea . . . okay."
"That's my suggestion."
"Sorry. I'll stop talking now."
"That's what I think. What do you think?"

4. Summarizing Others' Ideas
Born Leaders often have trouble really listening to others — especially others who disagree with them. When other children are speaking, Born Leaders are usually just waiting for their turn to talk so that they can continue to argue for their point of view. The more determined, excited, or vehement they feel, the more trouble they have listening. Learning to listen fully will help them relate better to others. As a side benefit, it could even help them get their way more often. In general, other kids will be more willing to listen to your child's ideas if they feel that your child has heard and understood their views.

Summarizing is a technique that can help your child learn to give a speaker his or her full attention. It helps your child focus on trying to understand the speaker's perspective without criticizing, arguing, or planning how to respond. It involves listening carefully and then stating the main ideas expressed by the speaker. The following table shows some examples of summarizing. The first two summaries for each statement refer only to the content. The third summary, written in parentheses, refers to both content and feelings. Start by having your child learn how to summarize just the facts of what a speaker says. Once your child is comfortable doing this, he or she can also try summarizing feelings.

SUMMARIZING

Statement: "I hate fractions! I've read this stupid unit three times, and I still don't get it!"

Summary:

"You're really having trouble with the math homework."
"Fractions are hard for you."
("You're feeling frustrated with this unit on fractions.")

Statement: "My sister is always borrowing my clothes without asking and then leaving them in a lump on the floor."

Summary:

"Your sister keeps messing up your clothes."
"Your sister takes your clothes without asking."
("You sound annoyed with your sister.")

Statement: "I don't want to play Monopoly. We always play Monopoly. Why can't we play something fun, like Battleship?"

Summary:

"So, you think we should play Battleship instead of Monopoly."
"You want to play Battleship."
("You're sick of playing Monopoly. You'd rather play Battleship.")

Look for opportunities to practice using this technique at home. You may want to plan a discussion of a topic that is likely to elicit disagreement among family members. For instance, you could discuss ideas on the best place to go on a family vacation, the best thing to collect, the best sports team, or the best kind of music. Have one family member state his or her opinion and then have another family member summarize that speaker's views. Be sure to check with the speaker to make certain that the summary is accurate. Family members should take turns speaking and summarizing so that no one feels singled out.

Alternatively, you could try having family members use summaries during ordinary conversation. Let your child hear you summarizing people's comments throughout the day. Try making a game out of seeing how many summarizing statements the family can make during dinner. You may want to keep a running tally and plan a special dessert to celebrate the family's good listening skills when you reach a certain goal.

You may need to clarify that direct requests from parents or teachers require action, not summarizing. When you tell your child not to leave shoes lying around in the middle of the hallway, you don't want to hear, "So, it really bothers you to have the hallway blocked" — you want the shoes picked up.

If your child gets very comfortable making summarizing statements, he or she can try using them with peers. These statements can be especially helpful during a disagreement. But even if your child feels too awkward to say them to peers, just thinking them can be helpful. The main purpose of these statements is to teach your child to listen. Having to come up with a summary forces your child to pay attention and to process what a speaker is saying — even if your child never says the summary aloud.

For older children, a good time to practice summarizing is when a friend is talking about a problem. Born Leaders usually leap in with advice as soon as they have the gist of the problem. Their well-intentioned suggestions — "You really should . . ." or "Why don't you just . . ." or "I know just what you should do!" — leave their friends feeling annoyed. If the problem were that simple to solve, the friend would have done so already! Explain to your child that people don't want to hear advice unless they specifically ask for it. Even then, advice should be offered as a tentative suggestion ("What do you think about . . . ?") rather than a direct command. Try role-playing some problems that a friend might confide. Have your child refrain from offering advice and instead respond sympathetically with a summarizing statement. For instance, you could start off by saying, "I failed the math test again. I don't know what I'm going to do!" or "My little brother is such a pest! He's always following me around."

5. Listening to and Remembering Others' Ideas: The Imagine Ten Game

Because Born Leaders are so full of their own ideas, it's hard for them to listen to other children's ideas. The Imagine Ten Game is a fun way to help them learn to listen. This is a great game to play with your child when you are driving in the car or sitting in a waiting room. One player states a scenario, such as "I'm going on vacation and I packed . . . ," "I had a terrible day yesterday because . . . ," or "I'm feeling very full because I ate . . ." That player then lists ten items to fit the scenario. Coming up with silly or outrageous items adds to the fun of the game. For instance, someone could say, "I had a terrible day yesterday because three prickly warthogs decided to sleep in my bed!" or "I'm feeling very full because I ate six banana and prune sandwiches!" The other player listens carefully to the ten items and then tries to recall as many as possible. (For younger children, or children who have trouble remembering spoken words, you can use fewer items.) Players get a point for each item they recall, and they take turns having the speaking and remembering roles.

6. Brainstorming

Born Leaders believe that there is one best way — their way. Not only is this irritating to other people, it also hurts Born Leaders themselves because they can become locked in to an idea too quickly. Brainstorming means letting ideas pour out without criticizing or censoring. You can try it with just you and your child or with the whole family.

Place a brick in the center of a table. Have everyone come up with as many ideas as possible of how that brick could be used. Tell players to say anything that comes to mind. No idea is too silly or too weird. Write everyone's responses on one sheet of paper. Be sure to treat one another's comments with respect.

Brainstorming can be a very freeing experience. It's amazing how many ideas we can come up with when we don't censor ourselves. It's fascinating how one person's notion can trigger someone else's, how building on one another's concepts can develop and enhance them, and how the best ideas often emerge when we think we have run out of them. Creating a page full of brainstorming responses is a vivid way of showing that there is often more than one "right" answer.

7. Creatively Collaborating: Add-a-Sentence Stories

Because Born Leaders prefer to act unilaterally, they haven't had much practice with creative collaboration. They haven't experienced how exciting and satisfying it is when two or more people come together and do something that is greater than anything they could have done alone. Add-a-Sentence Stories are another fun way of showing your child how people can build on one another's ideas. Choose one of the following story starters (or one of your own) and have each family member add one sentence to continue the narrative. Tape-record the evolving story or write it down as you go.

Add-a-Sentence Stories

Story Starters

William was astonished by what was waiting for him when he opened the front door of his house.

The box contained a green ribbon, a snail shell, three gold coins, and a key.

The girls were walking home from school when they heard it — a little voice calling, "Is that you, Mavis?" — and it seemed to be coming from down in the rain gutter.

Norman was trudging past the painting of Admiral Thisby, when, out of the corner of his eye, he saw the admiral stick out his tongue.

It all started when Claudia woke up to find that she had grown three feet taller during the night.

Jack: Acting Like the Rule Police

"Darn!" Peter said, pulling his sandwich out of his lunch bag. "I got bologna again! I keep telling my mom that I hate bologna sandwiches, but she keeps giving them to me. Does anybody want to trade?"

Before anyone could respond, Jack pronounced, "We are not allowed to trade food." Peter rolled his eyes but threw his sandwich back in the bag.

"Oh, cool! I got Lunchables today," George bragged, tilting back in his chair.

"You're not supposed to tilt back in your chair!" Jack insisted. "It's dangerous!" George banged his chair back down on all four legs with a disgusted snort.

Mitchell flicked a raisin at Jack. "Cut it out!" Jack whined. "The rule is No throwing food in the cafeteria."

"Nyah, nyah, nyah," Mitchell mimicked. The three boys quickly packed up the remains of their lunches and got up to go to the playground.

"Hey!" Jack called after them. "You didn't push your chairs in!" The other boys ignored him.

Some Born Leaders feel compelled to correct others when they break the rules, because infractions violate their sense of how things ought to be. Our colleague Jed Baker, Ph.D., says these children act like "Rule Police." In the story above, Jack found the other boys' minor misbehavior so disconcerting that he took it upon himself to enforce the law of the land. He was completely focused on what the other boys were doing wrong, and he failed to recognize how annoying his behavior was to them.

Children like Jack need to learn that it is not their responsibility to make other kids behave. Children resent having a peer reprimand them. It is extremely unlikely that they will respond by saying, "Oh, thank you for pointing that out." They are much more likely to respond with a rude dismissal, such as "Who asked you?"; "Get lost!"; or worse. Other kids don't want or need reminders about the rules. Elementary school kids already know the rules, so if they break them, it's usually because they choose to break them. Even if other kids comply with a Born Leader's scolding, there will be unpleasant repercussions. In Jack's case, he got everyone to follow the rules, but Mitchell mimicked him, and all of the boys rushed to get away from him.

Sadly, teachers often resent children who play the Rule Police as much as other kids do. When Born Leaders try to enforce the class rules, they are usurping the teacher's authority. Although their intentions are positive — they want to help — their actions imply criticism of the teacher. In effect, they are saying to the teacher, "You're not doing your job, so I will." If a teacher points out that it's the teacher's job to enforce the rules, Born Leaders are likely to argue, "But you didn't say anything . . ." These children need to understand that sometimes teachers have a good reason for ignoring misbehavior. Moreover, even if the teacher simply doesn't see the misbehavior, unless there is a serious safety risk, it is still not appropriate for Born Leaders to reproach another child.

In addition to being overly focused on rules, some Born Leaders are also sticklers for accuracy. If someone says, "There are ten kids on the playground," they will insist, "No, there are eleven." If their mothers say to a friend, "I tried to call you several times last night," they will interrupt with, "You only tried once, Mom!" Being contradicted in front of others is annoying and sometimes embarrassing. Born Leaders are just trying to make sure everyone knows The Truth (as they see it), but no one asked them and no one will thank them for it.

The Unwritten Rules and the following activities can help your child learn to refrain from correcting others.

THE UNWRITTEN RULES

- You are in charge of your own behavior, not anybody else's.
- If you correct or criticize other kids, they won't want to be around you.
- When you criticize someone, they remember it, even if you don't.
- It's not your job to "set the record straight."
- Correcting people in front of others makes them look bad. They will feel embarrassed and will probably be mad at you.

ACTIVITIES FOR LEARNING
THE UNWRITTEN RULES

1. Managing the Urge to Correct

Because of their strong need to have everything as it "ought" to be, Born Leaders feel very uncomfortable when people aren't following the rules or aren't being completely accurate. We can tell Born Leaders not to correct others, but that's not enough. We also need to give them some tools to manage their discomfort when they feel the urge to do so but know they shouldn't.

Talk with your child about why it's important not to correct others. Explain that in the long run it hurts your child, even if the other people comply with the reproach. Acknowledge how hard it is for your child to see people doing or saying something "wrong" and not say anything. Work together to come up with some strategies that will help your child keep quiet in these situations. We have found that some impulsive children actually need to put their hands or fingers over their lips — in a casual way — to keep from blurting out an inappropriate remark. Many children like to have a special phrase that they can repeat in their minds to help them keep quiet. We've listed a number of possibilities, but your child may prefer one that he or she invents.

Self-Statements to Manage the Urge to Correct Others
   "Let it go."
   "Let it slide."
   "Chill."
   "It doesn't matter."
   "It's not important."
   "It's not my job to correct them."
   "I'm not the one doing / saying the wrong thing, so I don't have to worry about it."

"If I correct them, they'll be mad."

"I can talk to him / her about it privately, later."

2. Learning to Let Go of Righteous Indignation

What fuels Born Leaders who act like Rule Police is their overdeveloped sense of justice. When they see someone misbehaving, they get all riled up inside, thinking, *That's not right! They're not supposed to do that! It's against the rules!* The following exercise acknowledges Born Leaders' righteous indignation but gives them a concrete way to let go of it.

Emphasize to your child the importance of *not* reacting when other children misbehave (unless there is a serious safety issue). Not reacting means not saying anything *and* not showing nonverbal signs of disapproval, such as rolling eyes or snorts of disgust. When your child gets home from school, make a game of having your child list all the misdeeds that he or she saw that day *but did not react to*. Give your child a small prize, such as a sticker or a plastic toy, for each item on the list. Go over the list with your child, clucking your tongue at the misbehavior and praising your child's restraint. You could say something like, "Oh my! That certainly is against the rules. It must have been very hard for you not to say anything." When you've read over the whole list, conclude by saying something like, "Good for you for not reacting to these. It's not your job to fix your classmates' behavior. You just have to let it go." Have your child rip up the list and throw it away.

Knowing that they will have a chance to report others' misbehavior when they get home can help Born Leaders refrain from reacting or tattling at school. You may need to remind your child that listing misbehavior should *only* happen at home and shouldn't be mentioned to classmates. Your child will have big problems if other kids see him or her gleefully recording their sins. Announcing, "I'm going to write that on my list when I get home!" will also cause problems.

Remind your child that only misbehavior that your child shows *no reaction* to at school can go on the list. Emphasize that the most important part of the game is ripping up the list at the end and letting go of concerns about other people's behavior. If your child can't resist the temptation to brag about this list at school, this is not a good activity for him or her.

3. Seeing Different Perspectives: The Inkblot Game

Born Leaders tend to get locked into their own views. They don't realize that people can have different but equally valid views of the same circumstances.

The Inkblot Game is a fun activity that helps children see different perspectives. You can play this game with just you and your child, with the whole family, or even with your child and his or her friends. First, make your own inkblots by dribbling some paint on a piece of paper, folding it in half, and squeezing the two sides together. Open the paper and have players quickly write down as many ideas as possible of what they see in the inkblot. When they've finished writing down responses, have each player explain to the other players one idea of what the inkblot could be. Make sure everyone sees what that player is describing before going on to the next player. After everyone has shared several ideas, turn the inkblot upside down and repeat the process. The upside-down inkblot will generate entirely different responses.

After doing this exercise, you can use the inkblot as a metaphor to help your child understand how different people can see the same thing in different ways. For instance, when your child corrects another person, your child sees this as being helpful. The other person is likely to interpret it as getting scolded. Both views are "true" — your child really was trying to help and the other person really does feel put down. The two views just come from different perspectives, like looking at the inkblot right-side up versus upside down. Your child needs to understand that his or her "helpful" efforts really do seem like criticism to the other person. Instead of working to convince the other person of the "rightness" of his or her perspective, your child needs to accept that that person has a different view of the situation and let it go.

4. Relating to Peers as Equals

Too often, Born Leaders surround themselves with children whom they can dominate. These may be younger children or children who are quiet and shy. These hierarchical relationships are comfortable for your child, but they shouldn't be the only kinds of relationships your child has. At some point, your child needs to learn to relate to peers as equals rather than followers. Spending time with other children who are as bright, capable, and assertive as your child will help your Born Leader build satisfying and stimulating friendships. Having more egalitarian interactions provides your child with practice and a necessary blueprint for building healthy adult relationships with a spouse, friends, and coworkers.

Try to get your child involved in activities that will allow him or her to get to know other dynamic leaders. Student government is an excellent way for Born Leaders to learn to work collaboratively with outgoing peers. Some towns even have clubs for "future leaders" that might appeal to your child. Enrichment programs, such as Destination ImagiNation, that explicitly teach brainstorming and teamwork skills can be extremely helpful and lots of fun for Born Leaders. Talk with other parents and teachers to find out what your community offers.

Francine: Arguing with Authority Figures

"Safe!" the umpire yelled.

Francine threw down her mitt and ran toward the umpire. "No way!" she yelled. "She was out! I tagged her before she touched the base! I saw it with my own eyes. I was closer than you."

"I said *safe,*" the umpire insisted.

"But you're wrong!" Francine protested.

The coach trotted over. "Francine, are you arguing again?" he asked.

"But, coach, I'm right! I saw it! I was there!" Francine howled.

"Francine, that's enough. If the umpire says she's safe, she's safe," the coach said.

"But, coach, it's not fair! The umpire is blind if he thinks she's safe! He's favoring their team," Francine said in a trembling voice.

"That's it," the umpire snapped. "You're out of the game."

"You heard him, Francine," the coach said. "Go sit on the bench."

Francine walked off the field with her head down, trying not to cry.

Francine was probably right. She probably did tag the other player before she reached the base. It doesn't matter. What the umpire says, goes. Arguing with the umpire didn't help, and it ultimately got Francine kicked out of the game.

Some Born Leaders have a great deal of difficulty with authority figures — mainly because they don't really recognize them as authority figures. Instead of doing what adults tell them to do, these children argue and insist on getting their way. They don't hesitate to correct a teacher or a parent in front of others. They pounce on any little mistake or inconsistency. They demand explanations and protest loudly and vehemently when things don't go their way: "But you said . . ."; "How come we have to . . . ?"; "It's no fair that . . ."

Adults find this public questioning of their authority extremely irritating. They are likely to respond sternly in an attempt to put Born Leaders in their place. They say or imply, "How dare you speak to me like that?" Other kids try to give a wide berth to children who frequently provoke adults, because they don't want to get hit by the fallout.

Born Leaders don't understand any of this. They are so focused on speaking up for their own versions of truth and justice that they don't see how their challenging behavior antagonizes people. They tell themselves, *But, I'm right!* and they keep pushing. In their minds, being right supersedes all other concerns. They don't realize that their arguing comes across as rude and disrespectful, so they feel hurt and confused when adults reprimand them and other children avoid them.

Born Leaders need to understand that sometimes it just costs too much to argue. They need to learn that "the boss is always right." This doesn't mean that the person in charge never makes mistakes. It does mean that Born Leaders need to treat authority figures with respect. This is a very difficult but very important lesson for Born Leaders to learn. The Unwritten Rules and the following exercises can help your child understand it.

THE UNWRITTEN RULES

- The boss is always right (even when he or she is wrong).
- Parents, teachers, coaches, and Scout leaders are authority figures. It's their job to call the shots.
- Publicly challenging an authority figure never works.
- Adults resent it if you try to tell them what to do.
- Just because you think someone is wrong doesn't mean you should say it.
- Sometimes it costs too much to argue.
- Some things are best left unsaid — even if they are true.
- Life is not always fair.

ACTIVITIES FOR LEARNING
THE UNWRITTEN RULES

1. Avoiding Public Confrontations

Born Leaders need to understand that it is not appropriate to criticize or argue with an adult in public. For instance, if your child contradicts a teacher in front of the entire class, there is no possibility that the teacher will respond positively — even if your child is absolutely correct. Publicly confronting an adult is rude. It challenges the adult's authority. It implies, "I know more than you do, and I'm going to prove it to everyone!" No wonder adults respond so negatively.

So, what should your child do if he or she sees an adult making a mistake? Most of the time the answer is *nothing*. If the teacher makes a spelling error when writing on the board, let it go. If the coach doesn't put your child in the position he or she wants, too bad. If this year's teacher wants page numbers written at the top of the page instead of at the bottom, just do it. Parents, teachers, and coaches are in charge. It's their job to make the calls, and it's your child's job to go along with their decisions (at least most of the time). It is not worth antagonizing an authority figure over trivial issues.

What if it isn't a trivial issue? What if your child feels very strongly about some matter? If your child truly cannot let something slide, he or she should approach the adult privately and discuss the matter in a respectful way. Your child should ask rather than demand, suggest rather than criticize, and clarify rather than challenge. Tell your child to keep the tone positive and the discussion short. Badgering doesn't help. If the adult says no, that's it. A private discussion may not work — your child may still have to go along with the adult's decision, even if he or she doesn't like it. However, a respectful private discussion is much more likely to yield success than a strident public challenge is. The following examples illustrate confrontational and polite phrases. Help your child recognize the difference. Encourage your child to speak to you in a respectful way when raising concerns.

Confrontational	Polite
"You're wrong!"	"I think it might be . . ."
"No fair!"	"I was wondering . . ."
"You said we could!"	"Will we also have time to . . . ?"
"That's not what we did last year!"	"Could we . . . ?"

If your child finds that he or she has antagonized an adult by arguing or criticizing, your child should just say, "I'm sorry," then stop talking. Once the adult is angry, your child has no chance of winning his or her case. Trying to explain further at that point will only irritate the adult more. Your child should either drop the matter or wait for a better time to try to explain his or her ideas in a respectful way.

2. Understanding Expectations

Performance at school or in organized activities depends on three things: ability, effort, and understanding expectations. Born Leaders are usually good students (high ability), and they always try very hard (high effort), but they often have trouble because they discount what authority figures expect of them when they think they know a "better" way. They make up their own rules, and are then irate when they get penalized for not following the authority figure's instructions.

Go over the scenarios below with your child. Explain that no amount of ability or effort can make up for ignoring relevant expectations.

UNDERSTANDING EXPECTATIONS

Scenario A: Suppose you are really good at math (ability), and you study really hard for the test (effort). The teacher wants you to show your work (expectation), but you only write the final answers. How will you do on the test?

Scenario B: Suppose you are really good at social studies (ability), and you work really hard on a report (effort). The teacher wants the report on Friday (expectation), but you turn it in one week late. Will you get a good grade on the report?

Scenario C: Suppose you are the best player on the soccer team (ability), and you never miss practice and always try hard (effort). The coach wants everyone to play in position (expectation), but you run all over the field because you know you can get the ball and score. What does the coach think of your playing? How do your teammates feel about you?

If your child is like many of the Born Leaders we've worked with, he or she will probably have an argument for why the expectations in each scenario are wrong or unreasonable. ("It's not fair to take off points for not showing your work as long as the answer is right!" or "The coach should let me play forward! I'm the best one for that position.") It doesn't matter. The expectations are what they are, and your child won't do well unless he or she meets them.

If your child has a lot of trouble understanding the importance of meeting expectations, you may want to tell this story:

Once there was a man who had a beautiful garden. He especially loved growing roses. One day he decided that he would like to have a brick path around his favorite flowers. So he hired the best bricklayer in town and explained what he wanted. Then the man went out for the day.

While the man was gone, the bricklayer worked very, very hard, and he built neatly and carefully. When he was finished, an enormous brick wall, ten feet high and three feet wide, surrounded the garden.

When the man came home, the bricklayer said proudly, "Look at the beautiful wall I made for you! See how tall and wide and straight it is!"

Horrified, the man said, "But I wanted a path! No one will see my roses!"

"Well, I think a wall is better," the bricklayer insisted. "And this one is a beauty!"

The bricklayer worked hard and did a great job, but he didn't do the job the man wanted. So, the man wasn't happy with his work. You can use this story as a metaphor to remind your child of the importance of understanding expectations. "If the teacher wants a path, don't build a wall."

THE HOME-SCHOOL CONNECTION

Some teachers dote on Born Leaders, whereas others feel exasperated by their tendency to take over. You may need to help your child's teacher understand that although your Born Leader appears outwardly confident, he or she can be deeply hurt by criticism or rejection. In fact, you may need to do this every year to ease the way for your child. If your family has experienced some particularly difficult circumstances, describing these could help the teacher gain a more sympathetic view of your child. Explain how important the teacher's opinion is to your child and how much your child needs the teacher's praise. Ask for the teacher's help in nurturing your child's initiative and resourcefulness while also guiding your child to relate more appropriately to peers.

If the teacher is reacting negatively to your Born Leader, you should be especially careful not to come on too strong when you ask for the teacher's help. Keep in mind that teachers are trained professionals. They are likely to balk if a parent tries to tell them what to do in their own classrooms. Be sure to ask questions and listen carefully to the impressions of your child's teacher before you make any suggestions. It may be painful for you to hear that the teacher has trouble working with your vivacious child, but remind yourself that the teacher's reaction to your child (whether negative or positive) could give you important information about how other people view your child's behavior. Arguing or defending your child's actions won't help. Instead, try to create a collaborative atmosphere with the teacher, asking, "What can *we* do to help my child?" Be open to the teacher's views and offer your ideas as suggestions rather than demands. It may help to bring in a copy of this book to show the teacher.

Teaching Teamwork Skills: One of the best things the teacher can do to help your child develop true leadership skills and minimize bossiness is to talk explicitly to the class about *how* to work together on a group project. Given no guidelines, Born Leaders will do what they always do — take over. However, the teacher could make consensus-building part of the project. For instance, the teacher could emphasize the importance of listening to everyone's ideas and require groups to turn in a page of brainstorming topics. The teacher could also tell each group to write a description of who did what on the project to make sure that everyone contributes somehow.

Having a post-project discussion of how team members worked together can sometimes be helpful if it is done in a gentle and constructive way. For instance, your child's teacher may want to have partners assess each other's teamwork strengths. Before starting the project, the teacher could have students look over a set of teamwork skills, such as those in the following list. This list describes areas where Born Leaders excel as well as areas where they need improvement. Just having such a list helps Born Leaders understand what they should be trying to do. In rating their teammates at the end of the project, students should circle three things that the person does well and put a star next to one thing that that teammate needs to work on.

Teamwork Skills

Ideas

Contributes good ideas

Is a good problem-solver

Comes up with creative ways of doing the assignment

Helps develop a plan for getting the work done efficiently

Listening / compromise

Asks others' opinions

Waits for his / her turn to talk, without interrupting

Listens respectfully to everyone's ideas

Seriously considers others' input

Is able to compromise

Contributes to win-win outcomes

Effort

Does his or her share of the work

Gives his or her best effort for the group

Contributes neat and attractive work

Morale

Shows enthusiasm

Expresses appreciation for others' contributions

Makes positive statements about others' ideas

Follows group decisions with good cheer
Graciously gives in if the group vetoes an idea
Keeps group ideas and disputes confidential

Some teachers like to use cooperative learning activities, in which each child has an assigned role and children take turns playing different roles at different times. This way, every child gets an opportunity to be a leader and a follower.

Supporting Partnerships: The teacher can also help by carefully choosing which classmates your child is assigned to work with on group projects. If your Born Leader is placed in a group with passive or shy children, it is inevitable that he or she will take over. At the other extreme, if your child has to work with very independent or confrontational children who resent your child's bossiness, your child will end up feeling hurt and rejected. The ideal scenario is to have your child work with one or two other bright, capable children who are confident and assertive enough to stand up for themselves when your child acts too pushy but who also like and respect your child. Working with these kinds of children gives your Born Leader a chance to experience the joy of true collaboration.

IF YOU TOO . . .

If you are also a Born Leader, you probably have strong opinions about how things should be done. Maybe you and your child have clashed a few times over this. If you haven't yet, you undoubtedly will when your child becomes a teenager — neither one of you could ever be described as "docile."

As a Born Leader, you probably know how crushing it is to have one's enthusiastically offered plans completely rejected. Drawing from your own childhood experiences may help you understand how hurt your child feels when other kids say, "You're too bossy!" and won't even listen to his or her well-intentioned suggestions.

To counterbalance the stinging rejection that your child too often receives from teachers and peers, you need to go out of your way to acknowledge and appreciate your child's ideas. You should also emphasize the positive aspects of the personality that you and your child share, such as your zest, your enthusiasm, your quick thinking, and your ability to "get things done."

At the same time, you can use the way that you interact with your child to help him or her learn less domineering ways of relating. Try to model a nonbossy way of talking. As much as possible, you should use respectful requests, ask for suggestions, and offer choices rather than issue direct orders. Go out of your way to express respect for opinions that are different from your own. Let your child see you give in gracefully sometimes. You may even want to explain that you are giving in out of consideration for other people's feelings. For instance, you could say, "Well, it's not what I would choose, but I can see that this is very important to you, so that's what we'll do." You could also point out the times when you compromise. "Daddy let me pick the movie last time, so this time, I'll let him pick."

You may also want to look at your family situation. Is your Born Leader frequently placed in charge of younger siblings? Does your child have more responsibility than most kids that age? Sometimes, circumstances make this unavoidable. In general, giving children responsibility is a good thing. It builds confidence and resourcefulness. However, too much responsibility can be burdensome for a child and can contribute to some of the social problems described in this chapter. Just because your child can handle a lot of responsibility and even seeks out leadership roles, doesn't mean that he or she should always be in charge. Make sure that your child has some time off to just be a kid. When you are around, tell your child, "I'm in charge now." Don't let your Born Leader reprimand younger siblings. Say, "That's my job." Your child enjoys being "the boss," but to get along with other children, he or she also needs to practice being "one of the gang."

SUMMARY

Born Leaders are little bundles of energy and enthusiasm. They run into trouble socially because they try to impose their ideas on other children. They are determined to have everyone go along with their vision of how things ought to be. They want to be helpful and to win the approval of their peers, but their domineering style makes other kids resistant and resentful.

Born Leaders need to learn how to relate to other kids as peers. They need to learn to really listen, to consider respectfully other children's thoughts and feelings, and to present their own ideas as suggestions rather than direct orders. They must learn to temper their tendency to be overly responsible. They shouldn't try to enforce the rules or "set the record straight" when it isn't their job to do so. The goal with Born Leaders is to teach them to collaborate and to help them to develop their true leadership skills without dampening their zest.

You Will Also Want to Read:
Chapter 3, "The Intimidating Child"
Chapter 6, "The Short-Fused Child"
Chapter 7, "The Little Adult"

THE UNWRITTEN RULES FOR THE
BORN LEADER AT A GLANCE

- How you say it matters as much as what you say.
- There is always more than one path to the same goal.
- People find it easier to listen to you when they know you have heard and understood their point of view.
- Everyone needs to feel that his or her input is worthy.
- A good negotiation means everybody wins something.
- If you push people into doing something, they will resent you, even if you are right.
- You don't always have to come up with an answer — just listening is often enough.
- Getting along sometimes means giving in.
- It's usually better to lose an argument than to lose a friend.
- You are in charge of your own behavior, not anybody else's.
- If you correct or criticize other kids, they won't want to be around you.
- When you criticize someone, they remember it, even if you don't.
- It's not your job to "set the record straight."
- Correcting people in front of others makes them look bad. They will feel embarrassed and will probably be mad at you.
- The boss is always right (even when he or she is wrong).
- Parents, teachers, coaches, and Scout leaders are authority figures. It's their job to call the shots.
- Publicly challenging an authority figure never works.
- Adults resent it if you try to tell them what to do.
- Just because you think someone is wrong doesn't mean you should say it.
- Sometimes it costs too much to argue.
- Some things are best left unsaid — even if they are true.
- Life is not always fair.

CHAPTER 10

The Pessimistic Child

Does your child . . .

complain a lot?

talk in a whiny tone of voice?

let everyone know it if he or she is unhappy?

approach classmates with critical rather than friendly comments?

act disdainful while other kids are having fun?

constantly worry about not getting his or her fair share?

say, "Yes, but . . . ," every time you offer a suggestion about how to solve a problem?

predict doom and failure for every new endeavor?

Do you . . .

feel concerned that your child looks for the negative in every situation?

fear that your child's habit of criticizing and complaining is off-putting to peers?

find it draining to be constantly answering your child's complaints?

find yourself bending over backward to assure your child that things are exactly fair and equal?

feel exasperated because nothing seems to please your child?

wish your child would just *try* to make friends?

worry that your child's tendency to believe "it's never going to work" will cause him or her to miss out on life's adventures?

*P*essimistic Children focus on the negative. They notice everything that's wrong and interpret events in the most dismal light. "We have a substitute teacher today? I bet she's mean." "We're playing a new game in gym? I know I'll hate it." These children constantly complain about how frustrating or unfair things are. They feel like victims. If someone offers them a suggestion about how to make a situation better, they immediately reply, "Yes, but . . . ," and list the reasons why they are sure that suggestion will never work. Even if something good happens to them, they are quick to discount it, insisting that it was just a fluke; it's unlikely to happen again; it wasn't that good, anyway; and it certainly doesn't make up for the many bad things that have happened to them. Pessimistic Children are convinced that they will fail, so they rarely try to enter new relationships or seek out new experiences. They give up before they start. Their expectation of disappointment makes it hard for them to enjoy life. They are always aware of what is lacking or what could go wrong.

Pessimistic Children share every negative thought they have. They whine. They complain. They criticize and refuse to participate. They generally act like wet blankets, dousing the fun. Instead of adding to the positive energy of a group, they deplete it. Pessimistic Children's dour interaction style discourages their peers from approaching or including them.

The thing to keep in mind about Pessimistic Children is that they truly don't want to be this way, but they are stuck in their own negativity. They don't know how to break out of their role as prophets of doom and gloom. Because they are so focused on their own dissatisfaction, they don't pick up on other children's needs or reactions, and they end up annoying their peers. Because they believe they never get their fair share of anything, they don't enjoy what they have. Because they can so easily imagine being rejected, they don't dare reach out to potential friends.

Helping Pessimistic Children to relate better to their peers requires three essential steps: (1) minimizing their negative social behavior, (2) increasing their positive, friendly behavior, and (3) helping them find the courage to take appropriate social risks.

ON THE POSITIVE SIDE

Pessimistic Children have a cautious attitude, which enhances their capacity for methodical decision-making and careful planning. They may become adept at not only anticipating but also forestalling future difficulties. They can foresee possible pitfalls or worst-case scenarios that others might overlook. In work situations, they can be excellent devil's advocates who help counterbalance other people's impulsiveness. Ideally, as these children grow, they can learn to use their pessimism as a planning tool. Rather than being an obstacle to progress, their pessimism can help them build a safety net that enables them to reach their goals.

SO, WHAT CAN WE DO?

Pessimistic Children need to learn the Unwritten Rules concerning how other people react to whining complaints and criticism. They need to become aware of the negative messages they might be sending, through not only their words but also their tone of voice and body language. They also need to learn positive ways of relating to others. These children need to understand that social failure is guaranteed if they don't try. Most of all, they need opportunities and gentle encouragement to break out of their victim role.

In this chapter we describe three children with pessimistic styles of relating. Meredith's habit of constantly complaining is infuriating to her mother and is undoubtedly unattractive to her peers. Nadia's preoccupation with how she is always being shortchanged clouds her enjoyment of social situations. Zack's tendency to expect the worst is annoying, and it prevents him from trying to befriend others.

Meredith: Constantly Complaining

Meredith's mother had barely pulled the van out of the driveway when the complaining began. "I don't want to go skating. It's the first day the rink is open. The ice won't be thick enough."

Striving for patience, Meredith's mother reassured her, "The ice is plenty thick. They wouldn't have opened the rink unless it was safe."

"Well, my blades aren't sharp enough," Meredith said.

"Meredith," her mother began, "I told all three of you kids yesterday afternoon that we would be going skating today. If you chose not to sharpen your skates beforehand, that's your problem. Just use them the way they are today. You can sharpen them more tonight if you want."

"The last time I went skating, I fell and hurt my knee."

Meredith's mother decided to ignore her. She turned on the radio.

"Besides, my gloves are too small. I can't even straighten my fingers."

No response.

"Tracey Mendleson got food poisoning from the pizza at the skating rink. She threw up in the parking lot. We'll probably all get sick."

Still no response.

"And anyway, I hate skating. I always get cold. Let's just go home."

"That's it, missy!" Meredith's mother snapped. "I've had it with your complaining! I want to go skating. Your sister and brother want to go skating. We're going skating. If you want to sit on a bench and sulk while we're having fun, that's your choice. But I don't want to hear another peep out of you for the rest of the trip!"

No matter what the situation, Pessimistic Children can find something to complain about. Their creativity in finding grievances can be impressive. Once they begin thinking about what is wrong, it opens the floodgates. Like Meredith, they may complain about current circumstances, past troubles, or future calamities. Their constant litany of complaints irritates others, and it also prevents Pessimistic Children from enjoying themselves. When they focus continually on what is, was, or might be wrong, they close themselves off to positive experiences.

Pessimistic Children frequently complain to adults, and they don't hesitate to voice their dissatisfaction in front of other children. Unfortunately, their peers are generally even less tolerant of this behavior than adults are. Complaints are simply not interesting or appealing. Other kids might listen to a Pessimistic Child describe how his foot hurts because his sock is bunched up, but not for long.

According to Dr. Robin Kowalski of Western Carolina University, two factors lead people to complain a lot: (1) they feel distressed often, and (2) they readily talk about their distress. It may be that Pessimistic Children are especially vulnerable to feeling unhappy because little things — things other people might ignore or brush off — really bother them. However, just experiencing discomfort doesn't necessarily lead to complaining. Most kids ignore minor irritations and keep playing. Pessimistic Children, however, have to share every little annoyance. They never suffer silently. Because they are so focused on their own woes, they fail to pick up on social cues. They seem either unaware of or unconcerned about how off-putting their complaints are to other people.

For many children, complaints are just a habit. They are so used to pointing out everything that is wrong that they do it automatically. They can't imagine acting any other way. It's almost as if griping has become their job.

The Unwritten Rules and the following exercises focus on helping your child to understand the negative social impact of complaining and to learn alternative ways of dealing with difficulties.

THE UNWRITTEN RULES

- No one likes to hear complaints.
- If you complain too often, people stop listening.
- If you can't say something positive, say nothing at all.
- When someone asks, "How are you?" answer by saying something positive.
- Save your physical complaints for your parents or your doctor.
- Try to solve the problem yourself, before you complain.
- When everyone is experiencing the same difficult circumstance, whining about it doesn't make it easier.
- Your comments should match the emotional tone of the group.

ACTIVITIES FOR LEARNING THE UNWRITTEN RULES

1. Minimizing a Whiny or Critical Tone of Voice

Many Pessimistic Children don't even realize when they sound whiny or critical. It's essential to teach these children to be more aware of their tone of voice so that they don't unintentionally push people away. However, just saying, "Stop whining!" won't help if a child doesn't know what *whining* means.

Using a tape recorder, tape yourself saying the following phrases. First demonstrate a whiny tone of voice, then a sullen or hostile tone, and then a friendly tone.

"I want to go out."
"It's raining."
"What time is it?"

Once your child can hear the difference in your voice, see if he or she can produce each of these tones. Talk about what kinds of impressions each tone creates.

To help your child break the whining habit, follow up by insisting that your child speak to you in a normal tone of voice. In general, you should try to ignore whining and to respond promptly to non-whining remarks or requests. You may want to have an unobtrusive nonverbal signal, such as touching your chin, to remind your child not to whine. If necessary, you can set up a system of small rewards for going a specified amount of time speaking only in a pleasant manner. The time period should be short enough that your child can succeed in refraining from whining (an hour? a morning? during one meal?). As your child gets better at using an acceptable tone of voice, you can gradually increase the time requirement for a reward.

2. Matching the Emotional Tone of a Group

Pessimistic Children blurt out any negative thought that comes to mind without thinking about the social impact of their words. When other kids are happy, excited, and having fun, Pessimistic Children's complaints can be as jarring as a wrong note in music. These children need to learn to pick up on the emotional tone of a group and to make comments that match that tone. If everyone else is complaining, it's okay if they also voice a complaint. But if everyone else is saying positive things, they need to find something positive to say as well.

Following is a list of remarks from four sample conversations. Read the first three statements in each conversation and then see if your child can come up with a comment that fits the emotional tone of the preceding remarks. If you can use real examples of conversations from your child's social interactions, that's even better.

Matching the Emotional Tone of a Group

Conversation A

Child 1: My favorite candy bar is Milky Way.

Child 2: I like Snickers the best.

Child 3: I still have some candy left over from Halloween.

Your Child:

Conversation B

Child 1: The Yankees have an amazing lineup this year!

Child 2: Yeah, even the pitcher can hit.

Child 3: They are definitely going to win the pennant again this year.

Your Child:

Conversation C

Child 1: I'm going to have to spend all weekend working on that social studies report.

Child 2: It's no fair that Mr. Clements gives us so much work.

Child 3: Yeah, the kids in the other class don't have to do as many reports as we do.

Your Child:

Conversation D

Child 1: I can't wait for summer.

Child 2: Me too. I'm going to go to the pool every day.

Child 3: I want to go to the beach.
Your Child:

3. Seeing the Silver Lining

Explain the saying "Every cloud has a silver lining" to your child. Working together with your child, place a sheet of aluminum foil on top of a sheet of black construction paper. Cut through both sheets to make six cloud shapes. Tape the black and silver pieces together so that the clouds are dark on one side and shiny on the other side. Write the "dark side" events listed in the following table on index cards and tape each card onto the black side of a cloud. See if your child can come up with some "bright side" ideas about something positive that might come from the negative event. Write these on index cards and tape them to the shiny side of the clouds. (If you don't want to use aluminum foil, you can use white paper and a silver pen for the bright side.) If your child can't think of a bright side, you can use our examples to explain the concept. Do the same thing with the remaining three clouds, using actual events from your child's life. Have your child list three negative events that happened in the past week, then think of a bright side for each of these events.

Dark Side	Bright Side
I lost my pencil.	I'll get a new, colorful pencil to replace it.
My friend can't come over after school.	My friend is coming over on Saturday, and we'll have more time to play.
The big game was rained out.	My team will have extra time to practice.

4. Using a Complaint Box

Having a complaint box can be a useful way of changing the habits of children who tend to complain constantly. Tell your child to write any complaints he or she has on a piece of paper and place each one in the box. Promise that you will discuss them at the end of the day. If your child starts to tell you a complaint, direct him or her to the box. This technique is helpful for several reasons. First, it interferes with your child's tendency to automatically voice complaints. Second, it may cut down on the actual number of complaints because your child has to make an extra effort to write them down. Third, knowing that you will consider your child's concerns at a specified time can help your child feel cared for and understood. Finally, the fact that the discussion is delayed may encourage your child to deal with the situation him- or herself rather than wait until the end of the day for you to solve it.

When you discuss the notes in the box, take your child's complaints seriously. Say, "I can see why that would bother you." Sometimes your child is only looking for a little understanding, but other times, he or she wants help solving a problem. Don't immediately offer advice or solutions. Ask your child questions such as "What do you suggest we do about this?"; "How have you tried to deal with this so far?"; or "What can we do to make it less likely that this will happen again?" Decide together what action should be taken to address the complaint.

5. Asking for Help Effectively

All children sometimes find themselves in situations in which they truly do need help from others to solve their problems. But Pessimistic Children complain so frequently that adults may tune them out or dismiss their concerns by saying, "It's fine" or "Go, sit down." This means that Pessimistic Children may not get the help they really need.

In the following box, we've outlined a formula for effective requests for help. Unlike complaints, which merely describe dissatisfaction and annoy people, effective requests for help usually elicit support. Go over the formula with your child. Emphasize that your child should say each statement without whining and should only use this formula when he or she truly can't solve the problem alone.

> ## FORMULA FOR EFFECTIVE REQUESTS FOR HELP
>
> **"I tried . . . ,"**   (What did you do to try to solve the problem?)
>
> **"but . . ."**   (How is the problem continuing?)
>
> **"I really need help."**

The first part of this formula, the "I tried . . ." statement, describes your child's efforts to solve the problem. Starting with this statement shows initiative and gets the adult's attention. It explains that your child has made some attempt to work things out on his or her own rather than just dump the problem in somebody else's lap. The "but . . ." statement allows your child to explain that the problem is continuing despite his or her efforts to solve it. Following these statements by saying, "I really need help," almost always gets a sympathetic response from a caring adult.

Have your child practice using the formula to restate the common complaints in the following list. We've provided some sample answers. Also be sure to have your child practice restating the complaints that you hear most frequently. Post the formula for effective requests in a prominent place in your home and insist that your child use it with you. If your child starts whining or complaining, don't respond. Just point to the formula. This reminds your child not only how to ask for help but also that he or she needs to try to solve the problem first. If your child uses the formula appropriately, praise him or her ("I like how you said that!") and try to respond immediately.

CHANGING COMPLAINTS TO EFFECTIVE REQUESTS FOR HELP

Complaint: "This thing is too big."

Polite Request:

> **"I tried** pouring a glass of milk for myself,
> **but** the gallon is too heavy for me to lift.
> **I really need help."**

Complaint: "He's bothering me."

Polite Request:

> **"I tried** asking Jim not to blow on me with his straw,
> **but** he keeps doing it.
> **I really need help."**

Complaint: "She's picking on me."

Polite Request:

> **"I tried** ignoring Gretchen,
> **but** she keeps calling me 'stupid' and pushing my paper
> on the floor.
> **I really need help."**

Complaint: "He's not taking turns."

Polite Request:

> **"I tried** asking him if I could have a turn playing with the ball,
> **but** he keeps running away from me.
> **I really need help."**

Complaint: "He's not sharing."

Polite Request:

> "**I tried** asking him to put the bowl of popcorn in the middle
> of the table,
>> **but** he's keeping it where I can't reach it.
> **I really need help.**"

Complaint: "I hate math. This homework is so stupid."

Polite Request:

> "**I tried** doing these homework problems,
>> **but** I don't understand them.
> **I really need help.**"

Nadia: Feeling Shortchanged

The birthday party was in full swing. The children had just finished eating pizza and were about to start on the cake and candy.

"No fair!" Nadia yelled. "She got more jelly beans than I did!"

"Who cares!" Melissa snapped. "You got a bigger piece of cake. It doesn't matter."

"Yeah, well, you got a longer turn on the tire swing, and I only got to do it for a little while before we had to come in. I'm always the last one in line."

"Oh, quit complaining and eat your cake," Kathy said. The other girls giggled.

"My mom's coming to get me any minute," Nadia groused. "I'm probably not even going to have a chance to eat my cake."

*   *   *

Even in the midst of a birthday party, the highlight of elementary school social life, Nadia manages to feel unhappy. While everyone else is enjoying the cake and candy, Nadia feels unfairly deprived.

Pessimistic Children often feel disappointed. Even when something good happens to them, it's never enough. If they get an A on a test, they torture themselves because someone else got an A+. If they are chosen for a team, they are miserable because they weren't chosen first. If three quarters of their classmates voted for them in a class election, they stew over the one quarter who didn't. If they are given a gift, they focus on the fact that someone else has a bigger or better version of it. Their lot is always second-best and somehow lacking.

In social situations, their vocal protests of unfairness come across as petty quibbling and project an attitude of entitlement. Their constant discontent seems to announce, "I never get what's due to me. People are always unfair to me." Not surprisingly, both children and adults quickly tire of trying to please someone who is never satisfied.

Underneath Pessimistic Children's demanding style of relating is a sense of neediness and insecurity. They believe that they have to insist on their fair share, or they won't get it. The problem is that focusing on getting their due highlights what is missing rather than what is there. They end up feeling constantly dissatisfied. As their mental list of times they have been "wronged" grows, they grow less trusting of other people's benign intentions. They become preoccupied with how they have been hurt or cheated again and again. They struggle harder and become more demanding, and this makes people less inclined to treat them generously. In fact, other children are likely to avoid them, making them feel even more insecure.

Pessimistic Children often experience intense sibling rivalry because they are constantly keeping score. "He got a bigger piece." "You let her, but you didn't let me." To keep the peace, you may find yourself reduced to counting sprinkles on cupcakes to make sure each child get exactly the same amount. This is a no-win game.

Refuse to play it. It is impossible to make every situation exactly equal for every person. Life just doesn't work that way. Even if you count sprinkles, the frosting will be slightly different. Moreover, going along with your child's insistence on keeping score encourages an unhealthy way of relating to others because it focuses on dissatisfaction rather than appreciation. Teach your child that the appropriate response to a gift is a sincere thank-you, not "Hers is better." Of course you want to avoid gross inequity when possible, but help your child understand that *fair* doesn't necessarily mean *equal*. It's okay to buy one child a present, just because you see something he or she would enjoy, without buying an item of identical value for the other child. You'll do something special for the other child some other time. You don't love your children equally; you love each of them in his or her own special way. That's much better than equal.

Pessimistic Children need a lot of nurturing, but it can be hard to give it to them. Their tendency to complain, criticize, and compare can undermine their parents' best attempts to show caring. You take time off from work to visit the zoo with them, and they spend all day complaining about every little thing. You buy them a nice present, and they say it's not as good as someone else's. You spend the entire evening helping them with their science project, and they dismiss the whole thing by saying, "It's stupid." Too often, parents of Pessimistic Children end up thinking or saying, "I'm giving my time and effort trying to do this nice thing for you, and you don't appreciate it! Forget it! I'm never going to do this again." This is a perfectly understandable reaction. When we do something nice for someone, we'd like to see a little acknowledgment or at least not constant complaints and criticism. However, for your child's sake, you need to persist. Even though it appears that your child is trying to push you away with these negative comments, he or she really needs you.

It will be easier on both of you if you focus on small signs of affection rather than grand gestures as a means of reaching out to your child. Find a way to give your Pessimistic Child a little bit of one-on-one time with you. Rather than taking a whole day off from work to spend with your child, spend an extra hour with him or her. Hang out together. Bring just him or her along when you do an errand. Write a friendly little note and leave it on his or her pillow. Don't forget the power of touch — our most basic way of connecting with others. If your child is "too cool" for hugs, you can try casually squeezing a shoulder, stroking his or her hair, or making back rubs part of the bedtime routine. Regardless of how your child responds, think of these little signs of affection as gentle waves that keep coming and coming, gradually smoothing away his or her rocky resistance.

The Unwritten Rules and the following exercises can help your child step out of the dissatisfaction trap by focusing on giving rather than receiving in social situations. They can help your child learn to behave in friendly rather than critical or demanding ways and to become more actively engaged with peers.

THE UNWRITTEN RULES

- *Fair* doesn't necessarily mean *equal.*
- Don't keep score about who gets what in social situations.
- Focus on what you have rather than what you don't have.
- You can't build a friendship tit for tat.
- If someone gives you something, say, "Thank you." Don't criticize the gift.
- Add to the positive energy of a group with your good ideas and enthusiasm.

1. Keeping a Gratitude Journal

Buy your child an attractive notebook to use as a gratitude journal. Each day, have your child spend about fifteen minutes listing all the positive things that happened that day. At first, your child may have trouble thinking of anything positive to write down, sullenly insisting, "Nothing good happened today." So, you may need to prime the pump. Every day is filled with simple pleasures: sunshine, a cool breeze, a special dessert, a good grade, a phone call from a friend, a favorite song on the radio, sitting next to a pal at lunch. You need to open your child's eyes to these things. If your child resists writing in the gratitude journal, a small reward system may be necessary to get things started. You may want to set up a daily target number of gratitude items for your child and reward him or her for coming up with that number of items, or you may want to offer a small prize (e.g., a sticker) for each item your child writes in the journal. Once your child begins looking for gratitude items, it will change how he or she sees the world.

2. Reaching Out to Others

Community service can be a wonderful way of breaking through your child's pessimism because it places your child in a situation in which it is clearly his or her role to *give* rather than to sit back and receive. Moreover, your child may come to view his or her complaints as trivial after seeing someone who doesn't have a home or who is confined to a wheelchair.

Investigate service opportunities in your community and help your child choose one that appeals to him or her. Focus on activities that involve direct personal interaction, such as entertaining sick children at a nearby hospital, helping run a bingo game at the local nursing home, being a supporter for a Special Olympics athlete, or tutoring younger children. Look for an activity with some structure because your child will feel less uneasy if he or she knows what to do (e.g., play Candy Land with these three children; help Mrs. Clark put the markers on her bingo card). To smooth the way for your child, plan on participating in the outreach activity with him or her. Ideally, the activity should not be a one-time event. Look for something that provides an opportunity for ongoing involvement. Helping others can boost your child's social confidence and build a base of successful interactions so that your child may be more willing to extend him- or herself with peers. It could also be a topic of conversation for your child to share with classmates. If the service activity becomes an important part of your child's life, he or she may even want to invite a potential friend to come along sometime.

3. Giving Gifts to Family Members

Be sure to give your child the chance to give presents to other family members. Selfless parents who say, "Oh, my child doesn't have to give me anything," are actually depriving their children of experiencing the joy of giving. Make it part of your family's normal rituals that all children over three years of age give gifts on birthdays, holidays, and Mother's and Father's Day. The gift doesn't have to be elaborate or expensive, but your child should be the one to choose it. Often, the best gifts are homemade. Your child could draw a special picture or even make something out of an egg carton. Coupons that family members can redeem for special favors are a great gift idea. For instance, a younger sibling might like a coupon for "Reading One Story to You" or "Playing One Board Game with You." An older sibling might like a coupon for "Cleaning Out the Hamster Cage When It's Really Not My Turn." Moms and Dads appreciate coupons like "Cleaning Up My Room Once Without Fussing" or "Stopping One Argument with a Sibling Without Being Told." With gifts from children, it really is the thought that counts.

4. Showing Friendly Interest

Pessimistic Children are often so used to complaining and criticizing that they don't know what else to do. They've never really learned how to show sincere interest or to contribute to the positive energy of a group.

Explain to your child that social interactions are like two or more people carrying a large load. If everybody does his or her bit to help, things proceed smoothly and the load is easily carried. But if one person complains and drops his or her end, the load teeters off-kilter. The other people carrying the load feel resentful and find a way to go on without the slacker. Your child needs to do his or her part to make social interactions work. This means behaving in friendly, involved, and upbeat ways.

Talk with your child about what kinds of behaviors communicate friendly interest. Possibilities include smiling, nodding, making eye contact, using a welcoming tone of voice, asking interested questions, and having a relaxed, open body posture. Tell your child to be aware of the goals of the group and to make sure that his or her words and actions fit with these goals. For instance, if the group is playing basketball, your child should either join in or cheer on the participants. If the group is talking about the latest rock star, your child should listen, comment agreeably, or ask questions.

Help your child observe people using friendly behaviors in the ordinary course of a day so that he or she can see what an integral part these behaviors play in social interactions. You may want to try having your child watch a television talk show. How does the host communicate interest to the guest? If you have a videotape of a family gathering, you can also try watching that. Which relatives seem to be enjoying themselves the most? How can your child tell? How do they show interest in others?

Have your child practice acting friendly with you at home and then with one or two classmates at school. Tell your child not to expect an immediate change in how other kids perceive him or her. It takes awhile to get the message across that your child is now open to friendship. You need to reassure your child that friendly behaviors elicit friendly responses and that with persistent effort, things are likely to improve.

5. Learning and Enjoying Jokes

Elementary school children love jokes. Even when they don't really "get" the punch line, they love the ritual of saying something, having people ask for more, finishing the joke, and having everyone laugh about it. Cultivating an interest in jokes and learning some jokes that he or she can tell can be great ways for your child to interact positively with peers.

Go to the library and check out some books of children's jokes — the sillier, the better. Have all family members who are old enough to read and write go through these books and select five jokes to write on index cards. Place everyone's index cards in a box and mix them up. Make it part of your child's daily routine to select a Joke of the Day from the box. Your child should read the joke aloud (with your help, if necessary) so that the whole family can enjoy it. Be sure to add to the fun of this activity by being enthusiastic about it and laughing or commenting appreciatively about the jokes ("That's a good one!"; "That's very silly!"). Your responses demonstrate for your child how to react to humor. Before long, your child will have a whole repertoire of jokes he or she can share with other kids, as well as an interest in hearing the jokes other children tell.

6. Finding Flow

Pessimistic Children's tendency to focus on dissatisfaction interferes with their ability to experience flow. Dr. Mihaly Csikszentmihalyi (*chick-SENT-me-hi*) of the University of Chicago coined the term *flow* to refer to a state of active involvement in a process. During flow, people are completely absorbed in what they are doing at that moment. They lose track of time and are totally unself-conscious. Flow is most likely to occur when the challenge of an activity matches our ability. If it's too easy, the activity doesn't engage us sufficiently. If it's too hard, we're likely to give up or feel overwhelmed. Dr. Csikszentmihalyi found that the more flow people experience, the happier they are.

Most people think of happiness as a lack of distress. They see it as some future state that will occur when all their problems are resolved or when they meet some specified goal. They tell themselves, *I'll be happy when this is over,* or *I'll be happy after I get that.*

The concept of flow gives us a totally different way of looking at happiness. It suggests that the key to happiness has nothing to do with ease or comfort and everything to do with being actively engaged in the *now*. Happiness is a process rather than an outcome. It's a matter of enjoying the journey rather than reaching the destination.

Many different kinds of activities can lead to a state of flow. Artists, writers, musicians, runners, rock climbers, and even avid gardeners experience flow. We believe flow is an important concept to teach children. Explain this idea and help your child find an activity that he or she can become passionate about. Experiencing flow can help your child feel more animated and energetic, feelings that are likely to carry over into his or her social relationships. Just as acting sullen or critical pushes people away, being enthusiastic attracts people.

Many people experience flow when they are involved in creative activities, so you may want to help your child develop some interests that involve using imagination and making things. Possibilities include knitting, drawing, woodworking, or poetry writing. Athletic activities can also be a source of flow, but until your child is able to have a more positive perspective, it's probably best to avoid competitive sports. Pessimistic Children often have an especially hard time dealing with losing — it's just too painful for them. Good alternatives might be hiking, noncompetitive swimming, yoga, or dance. Many elementary school children enjoy collecting things. Stamps or baseball cards might be engrossing choices for your child. Sometimes an interesting topic can inspire enthusiasm. Your child might like trying to learn everything he or she can about insects, birds, ancient Egypt, or magic tricks. If you can find a club related to your child's special interest, it can serve as a bridge to befriending others.

Zack: Expecting the Worst

Zack walked into the kitchen and plopped down on a chair. "I'm bored," he announced. "There's nothing to do in this stupid house, and I have no one to play with."

"Why don't you call Joey and see if he can come over?" his mother suggested.

"No, he won't want to come over."

"Why do you say that?"

"I just know he won't."

"But you two had such a good time together at Scouts this week," his mother argued.

"No, we didn't. You don't know." Zack sprawled his arms across the table and put his head down.

"I *saw* you two playing after the meeting," his mother said. "You looked like you were having a great time."

"It wasn't that fun," Zack muttered.

"Why don't you just give him a call?" his mother suggested.

"He'll be busy. He's always busy."

"Well, honey, you can't know unless you try."

"No. I don't want to play with him."

"So, call someone else!" his mother said in an exasperated voice.

"I'm sure everybody is busy. They're always busy," Zack whined.

"Well, if you don't like my suggestions, you think of something," his mother snapped, walking out of the room.

Zack's friend might have been home. He might have been eager for a play date. Even if that friend was unavailable, surely someone else was around. But, because Zack expected the worst, he didn't even try to call anyone. What's the point of trying if you're convinced nothing will work?

Pessimistic Children are often very lonely, but they don't dare extend themselves, because they see no possibility of success. The task of making friends feels so daunting to them that they can't even begin to attempt it. It seems easier not to try than to try and fail. They have such a clear picture of how things will go wrong that they can't imagine things going right.

Sometimes Pessimistic Children bring about the social failure that they fear because their negative style of interacting aggravates others. However, their predictions of doom often *don't* come true. The test in school that they're sure they'll fail, they actually pass with flying colors. The party where they know they'll be miserable, they actually love. The new game they are sure they'll hate, they actually enjoy. But, somehow, even when things go well for Pessimistic Children, they don't seem to learn from their successes. They never recognize how many times their dire predictions are wrong because their selective memory focuses only on their failures. They dismiss positive outcomes as isolated incidents, and when the same situation comes up again, they are back to square one, convinced that failure is imminent.

The Unwritten Rules and the following exercises encourage your Pessimistic Child to find the courage to take appropriate social risks.

THE UNWRITTEN RULES

- You can't succeed unless you try.
- If you believe you can't, you won't.
- Focus on the process rather than the outcome.
- Trying something new is often scary.
- Sometimes you have to ignore your misgivings and try anyway.

ACTIVITIES FOR LEARNING
THE UNWRITTEN RULES

---

1. Putting the Emphasis on the Process Rather than the Results

Pessimistic Children think that failure is something that should be avoided at all costs. Because they can vividly imagine everything that could go wrong, they don't even try. They automatically decide, "I can't do it," or "It won't work." They prejudge the outcome, and this keeps them from moving forward.

When your child seems stuck and is turning a decision into a problem, encourage him or her to concentrate on the process rather than the outcome. Your child's job isn't necessarily to succeed but rather to discover him- or herself by developing skills and abilities; seeking out new, positive experiences; and building healthy relationships. Try making a list with your child of all the good things that could come from a new undertaking. Maybe your child will meet new friends or try a new food he or she really likes. Maybe your child will gain a new hobby or find a new favorite author. Your child might even discover a new talent. Whatever the outcome, trying something new will move your child one step farther along the path of self-discovery. Focusing on process makes the success or failure of an activity secondary. Because our culture is geared toward prizing out-come, it takes practice to learn to value process. But it's worth the effort. Helping your child adopt a positive step-by-step approach to life lessens worry, decreases pressure, and enables your child to be open to new experiences.

You may want to read Joey Green's *The Road to Success Is Paved with Failure* with your child. This book describes the bumpy paths that many famous people took before they realized their goals. It points to the value of persevering and rallying after setbacks. Interest-ingly, many of the people described in the book only found their true calling when their original plans went awry. For them, initial failure wasn't an ending; it was a pivotal event in their life's journey that sent them in an unanticipated but very satisfying direction.

2. Inspiring Your Child to Change: The Language of Becoming

Pessimists are trapped in a naysaying role. They are so used to hold-ing back, saying, "It'll never work," that it's very difficult for them to try new ways of relating. As a parent, it's your job to help give your child room to grow and change. This means that you need to be very careful about the messages you give your child about him- or herself.

Avoid talking about your child's pessimistic attitude as an im-mutable part of his or her personality. Remarks such as "You're at it again! Why are you always complaining? You're just like your Uncle Melvin!" cause your child to think, *That's the way I am; that's the way I'll always be.* These comments suggest that pessimism is bone-deep and unchangeable. It's not. Pessimism, as we've described it in this chapter, is a negative way of thinking and interacting with the world. Without intervention, it tends to be self-perpetuating, but it's definitely changeable. Your child is unlikely to turn into a little

Pollyanna, skipping merrily through life, but he or she can certainly learn to relate to others in a more positive way, to counter his or her automatic tendency to say "no" or "no fair," and to take appropriate social risks.

Also be careful about taking credit for the times that your child manages to step out of the pessimistic role. Although it might be very tempting to say, "See? Wasn't that fun? I told you you'd like it!" try very hard not to do so. Even if you're right — especially if you're right — your child will feel the need to defend his or her previous reluctance. Your child will respond by grumbling, "It wasn't *that* fun," and it could be harder to encourage him or her to do the activity again.

So, what can you do for your child to open the doors for change? One of the most powerful techniques for helping your child see him- or herself differently was developed by the noted family therapist Dr. Ellen Wachtel. She calls it the "language of becoming." This technique allows children to let go of their rigid and limiting definitions of themselves ("That's just the way I am") and to see themselves instead as evolving. First, be on the lookout for times when your child manages to act in a nonpessimistic way. Then, hold up these exceptions to your child as a sign that he or she is growing, changing, and developing, by saying "I've noticed you are becoming . . ." The following list gives some examples of remarks about becoming, based on Dr. Wachtel's work, that might be appropriate for your child.

The Language of Becoming

"**I've noticed that you are becoming good at** getting yourself to try new things."

"**I've noticed that you are becoming more** friendly around your classmates."

"**I've noticed that you are becoming better able to** see the bright side of things and keep going after a setback."

"I've noticed that you are becoming the kind of person who can make the best of a tough situation."

"I've noticed that you are becoming a really good listener."

You should make comments about your child's 'becoming' directly to your child, but you may also want to make them to other people. Children often absorb more from what they overhear than from what they are told directly. Use this to their advantage. Let your child overhear you expressing delight about how he or she is changing to your spouse, relatives, or friends.

Comments about becoming carry a message of hope that seems especially appropriate for Pessimistic Children. Because of their habitual negative outlook, these children are quick to deny ordinary praise. If you tell them, "You're great!" they answer, "No, I'm not." If you say, "You did a great job!" they say, "No, I didn't. I was just lucky. It'll never happen again." But statements about becoming are much harder to deny. Statements of becoming say "Never mind all the times that you might have failed before or might fall short in the future, I see that you are developing in this wonderful way. I see evidence for hope."

THE HOME-SCHOOL CONNECTION

Your child's teacher can play a very important role in helping your child relate to others in more positive ways. Tell the teacher about the strategies that you are using at home and ask for his or her patience and support in encouraging your child to use a more optimistic social style. The teacher might be interested in using some of the activities in this chapter in the classroom. The formula for polite requests and the gratitude journal, in particular, are activities that many children might find beneficial.

Minimizing Complaints: Ask for the teacher's help in decreasing your child's habit of complaining. The teacher may be willing to ignore complaints and praise or reward your child for positive comments or productive suggestions.

Focusing on Process: Explain that you are trying to teach your child to focus on process rather than outcome — on *how* your child does things rather than *how well.* The teacher could support this focus by showing special interest when your child displays effort, helps others, attempts new things, or generally shows a positive attitude.

Supporting Enthusiasm: If your child develops a special interest, the teacher may be willing to give your child the opportunity to share his or her enthusiasm about this topic with the rest of the class.

The teacher may also be willing to pair your child with more optimistic classmates. He or she may also identify upbeat children you could invite over for play dates with your child.

IF YOU TOO . . .

Pessimistic parents often have Pessimistic Children. Some researchers believe that pessimism is an inherited trait, whereas others see it as a learned response. You may have come from a family in which one or both of your parents were pessimistic. But even if you didn't grow up with a positive model of parenting to emulate, you can take steps now to make sure that the pattern doesn't continue with your child.

Your own style of interacting can intensify, minimize, or redirect your child's pessimistic tendencies. If you have a pessimistic streak yourself, you will have to work extra hard to help your child step out of his or her usual negative role. You may feel awkward urging your child to look on the bright side or express friendly interest when that's not how you usually respond. It may be especially difficult for you to encourage your child to take appropriate social risks when you can so easily envision unhappy outcomes. You may have to bite your tongue to refrain from making a negative comment. You may have to draw upon all your reserves of love and patience to keep reaching out to your child, even when he or she is pushing you away. But all of this extra effort can really pay off. It will enable you to provide a good example for your child, and in time, you may find your own pessimism receding. The old adage "Teaching something is the best way to learn it" is very true. Forcing yourself to see things positively in order to help your child could also help you expand your own horizons.

If the exercises in this chapter seem daunting to you, start slowly. Little changes really do add up. Also, keep in mind that you don't have to do it all yourself. A close adult relative or friend, or even a caring baby-sitter with an optimistic style, may be able to help you teach your child a more positive way of looking at the world.

WHEN IT'S TIME TO DO MORE

If your attempts to help your child think and act more positively just don't seem to be working, it may be time to seek another path.

Pessimistic Children are at risk for depression. Depression is more than just sadness — it's a serious condition that affects mood, thoughts, and behavior. It's also very treatable. The following list shows possible symptoms of depression (adapted from the *Diagnostic and Statistical Manual of Mental Disorders,* fourth edition). Don't panic if your child occasionally has a few of these symptoms — we all have off days sometimes. However, if your child is consistently in a negative or uninterested mood and also shows several other symptoms for two weeks or more, he or she may be depressed. Visit your pediatrician to rule out any physical problems and then seek the help of a mental health professional.

If the following symptoms also seem to apply to you, it's essential that you get professional help — for your child's sake as well as your own. You may also want to read Dr. William R. Beardslee's *Out of the Darkened Room,* which talks about ways of protecting children and strengthening families when a parent is depressed.

Possible Symptoms of Depression
  Sad or irritable mood most of the time
  Lack of interest or enjoyment in almost all activities
  Changes in appetite
  Changes in sleep habits
  Restlessness or lethargy
  Feeling tired or having very little energy nearly every day
  Feeling worthless
  Trouble concentrating or making decisions nearly every day
  Thoughts of death (not just fear of dying) or attempts to hurt
    oneself

SUMMARY

Pessimistic Children are stuck in a negative style of relating to others. Their tendencies to complain, criticize, and predict doom can be very annoying. They need guidance and support to break out of the victim role so that they can enjoy life and reach out to their peers in appropriate ways.

You Will Also Want to Read:
  Chapter 4, "The Different Drummer"
  Chapter 6, "The Short-Fused Child"
  Chapter 8, "The Sensitive Soul"

THE UNWRITTEN RULES FOR THE PESSIMISTIC CHILD AT A GLANCE

- No one likes to hear complaints.
- If you complain too often, people stop listening.
- If you can't say something positive, say nothing at all.
- When someone asks, "How are you?" answer by saying something positive.
- Save your physical complaints for your parents or your doctor.
- Try to solve the problem yourself, before you complain.
- When everyone is experiencing the same difficult circumstance, whining about it doesn't make it easier.
- Your comments should match the emotional tone of the group.
- *Fair* doesn't necessarily mean *equal.*
- Don't keep score about who gets what in social situations.
- Focus on what you have rather than what you don't have.
- You can't build a friendship tit for tat.
- If someone gives you something, say, "Thank you." Don't criticize the gift.
- Add to the positive energy of a group with your good ideas and enthusiasm.
- You can't succeed unless you try.
- If you believe you can't, you won't.
- Focus on the process rather than the outcome.
- Trying something new is often scary.
- Sometimes you have to ignore your misgivings and try anyway.

CHAPTER 11

Frequently Asked Questions

Q: How do I know my daughter won't just outgrow her current social difficulties?
A: She probably will. We all somehow managed to muddle our way through the social maze of elementary school, and your daughter probably will too. But wouldn't it be great if you could make the journey a little easier for your child? Looking back, most of us can remember times that make us think, *Oh, I wish I had known then what I know now!* The majority of children do eventually figure out a lot of the Unwritten Rules on their own. But teaching your daughter these rules directly can smooth the way for her now.

Q: How can I make sure that my son really wants to have more friends and that it isn't just my need?
A: Not everyone can or wants to be the life of the party. Some children prefer to have one or two close friends rather than a large circle of acquaintances. Many children genuinely enjoy spending time by themselves. This is fine. In fact, the ability to entertain oneself is a wonderful gift. But you should make sure that your child's tendency to spend a lot of time alone is really a preference rather than a default position. Sometimes children avoid social situations because they

don't know how to make friends or because they're convinced no one will like them. They resign themselves to being alone because they don't see any alternative.

Does your son have the necessary skills to do what he wants to do socially? Look at how your son acts when he's around other kids. Does he seem comfortable or awkward? Is he able to relate to other children in a friendly way? How do other children respond to him? Also, look at your son's mood. Does he generally seem content or lonely? Interested or irritable? If you're in doubt, it's probably better to err on the side of overfortifying your son's social skills rather than leaving him lacking and feeling lost.

Q: How do I know if my six-year-old daughter is developmentally ready to learn the material in this book?
A: Your daughter has already started learning about some of the ideas we discuss in this book. Learning to get along with other people is a lifelong process that starts in infancy and continues on through adulthood. For instance, young babies quickly learn that smiling elicits warm responses from their parents. Your daughter probably learned about sharing, taking turns, and sitting in a circle during nursery school. The social developmental tasks for elementary school children involve learning to cooperate with peers and to build, maintain, and repair friendships. They involve an extension and elaboration of earlier skills, not something completely different. Children's individual aptitudes and experiences determine how quickly or slowly they learn these tasks, but usually it takes time and practice to develop these skills. Your daughter may not fully master the material in this book for several years, but exposing her to it again and again can help her move in the right direction.

Q: You talk a lot about how important it is for children to follow the Unwritten Rules and to know how to blend in to a group.

Does this mean my child has to become a conformist and be just like everybody else? What if everybody else is doing drugs? Is my child still supposed to "blend in"?

A: Of course not. This book is about giving children knowledge so that they can make appropriate *choices*. When children don't know how to get along with others, their choices are limited. They *can't* blend in with a group. They are always outsiders.

Research tells us that it's not the socially well adjusted children who tend to turn to drugs and alcohol — it's mostly the children who are unhappy and feel disconnected from their peers. They may resort to using these dangerous substances to gain acceptance or to seem "cool" because they don't know any other way to fit in. Learning the Unwritten Rules can give children the ability to build good friendships and to make healthy choices.

Q: My two children are so different. The younger one is a little ambassador. He goes to a playground, and the next thing I know, he's got all the kids involved in some great game. But my older son is a different story. He really struggles to make friends. I don't get it. I brought both of them up the same way, in the same home. Why didn't my older son learn the same skills that my younger one did?

A: Some children are born sociable. They seem to pick up on the Unwritten Rules of social relationships automatically. It's like they pluck them out of the air. Other children, like your older son, need to be taught these skills directly. Just like some kids need extra help learning how to read, some kids need extra help learning how to get along with their peers.

Our goal with this book is to enable children like your older son to learn skills, gain confidence, and draw on their particular strengths in relating to others. This means different things for different children because each child is unique. Some children need to learn to speak up; others need to learn to tone down their responses. Your older son may never become a "little ambassador," but he has other good qualities that he can bring to a friendship. Maybe he is extremely loyal or very thoughtful or wonderfully exuberant. We talk about nine prototypical children so that you can find the special combination of strengths and difficulties that describes your child and build from there.

Q: Aren't social skills about being "fake"? Aren't you teaching children to act in a certain way just so other kids will like them?
A: Definitely not. Our focus is on helping children to be true to themselves while also being able to see other people's perspectives. We talk about assertiveness, kindness, and genuine empathy. Too often, children have off-putting habits that get in the way of forming authentic friendships. The Unwritten Rules and the exercises in this book are about giving children the opportunity to connect with others so that other people can get to know who they really are.

Q: I found a chapter, actually several chapters, that describe my son exactly. I'm sure the exercises would be helpful for him, but he refuses to do them. What should I do?
A: First, you need to understand why your child is reluctant to do the exercises. Maybe your son doesn't realize that he needs to learn to get along better with other kids. Children with social skills deficits are often the last to know that their behavior pushes others away. They may be upset when they're not invited to a party or when another child is mean to them, but they often don't see their own role in contributing to that rejection. When your child is upset about being left out, help him to understand that there are things he can do to make it more likely that other kids will want to play with him.

Sometimes children are reluctant to do the exercises because they feel overwhelmed. They may be trying to do too much, too fast. It's important to do the exercises gradually so that your child has a chance to master each concept and to build on success.

Sometimes children's reluctance stems from picking up on their parents' anxiety about their lack of friends. As much as you can, you need to keep your worries to yourself. Try to create a fun and relaxed atmosphere as you work on the material in this book with your child. Tell your child that the Unwritten Rules are like a secret code. Even adults have to figure them out every day as they relate to their spouse, their children, their friends, and their coworkers. By becoming aware of Unwritten Rules now, your child will be ahead of the game. Assure your child that, with a little time and effort, he will be able to make friends and to feel more comfortable in social situations.

Q: I've tried a number of the exercises with my son, and I can really see a difference, but things at school haven't improved. My son is feeling discouraged. What should I do?
A: Unfortunately, reputations die hard. It may take awhile for the kids at school to notice the changes your child makes. Help your son understand that he can't do a friendly behavior just once and expect everyone to see him differently — he may have to do it fifty times to make an impact. When change does come, it might be subtle. Other kids are not going to come up to your son and say, "My, how you've improved!" They'll just like him better and include him more.

You can help your son during the transition period by giving him lots of support and encouragement for the positive changes you see. Reassure him that if he keeps trying, other kids will eventually notice. Also, try arranging one-on-one play dates to give your son's classmates an opportunity to get to know him better.

It may also help to provide your child with other social settings where he might meet friends. Your son may find it easier to get along with kids he hasn't met before. So, seek out a new Scout troop or a special-interest club not based at school. Sometimes, changing classes or schools at the beginning of a new school year gives children a fresh start.

Q: Will learning the Unwritten Rules make my child popular?
A: This book is not a formula for making children popular. The Unwritten Rules are explicit guidelines, kind of like social crib notes, meant to help children get along better with their peers. They could certainly enable a child with social skill problems to become more accepted, but they won't necessarily lead to popularity. Our emphasis is on helping children gain a sense of social comfort and the ability to connect with other people. We believe these are much more important, in the long run, than popularity.

Q: Now that my daughter knows how to act in social situations, how can I get the other kids, who don't know the Unwritten Rules, to behave appropriately? My daughter gets very upset when she sees other kids doing the wrong thing.
A: One of the most important lessons we can teach our children is that we are each in charge of our own behavior, no one else's. This can be a tremendously freeing message. If we understand that other people are going to do what they're going to do and that we have very little control over this, we're less likely to become upset when they don't behave as they "should." It's their problem, not ours. We don't need to take it personally.

We can't make other people do the "right thing," but we can choose how we respond to them. Sometimes, the best response is no response. Your daughter may need to learn to overlook other children's misbehavior. You don't want her to become the Rule Police or the official teacher of the Unwritten Rules. That's not her job. If it's an ongoing problem, your daughter may want to try to resolve the conflict in positive ways, making sure that she understands and acknowledges the other child's point of view. If neither ignoring nor talking works, the best response may be to leave the situation and find different playmates.

Q: Will my daughter ever really be at ease socially?
A: We hope so. We can't guarantee that your child will become a social butterfly after using the material in this book, but providing her with knowledge and strategies can only help. She will definitely have an easier time getting along with others if she understands the Unwritten Rules about how to interpret social cues and how to act appropriately in social situations.

Q: I've read a lot lately about Asperger's syndrome. How can I tell whether my child has this disorder? Is this book helpful for children with Asperger's?
A: Asperger's syndrome involves significant impairment in social interaction. Children with Asperger's have trouble understanding other people's feelings and communicating nonverbally. They don't know how to have give-and-take conversations, and they generally don't try to engage others in shared activities. These children also may engage in repetitive behaviors, involving odd movements, rituals, or an intense interest in a particular subject. Many children occasionally show some of these symptoms, but for children with Asperger's, these symptoms are persistent and seriously interfere with their ability to relate to others.

There are a lot of differing opinions right now about Asperger's syndrome. Some experts believe that it is a high-functioning form of autism. Others insist that it's really a temperament or a social learning disability. Still others claim that it isn't helpful to see social difficulties as a "syndrome" and that we should just concentrate on helping children learn the skills they need to interact with their peers.

We don't have the data to answer the diagnostic question either for your son in particular or for children in general. But based on our clinical knowledge and experience, we can say that a wide range of social difficulties exist, from occasional awkwardness to more enduring and pervasive deficits in social understanding and self-control. At the milder end of this spectrum, kids just need some pointers and maybe a bit of practice. At the more severe end, they need more intensive coaching for a longer period of time.

Teaching your son the Unwritten Rules is very likely to help him because these rules describe precisely the information that socially struggling children don't manage to pick up on their own. You may find chapter 4, "The Different Drummer," chapter 7, "The Little Adult," and chapter 10, "The Pessimistic Child," particularly relevant. However, if your son's difficulties are extensive, this book is probably not enough to help him. A social skills group and / or a psychotherapist specializing in Asperger's syndrome could provide additional assistance.

While it's very important for your son to learn to get along with others, keep in mind that socializing is likely to be very stressful for children who have Asperger's symptoms. So, use a balanced approach. Give your son some social exposure but also let him have the solitary time that he probably craves. Encourage him to learn new social skills but, most of all, let him know that you love and appreciate him for exactly who he is.

Q: How do I know if my child needs professional help?
A: You may need to seek professional help for your child if

- you've tried the exercises in this book, and they're just not enough
- your child is extremely resistant to working with you on these problems
- your child's problems seem to be getting worse rather than better
- your child has been very distressed for weeks or months

A social skills group can provide an ideal opportunity for your child to practice getting along with others. These groups can teach your child social fundamentals while also giving him or her a chance to try out new behaviors in a safe environment. A trained group leader can also observe, from an objective perspective, your child interacting with other kids and intervene on the spot if necessary. Feedback from peers plus direction from the group leader make a powerful combination for change. Professionally led social skills groups can also take the pressure off Mom or Dad to teach the necessary skills. Be sure to look for a group that uses a cognitive-behavioral or teaching approach that focuses on helping children learn how to act appropriately.

In addition, if your child is experiencing emotional reactions that interfere with his or her daily functioning, such as depression, excessive anxiety, or frequent angry outbursts, or if your family has been struggling with very stressful circumstances, consulting a mental health professional may be necessary.

CLOSING MESSAGE

We have stressed two main themes throughout this book. First, we've talked about the importance of teaching your child the Unwritten Rules that guide social interactions so that he or she can relate appropriately to others. Second, we've talked about the importance of knowing and treasuring who your child really is. Drawing from clinical experience, we've described nine prototypical children, but your child is undoubtedly a combination of several of the children whom we have discussed. Our intention isn't to label children but to illustrate the kinds of thoughts, feelings, and behaviors that underlie children's social difficulties. Our hope is that this book will give you a practical but compassionate view of your son's or daughter's social struggles so that you can help your child to grow and develop in his or her own special way.

LIST OF ACTIVITIES

Chapter 7: The Little Adult

Chapter 8: The Sensitive Soul

Chapter 9: The Born Leader

Chapter 10: The Pessimistic Child

RECOMMENDED READING FOR PARENTS

On Social Skills

Duke, Marshall P., Stephen Nowicki Jr., and Elisabeth A. Martin. *Teaching Your Child the Language of Social Success*. Atlanta: Peachtree Publishers, 1996.

Frankel, Fred. *Good Friends Are Hard to Find: Help Your Child Find, Make and Keep Friends*. Glendale, CA: Perspective Publishing, 1997.

Nowicki, Stephen Jr., and Marshall P. Duke. *Helping the Child Who Doesn't Fit In*. Atlanta: Peachtree Publishers, 1992.

Shapiro, Lawrence E. *How to Raise a Child with a High EQ: A Parent's Guide to Emotional Intelligence*. New York: HarperCollins, 1998.

Thompson, Michael, and Catherine O. Grace, and with Lawrence J. Cohen. *Best Friends, Worst Enemies: Understanding the Social Lives of Children*. New York: Ballantine Books, 2001.

Wallace, Carol McD. *Elbows Off the Table, Napkin in the Lap, No Video Games During Dinner: The Modern Guide to Teaching Children Good Manners*. New York: St. Martin's Press, 1996.

On Parenting

Coleman, Paul. *How to Say It to Your Kids: The Right Words to Solve Problems, Soothe Feelings and Teach Values*. Upper Saddle River, NJ: Prentice Hall, 2000.

Crary, Elizabeth. *Help! The Kids Are at It Again: Using Kids' Quarrels to Teach "People" Skills.* Seattle: Parenting Press, 1996.

Elkind, David. *The Hurried Child: Growing Up Too Fast Too Soon.* Cambridge, MA: Perseus Publishing, 2001.

Faber, Adele, and Elaine Mazlish. *How to Talk So Kids Will Listen and Listen So Kids Will Talk.* New York: Avon Books, 1980.

———. *Siblings Without Rivalry.* New York: Avon Books, Inc., 1990.

Goleman, Daniel. *Emotional Intelligence: Why It Can Matter More than IQ.* New York: Bantam Books, 1995.

Krane, Gary, and John Bradshaw. *Simple Fun for Busy People: 333 Free Ways to Enjoy Your Loved Ones More in the Time You Have.* York Beach, ME: Conari Press, 1998.

Kurcinka, Mary S. *Kids, Parents, and Power Struggles: Winning for a Lifetime.* New York: HarperCollins, 2001.

———. *Raising Your Spirited Child: A Guide for Parents Whose Child Is More Intense, Sensitive, Perceptive, Persistent, and Energetic.* New York: HarperPerennial, 1992.

MacGregor, Cynthia. *Everybody Wins!: 150 Non-Competitive Games for Kids.* Avon, MA: Adams Media Corporation, 1998.

Pollack, William S. *Real Boys: Rescuing Our Sons from the Myths of Boyhood.* New York: Random House, 1998.

Wolf, Anthony E. *The Secret of Parenting: How to Be in Charge of Today's Kids — From Toddlers to Preteens — Without Threats or Punishment.* New York: Farrar, Straus and Giroux, 2000.

About Specific Difficulties

Anderson, Jill. *Thinking, Changing, Rearranging: Improving Self-Esteem in Young People.* Memphis: Metamorphosis Press, 1993.

Beane, Allan L. *The Bully Free Classroom: Over 100 Tips and Strategies for Teachers K-8*. Minneapolis: Free Spirit Publishing, 1999.

Beardslee, William R. *Out of the Darkened Room: When a Parent Is Depressed*. Boston: Little, Brown and Company, 2002.

Fried, Suellen, and Paula Fried. *Bullies and Victims: Helping Your Child Through the Schoolyard Battlefield*. New York: M. Evans & Company, 1996.

Green, Joey. *The Road to Success Is Paved with Failure: Hundreds of Famous People Who Triumphed Over Inauspicious Beginnings, Crushing Rejections, Humiliating Defeats, and Other Speed Bumps Along Life's Highway*. Boston: Little, Brown and Company, 2001.

Greene, Ross W. *The Explosive Child: A New Approach for Understanding and Parenting Easily Frustrated, Chronically Inflexible Children*. New York: HarperCollins, 1998.

Levine, Mel. *All Kinds of Minds: A Young Student's Book About Learning Abilities and Learning Disorders*. Cambridge, MA: Educators Publishing Service, 1993.

———. *Keeping a Head in School: A Student's Book About Learning Abilities and Learning Disorders*. Cambridge, MA: Educators Publishing Service, 1990.

———. *A Mind at a Time*. New York: Simon & Schuster, 2002.

Seligman, Martin E. P. *The Optimistic Child*. Boston: Houghton Mifflin, 1995.

Swallow, Ward K. *The Shy Child: Helping Children Triumph over Shyness*. New York: Warner Books, 2000.

Voors, William. *The Parent's Book About Bullying: Changing the Course of Your Child's Life*. New York: Hazelden Information Education, 2000.

For Children

Barnes, Bob, and Emilie Barnes. *A Little Book of Manners for Boys*. Eugene, OR: Harvest House Publishers, 2000.

Bennett, William J. *The Children's Book of Heroes*. New York: Simon & Schuster, 1997.

Berry, Joy W. *A Children's Book About Tattling*. New York: Grolier Books, 1998.

Brown, Laurie K. and Marc T. Brown. *How to Be a Friend: A Guide to Making Friends and Keeping Them*. Boston: Little, Brown and Company, 1998.

Bourgeois, Paulette. *Franklin Is Bossy*. Tonawanda, NY: Kids Can Press, 1994.

Conari Press. *Kids' Random Acts of Kindness*. York Beach, ME: Conari Press, 1994.

Holyoke, Nancy. *Oops! The Manners Guide for Girls*. Middleton, WI: Pleasant Company, 1997.

Kaufman, Gershen, and Lev Raphael. *Stick Up for Yourself! Every Kid's Guide to Personal Power and Positive Self-Esteem*. Minneapolis: Free Spirit Publishing, 1990.

Kennedy-Moore, Eileen. *Twelve Ways to Get Your Parents' Attention (Other Than Hitting Your Sister)*. Seattle, WA: Parenting Press, 2004.

Shapiro, Lawrence E. *The Very Angry Day that Amy Didn't Have*. Plainview, NY: Childswork / Childsplay, 1994.

SELECTED PROFESSIONAL REFERENCES

Becker, J. A. "Bossy and Nice Requests: Children's Production and Interpretation." *Merrill-Palmer Quarterly* 32 (1986): 393–413.

Beidel, D. C., S. M. Turner, and T. L. Morris. "Psychopathology of Childhood Social Phobia." *Journal of the American Academy of Child and Adolescent Psychology* 38 (1999): 643–650.

———. "Behavioral Treatment of Childhood Social Phobia." *Journal of Consulting and Clinical Psychology* 68 (2000): 1072–1080.

Crick, N. R., and M. A. Bigbee. "Relational and Overt Forms of Peer Victimization: A Multiinformant Approach." *Journal of Consulting and Clinical Psychology* 66 (1998): 337–347.

Crick, N. R., and K. Dodge. "A Review and Reformulation of Social Information-Processing Mechanisms in Children's Social Adjustment." *Psychological Bulletin* 115 (1994): 74–101.

Crick, N. R., and J. K. Grotpeter. "Children's Treatment by Peers: Victims of Relational and Overt Aggression." *Development and Psychopathology* 8 (1996): 367–380.

———. "Relational Aggression, Gender, and Social-psychological Adjustment." *Child Development* 66 (1995): 710–722.

DeBaryshe, B. D., and D. Fryxell. "A Developmental Perspective on Anger: Family and Peer Contexts." *Psychology in the Schools* 35 (1998): 205–216.

Elman, Natalie, with Janet Ginsberg. *The Resource Room Primer.* New York: Prentice Hall, 1981.

Elman, Natalie. *The Special Education Almanac.* Center for Applied Research in Education, 1984.

Gottman, J. M. "How Children Become Friends." *Monographs of the Society for Research in Child Development* 48(3) (1983): [No. 201] 86.

Gottman, J. M., L. F. Katz, and C. Hooven. "Parental Meta-emotion Philosophy and the Emotional Life of Families: Theoretical Models and Preliminary Data." *Journal of Family Psychology* 10 (1996): 243–268.

Frey, K. S., M. K. Hirschstein, and B. A. Guzzo. "Second Step: Preventing Aggression by Promoting Social Competence." *Journal of Emotional and Behavioral Disorders* 8 (2000): 102–112.

Hart, C., ed., *Children on Playgrounds: Research Perspectives and Applications.* Albany, NY: SUNY Press, 1993.

Kagan, J. "Temperamental Contributions to Emotion and Social Behavior," in *Review of Personality and Social Behavior* (Newbury Park, CA: Sage, 1992), 14: 99–118).

Kennedy-Moore, E., and J. C. Watson. *Expressing Emotion: Myths, Realities, and Therapeutic Strategies.* New York: Guilford Press, 1999.

Kochenderfer, B. J., and G. W. Ladd. "Victimized Children's Responses to Peers' Aggression: Behaviors Associated with Reduced Versus Continued Victimization." *Development and Psychopathology* 9 (1997): 59–73.

Kowalski, R. M. "Complaints and Complaining: Functions, Antecedents, and Consequences." *Psychological Bulletin* 119 (1996): 179–196.

Ladd, G. W. "Peer Relationships and Social Competence During Early and Middle Childhood." *Annual Review of Psychology* 50 (1999): 333–359.

Landau, S., R. Milich, and M. B. Diener. "Peer Relationships of Children with Attention-deficit Hyperactivity Disorder." *Reading and Writing Quarterly: Overcoming Learning Difficulties* 14 (1998): 83–105.

Mahady Wilton, M. M., W. M. Craig, and D. J. Pepler. "Emotional Regulation and Display in Classroom Victims of Bullying: Characteristic Expressions of Affect, Coping Styles and Relevant Contextual Factors. *Social Development* 9 (2000): 226–245.

Mehrabian, A. *Silent Messages: Implicit Communication of Emotions and Attitudes* (2nd ed.). Belmont, CA: Wadsworth, 1981.

Menesini, E., E. Melan, and B. Pignatti. "Interactional Styles of Bullies and Victims Observed in a Competitive and a Cooperative Setting." *Journal of Genetic Psychology* 161 (2000): 261–281.

Miranda, A., and M. J. Presentacion. "Efficacy of Cognitive-behavioral Therapy in the Treatment of Children with ADHD with and without Aggressiveness." *Psychology in the Schools* 37 (2000): 169–182.

Nolen-Hoeksema, S. "Ruminative Coping with Depression," in *Motivation and Self-regulation Across the Life Span* (New York: Cambridge University Press, 1998), 237–256.

Olweus, D. *Bullying at School: What We Know and What We Can Do.* Cambridge, MA: Blackwell, 1993.

Patterson, G. R. *Coercive Family Process.* Eugene, OR: Castalie, 1982.

Putallaz, M., and J. M. Gottman. "An Interactional Model of Children's Entry into Peer Groups." *Child Development* 52 (1981): 986–994.

Roberts, W. B., Jr., and A. A. Moroti. "The Bully as Victim: Understanding Bully Behaviors to Increase the Effectiveness of Intervention in the Bully-victim Dyad." *Professional School Counseling* 4 (2000): 148–155.

Ross, D. M. *Childhood Bullying and Teasing: What School Personnel, Other Professionals, and Parents Can Do*. Alexandria, VA: American Counseling Association, 1996.

Schwartz, D. "Subtypes of Victims and Aggressors in Children's Peer Groups." *Journal of Abnormal Child Psychology* 28 (2000): 181–192.

Segrin, C., and L. Y. Abramson. "Negative Reactions to Depressive Behaviors: A Communication Theories Analysis." *Journal of Abnormal Psychology* 103 (1994): 655–668.

Shapiro, J. P., R. F. Baumeister, and J. W. Kessler. "A Three-component Model of Children's Teasing: Aggression, Humor, and Ambiguity." *Journal of Social and Clinical Psychology* 10 (1991): 459–472.

Spence, S. H., C. Donovan, and M. Brechman-Toussaint. "Social Skills, Social Outcomes, and Cognitive Features of Childhood Social Phobia." *Journal of Abnormal Psychology* 108 (1999): 211–221.

Stephan, W. G. "The Role of Empathy in Improving Intergroup Relations." *Journal of Social Issues* 55 (1999): 729–743.

Sutton, J., and P. K. Smith. "Bullying As a Group Process: An Adaptation of the Participant Role Approach." *Aggressive Behavior* 25 (1999): 97–111.

von Salisch, M. "Children's Emotional Development: Challenges in Their Relationships to Parents, Peers, and Friends." *International Journal of Behavioral Development* 25 (2001): 310–319.

Wachtel, E. F. "The Language of Becoming: Helping Children Change How They Think About Themselves." *Family Process* 40 (2001): 369–384.

———. *Treating Troubled Children and Their Families*. New York: Guilford Press, 1994.

Warm, T. R. "The Role of Teasing in Development and Vice Versa." *Journal of Developmental and Behavioral Pediatrics* 18 (1997): 97–101.

ACKNOWLEDGMENTS

This book would not have been possible without the help and support of our clients, colleagues, friends, and family. First and foremost, we thank the children and parents who have shared their struggles with us and trusted us to help. They are truly the inspiration for this book.

We thank our agent, Susan Ginsburg, for her perceptive comments and for being our advocate extraordinaire. We thank our editor, Deborah Baker, for being enthusiastic about this book from the start and for understanding and appreciating our vision of a guide to children's social relationships that is both practical and sensitive. We also thank Shannon Langone, our copyeditor, for her eagle eye, and the administrative assistants at the Summit Center for Learning, Nancy Pompan and Laurane Friedman, for giving above and beyond their stated duties.

The names of the children in this book have no relationship to any real children we know. We tried to use names other than those of our families, friends, colleagues, and clients. Any similarities to real people are coincidental.

𝒩atalie

To believe that the ideas for this book were generated by one or even two authors is folly. Years of learning from the children I've seen professionally have provided the inspiration and the largest contributions to this book. To all these beautiful, hopeful young people I say thank you. (I hope I have given them as much as they have given me.)

I am indebted to my primary family, Erwin, Sara, David, and Marilyn, my brothers and sisters, for the early training in how to get along with others, and especially in how to defend myself. Our continuing relationships are a tribute to that training.

My husband, Stanley, not only read every chapter but delivered each finished document, purchased books for us, and gave us ongoing support. He is a vital part of the completion of this book and truly my life partner.

Susan and Mitchell Mullen, Michael and Phyllis Elman, and Elisabeth Elman, my grown children, have brought me great pride. Their continuing encouragement and their ability to make me laugh at my trials and tribulations have sustained me. Bobby, Scott, and Sam Mullen, Gabriella and Isabella Elman, my grandchildren, bring me endless joy and always give me new insight into children's social interactions.

To my friends and colleagues Dr. Carol Lewis and Dr. Laura Weitzman, early readers of this book, I say thanks for your diligence and wonderful suggestions. Your input really enhanced this work.

The influence of Dr. Nancy Tomevi, my first supervisor and mentor, from whom I've learned so much, is expressed throughout the pages of this book. Her memory lives on.

To those who offered encouragement and support throughout the years: Joy Rodino, my friend, who always showed me the bright side of things; Dr. Dorothy Cantor, who has been an inspiring role model; Adele Ben Ary, Hanne Walsh, Lois Fisher, and Tom and Rosemarie Seippel, and to so many others, I say many thanks.

Susan Ginsburg (Webman), my good friend and agent, always believed that this book would be written one day. Her continuing encouragement and belief in my abilities are greatly appreciated.

*E*ileen

Several colleagues have helped me in important ways. Dr. Charlotte O'Tiarnaigh generously shared her personal and professional insights. Dr. Patricia Steckler has been a wonderful role model for me. Her encouragement, understanding, and faith in me have been invaluable, and she never fails to laugh at my stories. My clinical supervisor, Dr. Mark Lowenthal, has taught me a tremendous amount about being a therapist. His warmth, wisdom, and unwavering support have been sustaining.

My sister, Sheila Hickey, and my friends Donna Kulpan, Debbie Ingrassia, Julie Abrams, Lucy Harrington, Pam Reid, and Jill Degener Smith have encouraged me and shared with me their own and their children's experiences of learning to get along with others. I rely on them as sources of good sense and great fun.

My father, Ed Kennedy, is extremely optimistic and loves how-to books. He even read Dale Carnegie's *How to Win Friends and Influence People* to me when I was an awkward six-year-old. It wasn't terribly relevant for a first-grader — I recall a section on the importance of a firm handshake — but perhaps it planted the seed of my interest in social relationships. My mother, Mary Clark Kennedy, died several years ago, but I'm sure her influence comes through in this book. Within ten minutes of meeting my mother, most people found themselves confiding in her because she was genuinely interested in their experiences. She was very practical, but she laughed easily and had a wonderful appreciation for what she called the "ridiculousness of life."

My children, Mary, Daniel, Sheila, and Brenna, have brought me immeasurable joy. Through their strengths and their struggles, they have also taught me more about psychology than all the courses I ever took in graduate school.

Most of all, I want to thank my husband, Tony Moore. He helped with the kids, ignored or tackled the unfinished housework, chased down references, solved computer problems, and generally cheered me on. After sixteen years of marriage, he's still my true love, best friend, and favorite companion.

NATALIE MADORSKY ELMAN, PH.D. (education), has more than twenty years of experience as the director of the Summit Center for Learning in Springfield, New Jersey, where she evaluates children, directs appropriate remediation, and facilitates social skills training groups, using her unique, proprietary methods. She is a certified learning consultant and speech pathologist. Dr. Elman is also a national speaker and has consulted for the New Jersey Department of Education and many public and private schools.

A former special education teacher, Dr. Elman has taught children ages five through twelve and has served as a speech and language pathologist. She has directed resource room classes and has helped children with communication, neurological, and perceptual impairments.

Dr. Elman was a contributing editor to *Child Magazine,* cowriting several articles on children's learning and social skills. She is the author of three published books: *The Special Educator's Almanac: Ready-to-Use Activities for a Resource Room or a Self-Contained Classroom; Super Sayings: Super Ways to Teach Idioms to Kids;* and *The Resource Room Primer: Teaching Techniques for Developing, Implementing, or Improving a Resource Room Program.*

Dr. Elman lives in West Orange, New Jersey, with her husband.

EILEEN KENNEDY-MOORE has a Ph.D. in clinical psychology. She works with individual children, adults, and families. She is the coauthor, with Jeanne C. Watson, of *Expressing Emotion: Myths, Realities, and Therapeutic Strategies,* which has been praised as "the Michelin Guide to emotions." Dr. Kennedy-Moore received an American Psychological Association Dissertation Award for her work on causal explanations for daily mood, and she has published articles in professional journals on coping, emotions, and social behavior. She has written a children's book entitled *Twelve Ways to Get Your Parents' Attention (Other Than Hitting Your Sister)*. Dr. Kennedy-Moore lives in New Jersey with her husband and four children.